Cyber Law in India

Cyber Law in India

Talat Fatima

This book was originally published as a monograph in the International Encyclopaedia of Laws/Cyber Law.

Founding Editor: Roger Blanpain
General Editor: Frank Hendrickx
Volume Editor: Jos Dumortier

Wolters Kluwer

Published by:
Kluwer Law International B.V.
PO Box 316
2400 AH Alphen aan den Rijn
The Netherlands
Website: www.wklawbusiness.com

Sold and distributed in North, Central and South America by:
Wolters Kluwer Legal & Regulatory U.S.
7201 McKinney Circle
Frederick, MD 21704
United States of America
Email: customer.service@wolterskluwer.com

Sold and distributed in all other countries by:
Turpin Distribution Services Ltd.
Stratton Business Park
Pegasus Drive, Biggleswade
Bedfordshire SG18 8TQ
United Kingdom
Email: kluwerlaw@turpin-distribution.com

ISBN 97890-411-8743-7

e-Book: ISBN 97890-411-8766-6
web-PDF: ISBN 97890-411-8796-3

This title is available on www.kluwerlawonline.com

The Author

The author was a law teacher by profession and retired as the Principal, Government Law College, Dholpur, Rajasthan in January 2016. She followed her educational pursuits starting from Kolkata, her birthplace from where she moved to Aligarh Muslim University where she got her Gold medal in the Law degree and did her LL.M. She has been working as a dedicated law teacher since. She was awarded the PhD by the prestigious University of Delhi in the rare but latest subject of cybercrime in 2008. Her PhD thesis has been published as a book entitled CyberCrimes, by the leading law publisher of the country the Eastern Book Company, the second edition of which is on the stalls. Her book entitled CyberCrimes is being translated by her in Hindi, the dominant language of India. She has special crave for the silicon revolution vis-à-vis the legal responses.

The Author

Table of Contents

Table of Contents

List of Abbreviations

ADC	Access Deficit Charge
ADSL	Asymmetrical Digital Subscriber Line
AIR	All India Reporter
ARE	Annual Recurring Expenditure
BPO	Business Process Outsourcing
BSNL	Bharat Sanchar Nigam Limited
CAS	Conditional Access System
CCC	Common Criteria Certification
C-DoT	Center for Development of Telematics
CII	Critical Information Infrastructure
CLIP	Callers Line Identification Protocol
COAI	Cellular Operators Association of India
CP	Certificate Policy
CPS	Carrier Per Selection
CRL	Certificate Revocation List
CSR	Certificate Signing Request
DEITY	Department of Electronics & Information Technology
DoT	Department of Telecommunications
DSC	Digital Signature Certificate
DSL	Digital Subscriber Line
DTH	Direct To Home
GISFI	Global ICT Standardization Forum for India
GMPCS	Global Mobile Personal Communication by Satellite
GSM	Global System for Mobile Communication
IIP	International Infrastructure Providers
ILD	International Long Distance
ILDO	International Long Distance Operator
IP	Internet Protocol
IPLC	International Private Leased Circuits

IPTV	International Protocol Television
IDN	International Domain Names
ICANN	International Corporation for Assigned Names and Numbers
INSAIT	Indian Society of Agricultural Information Technology
ISDN	Integrated Services Digital Network
ISP	Internet Service Providers
ITU	International Telecommunications Union
IUC	Interconnection Usage Charges
INOC	Integrated Network Operations Center
KPO	Knowledge Process Outsourcing
LAN	Local Area Network
LDCC	Long Distance Charging Center
MTNL	Mahanagar Telephone Nigam Limited
MNVO	Mobile Virtual Network Operators
NIXI	National Internet Exchange of India
NAP	Network Access Points
NOC	Network Operations Center
NPE	National Policy on Electronics
NABARD	National Bank for Agriculture and Rural Development
NKN	National Knowledge Network
NIC	National Informatics Center
PBX	Private Branch Exchange
PCO	Public Call Office
PIN	Personal Identification Number
PKI	Public Key Infrastructure
POP	Point of Presence
PSTN	Public Switched Telecom Network
RBI	Reserve Bank of India
RSA	Rivest, Shamir & Adelman
SAFCA	Standing Advisory Committee on Frequency
SDCA	Short Distance Charging Area
SEBI	Securities and Exchange Board of India
SIM	Subscriber Identification Module
SLDC	Short Distance Charging Center

List of Abbreviations

STQC	Standardization Testing and Quality Certification
TCP	Transmission Connection Protocol
TDSAT	Telecom Disputes Settlement and Appellate Tribunal
TLD	Top-Level Domain
TRAI	Telecom Regulatory Authority of India
TTO	Telecommunications Tariff Order
UHF	Ultra High Frequency
U.K.	United Kingdom
UNESCAP	United Nations Economic and Social Commission For Asia and the Pacific
URL	Uniform Resource Locator
U.S.	United States of America
USO	Universal Service Obligation
USOF	Universal Service Obligation Fund
VAS	Value-Added Service
VOIP	Voice over Internet Protocol
VPN	Virtual Private Network
VSNL	Videsh Sanchar Nigam Limited
WAN	Wide Area Network
WLL	Wireless in Local Loop
WPC	Wing Wireless Planning and Coordination Wing
WTO	World Trade Organization

Preface

Ancient India goes digital. From an agrarian society 10,000 years ago to the information society of today, India's telecom revolution is a success story. The first ever ringtone rang in Kolkata in 1882 and the first cellular service started in Kolkata in 1995. Today India is an IT destination and the ICT prophets forecast a long stride for the country. Telecommunications, electronics, banking, Internet and consumer protection are flourishing well in the country so much so that the country has the third largest Internet population in the world after United States of America (U.S.) and China. The techno-legal upswing however does not complement each other. While the silicon landscape in the country is registering an untiring march, the legal scenario presents a dismal picture. Today in the country, it would be rare that someone is not using a cellular phone but the legal armor still lacks much-needed legislations. The overall approach has been piecemeal. The Information Technology Act formulated in 2000 is the only IT Act in the country while the Communication Convergence Bill and the Data Protection Bill are yet to see the light of the day. No law exists for information society services. In the area of electronic banking, a comprehensive law is yet to come. The country presenting world-class technocrats is still grappling with political will to get a viable and strong legal matrix.

October 2016
Talat Fatima
India

General Introduction

Chapter 1. General Background

§1. Geography

1. "India is the cradle of the human race, the birthplace of human speech, the mother of history, the grandmother of legend and the great grandmother of tradition. Our most valuable and most instructive materials in the history of man are treasured up in India only" (Mark Twain). Geographically too it is a rich country having all the indicia of a continent. From the snowcapped Himalayas in the north to sun-drenched coastal villages in the south from the green basin of the Brahmaputra in the east to the sand dunes of Rajasthan in the west, the country is geographically gifted by nature. It covers an area of 32,87,263 km^2 and is the seventh largest country in the world lying entirely in the northern hemisphere. The mainland extends between latitudes 8° 4' and 37° 6' north and longitudes 68° 7' and 97° 25' east. The country spreads over the mainland having land frontier of about 15,200 km and two sets of archipelagoes: the Andaman & Nicobar Islands and Lakshadweep Islands. It borders with Afghanistan and Pakistan in the north-west, China, Bhutan and Nepal in the north and Bangladesh and Myanmar in the east and the Far East. It tapers off into the Indian Ocean between the Bay of Bengal in the east and the Arabian Sea in the west. The mainland comprises four regions, namely the great mountain zone, plains of the Ganga and the Indus, the desert region and the southern peninsula. The geological regions are grouped into three – the Great Himalayas and their associated group of mountains, the Indo Ganga Plain and the Peninsular Shield. The country's climate is basically tropical monsoon type. It has rich flora and fauna being the tenth in the world and fourth in Asia in plant diversity. The country has a network of great rivers; the holy Ganges (Ganga), the Yamuna, the Brahmaputra, the Indus, the Tapti, the Chambal and many other providing a great source of water throughout the year.

§2. Demographic and Cultural Composition

2. Demographic of India-

INDIA'S DEMOGRAPHY

POPULATION	1,236,344,631 (JULY 2014)
GROWTH RATE	1.51% (2009)
BIRTH RATE	20.22 BIRTHS/1000 POPULATION(2013)
DEATH RATE	7.4 DEATHS PER 1000 (2013)
LIFE EXPECTANCY Female Male	68.89 YEARS (2009) 72.61 (2009) 67.46 years (2009)
FERTILITY RATE	2.44 CHILDREN BORN/WOMAN SRS 2011
INFANT MORTALITY	44 DEATHS /1000 LIVE BIRTHS

3. "Intangible Cultural Heritage." (ICH): Unity in diversity is the bottom-line of Indian culture. The forefathers, *the Aryans*, the Rulers, the *Mughals* and the mighty British left behind the footprints of their own culture and ethos. Predominantly, a religious society the country imbibes the cultural values not only of the ancient Hindu religion but also a tinge of Islamic culture and a dash of many other local cultures like *Punjabi, Gujarati* and *Bengali* that make it a culturally potent society. The Indus Valley Civilization (IVC) and the Vedic Age preceding it are the flag bearers of the cultural heritage. India has one of the world's largest collections of songs, music, dance, theatre, folk traditions, performing arts, rites and rituals, paintings and writings also known as the "Intangible Cultural Heritage." (ICH) Dancing in India has an unbroken tradition of 2,000 years. Its themes are derived from mythology, legends and classical literatures; two main divisions being classical and folk. *Bharatnatyam, Kathakali, Kathak, Manipuri, Kuchipudi* and *Odissi* are the various dance forms from different states of India and have religious and ethical importance as well.

4. Tangible Cultural Heritage: The National museums, the art galleries, the innumerable and grand edifices like the *Taj Mahal*, good number of ancient temples and mausoleums reflect the majestic past of the country. The mute and majestic specimen of architectures like the *Mohanjodaro*, the *Ajanta Ellora,* etc., speak volumes about the tangible cultural heritage of the country. To preserve this great heritage and to save it forever the Government of India (GOI) through the Ministry of Culture and the Zonal Cultural Centers (ZCC) takes care of it. The Ministry of Culture of the GOI is the highest body to preserve the cultural heritage of the country. The Archaeological Survey of India (ASI) established in 1861 is attached to the Department of Culture and it maintains and conserves the centrally protected monuments and buildings apart from performing many other functions to conserve the cultural heritage of the country.

§3. Political System

5. From a country that was for centuries under British dominion to a nation moving on the Information Superhighway, India proved to be a country that truly deserves independence and self-realization. For centuries the country longed for home rule (1600–1947), was an attraction for rulers and an object of lust for plunderers. After the fall of the Great Mughals, the country fell prey to the administrative acumen of the mighty British. Dependency, slavery and submission describe the plight of Indians under the British Rule. Though during this period India got its most viable legal and educational system, yet the social, religious, economic and cultural spirit was fully crushed. The First War of Independence in 1857 was a futile effort of disunited India, which proved to be a miscalculation on the part of the earnest fighters regarding the might of the British. There was bloodless fight for about fifty years thereafter when Mohan Das Karamchand Gandhi, the *Father of the Nation* became the flag bearer of the struggle for freedom. This fight of the ideologies, of philosophies, of minds and of thoughts though the sacrifices of the soldiers is unforgettable. Ultimately, on August 15, 1947 India awoke to the dawn of freedom and broke the shackles of slavery and submission. A new country was born with a political structure that was unsuitable for the rule by the natives. The Constitution of India, a dream house of the innumerable freedom fighters, of struggling natives and of hundreds of national leaders saw the light of the day November 26, 1949 which envisages a sovereign, democratic, socialist and secular Republic of India.

6. Political set-up: Although India became a federation under the Government of India Act 1935, yet its true spirit was yet to come. With the full enforcement of the Constitution of India on January 26, 1950, India adopted the democratic and responsible type of parliamentary system of government. India is a federal State in which the Constitution envisages that India shall be a Union of States (Article 1). As such there is a government at the center called the GOI and also local governments at the various state levels. Today there are twenty-nine States and seven Union Territories.[1] The First Schedule shows twenty-eight states while in the southern peninsula on June 2, 2014 *Telangana* has been added as the twenty-ninth state of the Indian Federation.[2] Following the fundamental principle of a federation there is division of power between the Center and the State in the legislative, administrative and financial spheres.[3] There are Three Lists containing the Union List with ninety-seven subjects of national importance on which the Central Legislature or the Parliament can make laws, the State List with sixty-six subjects on which the State legislatures can make laws and which are of local importance and then there is Concurrent List with forty-seven subjects on which both the Parliament and the State Legislatures can make laws regarding matters which require uniformity throughout the country.[4] The Executive power of the Center rests in the President of India who is the head of the Republic and who has executive, legislative, diplomatic, military, judicial and emergency powers to be utilized by the President on the aid and advice of the Union Cabinet headed by the Prime Minister.

1. First Schedule; Part XXII, Constitution of India
2. www.india.com
3. Article 245–276; Constitution of India.
4. Seventh Schedule; Part XXII, Constitution of India.

Thus, the real power lies in the Prime minister while the President is the *de facto* head of the State. At the state level, Governors, as the head of the State Executive, are appointed by the President who is the prototype of the President and the duly elected state government is headed by the Chief Minister and other ministers.

7. Judicial System: India also adopts the federal principle of having an independent judiciary. The country has a strong judicial set up continuing from the British Period although the Supreme Court of India was established on January 28, 1950. The Supreme Court is the symbol of the judicial independence in the country; it is not only the last appellate court in the country but serves as the final arbitrator between the Center and the various states. There is a Chief Justice of the Supreme Court known as the Chief Justice of India and thirty other *puisne* judges. It is the torchbearer of the fundamental rights of the citizens and upholds the concepts of justice, liberty, equality and fraternity so dearly cherished by the constitutional makers as well by all the Indians. At the state level, there are High Courts which are the last word in judiciary in the state though in some matters appeal can be taken to the Supreme Court of India. There are twenty-one High Courts in the country in all. The Constitution upholds the independence of the judiciary as the appointment and salary of the judges are kept out of political control. In every state, there is an established hierarchy of the subordinate courts to dispense justice at the grass-root level though the authority of courts is established at every level. Recently under the Legal Services Authorities Act 1987, *Lok Adalats* (People's Court) have been the trends which are organized by the district judicial officers to dispense with petty or family matters. There are also various consumer redressal forums to provide easy and fast relief to the aggrieved consumers established under the Consumer Protection Act 1986.

§4. Population and Vital Statistics

8. The population of India as on March 1, 2011 stood at 1,210.6 million (623 million males and 587.5 million females) although the country covers 2.4% of the world surface area of 135.79 million km^2 yet it supports and sustains a whopping 6% of the world population. The population density of India in 2011 was 382 per km^2- decadal growth 17.54%. Census 2011 is the fifteenth Census of India since 1872. It was held in two phases:

- House listing and Housing Census (April to September 2010) and
- Population Enumeration (February 9 to 28, 2011 with revisions round during March 1 to 5, 2011.

The Population: Persons 1210.6 million; Males 623 million and Females 587.4 million.

9. Vital Statistics: United Nations Estimates[5]

PERIOD	AVERAGE POPULATION	LIVE BIRTHS	DEATHS	NATURAL CHANGE	CRUDE BIRTH RATE	CRUDE DEATH RATE	NATURAL CHANGE	Total Fertility Rate
2006	1157039	27190000	8678000	18512000	23.5	7.5	`6.0	
2007	1173972	27119000	8687000	18432000	23.1	7.4	15.7	
2008	1190864	27152000	8812000	18340000	22.8	7.4	15.4	2.6
2009	1207740	27174000	8817000	18357000	22.5	7.3	15.2	2.6
2010	1224614	27064000	8817	18247000	22.1	7.2	14.9	2.5
2011	1242738	27092000	8823	18268000	21.8	7.1	14.7	2.44
2012	1261006	27237000	88270	18410	21.6	7.0	14.6	2.4

10. Sex Ratio: Sex ratio defined as the number of females per thousand males is an important social indicator to measure the extent of prevailing equality between males and females in a society at a given point of time. The sex ratio in the country favors the female gender. It was 972 at the beginning of the twentieth century and thereafter showed continuous decline until 1941. The sex ratio from 1901 to 2011 has registered a ten point increase at census 2011 over 2001; however child sex ratio has declined to 919 females per 1000 males.

11. Literacy Rate: Census 2011[6]

LITERACY RATE		LITERACY RATE
PERSONS	77 84,54,120 74.04	
MALES	44,42 03 762	82.14
FEMALES	334250 358	65.46

5. World Population Prospects -2010 Revision.
6. Provisional Population Totals – Office of the Registrar General and Census – Ministry of Home Affairs – Government of India. New Delhi.

12. India though an ancient country is robust and resilient, well equipped to survive in the contemporary world. The telecommunication story started centuries back with the introduction of the telephonic system by the British, but since then it has come a long way in this field. Being densely populated, telecommunication is its survival plank; consequently, in the present scenario the country has a honeycomb of legislations comprising not only of Acts but also of Rules, Guidelines and situation-specific Policies. The Indian Telecommunication Network has 302.35 million Internet connections and is the second largest in the world. The sector has seen a tremendous growth rate of 46–50% during recent years.

13. Liberalization started in 1981 with signing of contracts with Alcatel of France to merge with the State-owned Telecom Company (ITI) with the aim to set up 5 million lines per year. India made steady progress and in 1994, the *National Telecommunications Policy* (NTP) by the Indian Government changed ownership, business management and regulation of ITI. With the birth of the *Telecommunications Regulatory Authority of India* (TRAI) in 1997, the interference of Government in the field of tariff fixing and policy making was reduced. Although the World Bank advised the Indian Government to liberalize long-distance services to minimize the monopoly of the State-owned companies but the government first concentrated on liberalization of local services. During this period, the Government allowed two service providers and gave a fifteen-year license to each. Later in 1999, furthering the liberalization policy the ministry was bifurcated into two – the policy maker and the service provider. The service provider called the Department of Telecommunication Services (DTS) was later named as *Videsh Sanchar Nigam Limited* (VSNL). In 2002, the Government reduced its stake in VSNL from 53% to 26% and the private enterprises were invited. The Government's liberal attitude continued when in March 2000 the license fees was reduced for cellular service providers and a 74% stake was allowed to the foreign companies. The result was cheaper tariffs and the facility of cellular phones reaching more and more middle class and common Indians. The liberal and technology-savvy attitude of the government as well as enthusiastic participation both by the private and public sector has made possible the long strides in this field. Selective privatization and planned competition started as early as 1992 when private competition in value-added services was followed by opening of cellular and basic services for local area to private competition. As communication in the Internet age has assumed importance and usefulness as never before, India too responded to it instantly by building up an infrastructure not only of communicational hardware but also a galaxy of legislations to make such infrastructure not only viable but also safe and legal.

14. The former State-owned VSNL is the seventh largest telecom company in the world in terms of its number of subscribers. Companies like the *Vodafone, Bharti Airtel, Tata Indicom, Idea Cellular, Aircel and Loop Mobile* thronged the market in 2008–2009 making a big increase in rural subscribers as compared to the urban subscribers. The total number of telephones in India exceeded 543 million in October 2009 and the overall tele-density exceeded 44% in November 2009. Total wireless subscribers are now more than 543.20 million. As a common feature, the fixed line subscribers declined 0.13 million in November 2009. Thus, in the area of mobile services India has made significant progress and became one of the fastest growing mobile markets in the world. Mobile services were launched in August 1995 and in the start the monthly subscribers' additions were around 0.05–0.1 million and by December 2002 it stood at 10.5 million.

15. The telecommunication infrastructure of today is unimaginable without the Internet. To catch up with the latest communicational demands India's response has been commendable. The total subscriber base for Internet in India was 13.54 million in 2009. After 1992 many private Internet Service Providers (ISPs) have entered the market with their own local loop and gateway infrastructures. The number of broadband connections in India is on the rise since 2006, but it is more expensive compared to Western Europe and United Kingdom (U.K.) and the U.S. Towards the end of November 2009 total broadband connections in the country reached 7.57 million.

16. The Telecom Department has adopted new communicational means like the Cellular Telephones, Radio Paging Service, Fax Machines and Electronic Mail Service. TRAI is the linchpin of the entire telecom infrastructure. Steady fall in tariffs is the secret of India's big success in the in the field of telecommunications. This was made possible by the policy know as *PTB – Power, Tower and Backhaul*. India became a model for other countries so much so that the United Nations Economic and Social Commission For Asia and the Pacific (UNESCAP) urged member countries to learn from India's experience with infrastructure sharing and outsourcing of its IT infrastructure management as a way of leveraging additional services from already available facilities and ultimately maximizing productivity of the equipment. Outsourcing is the model pioneered by *Bharti Airtel* which outsources all information technology operations and customer care to IBM.

17. Infrastructure Sharing: Tower sharing which happens in Britain, America and China, etc., have made sharing compulsory and in India voluntary sharing has gone much further. In 2007, the three Indian Operators – *Bharti, Vodafone Essar and Idea Cellular* pooled 100,000 of their towers in one single company, *Indus Towers*. Reliance Communications too set up towers as a separate unit that offers tower capacity to other operators. Thus, India's market-led sharing has become its important feature, reducing cost and saving extra space. India also has yet another infrastructure innovation with the pre-paid "lifetime" scheme in which customers pay a one-off fee and can then receive incoming calls indefinitely. It is widely recognized that for rural subscribers as many as 80% of calls originate in cities or even overseas.

Chapter 3. Information and Communications Technology Market

§1. General Statement

18. The dawn of ICT sector in India has been a remarkable one and is all set to become a USD 225 billion industry by 2020. Since the adoption of the World Market Policy in 1988, India has shown great activity in the field of software development for export, telecommunications policy reform and the privatization of telephone companies. There are a number of governmental policies which aim at making the ICT market in India a promising one. Worth USD 79.737 billion, the ICT sector welcomes new business technologies like cloud, mobility, analytics, social media and vertical specific solutions. Quite recently, the adoption of IT in Retail, Healthcare and Utilities has shown increase in uptake.

19. The telecommunications services in India comprising fixed and mobile, data and voice services is the largest IT segment and the spending forecast is expected to reach USD 30 billion in 2014 (Gartner Inc.). The devices market including the PCs and tablets and printers is expected to go to a total of USD 23.5 billion in 2014, a probable 6% increase from 2013. IT services are in various segments and may grow by 13% to reach USD 11.2 billion in 2014.

20. Revenue: IT spending in India is projected to total USD 71.3 billion in 2014 which is about a 5.9% increase from the USD 67.4 billion forecast for 2013. Software will account for USD 4.1 billion in revenue. The year 2014 is promised to be the indicator of tremendous rise in revenue the overall strong growth of 12.1% with software revenue promising to grow by 10% and the telecommunication services to account for 2% rise in revenue. The IT market in India is the third largest in the growing economies and the fourth largest among developing and mature Asia/Pacific countries. Thus, the Indian devices market is also expected to be driven by sale of mobile phones, one of the fastest growing sub-segments within the Indian IT industry and the mobile phone revenue will total USD 26 billion by 2017 and will account for 76.4% of device revenue and 28% of overall IT spend in the year 2017 (Gartner Inc. 2013).

§2. Retail Markets

I. Fixed Communications Market

21. The two giants in the fixed Communications market are the *Mahanagar Telephone Nigam Limited* or MTNL and *Bharat Sanchar Nigam Limited* or BSNL. Both in terms of fixed lines and mobile communications, the BSNL has the lion's share in the market. The number of fixed lines was just 47 million in 2007. The BSNL's

Global System for Mobile Communication (GSM) began only in 2006. BSNL is said to have only 84 million subscribers in 2008. As for the fixed lines, there are 31.53 million subscribers as of May 2012. The broadband penetration was very low; the lowest in the world in 2008 covering about only 1% of the entire population, but in May 2012 it reached 14.31 million. The fixed line service is overshadowed by the rapid growth of the cellular phone and the landline service providers are trying hard for improvement in the quality of service and efficiency in this area.

II. Mobile Communications Market

22. Mobile communications in India has hit the market with a bang. It has received ever-increasing response from the masses. With a subscriber base of 929 million, the mobile telecommunications system has risen significantly from 350 million just forty months earlier. India has 736,654 base transceiver stations (2G GSM & CDMA and 3G), out of these 96,212 base transceiver stations provide 3G mobile and data services. Out of 640 districts in India, 610 have been covered by 3G services by November 2012.[7] India ranks the second largest in the world.

23. India is divided into multiple zones called "circles." The mobile subscriber base has grown by a factor of over a 130 from 5 million subscribers in 2001 to over 929 million in 2012. GSM is the main mobile technology working in this area and there are twenty-three service areas, nineteen telecommunications services areas and four metro police service areas. At present, certain operators also operate in the 1800 MHz band.

24. With regard to mobile operators in India, the operator Airtel owned by Bharti Enterprises (64%) and Singtel (36%) rank first among the mobile operators in India.

III. Interactive Services

25. In India Business Process Outsourcing (BPO), Knowledge Process Outsourcing (KPO), Domestic and International Call Centers, Network Operations Center (NOC), etc. are covered under the "Other Service Provider" category by Department of Telecommunications (DoT). "Application Services" means providing services like tele-banking, tele-medicine, tele-education, tele-trading, e-commerce, call center, network operation center and other IT-enabled services by using Telecom Resources provided by Authorized Telecom Service Providers. The "Telecom Resource" means telecom facilities used by the OSP including but not limited to Public Switched Telecom Network (PSTN), Public Land Mobile Network (PLMN), Integrated Services Digital Network (ISDN) and/ or the telecom bandwidth provided by authorized telecom service provider having license under the Indian Telegraph Act 1885. The "Company" means a company registered under the Indian Companies Act 1956 including foreign companies permitted by RBI under Foreign Exchange Management Regulations and registered under Part XI (section 591–608) of the Companies Act 1956 for setting up a place of

7. Bafna Sanjay (2012-12-21). "*India has 7, 36,654 Mobile Towers and only 96,112 BTSs are 3G enabled!*" Telecomtalk.info retrieved Apr. 22, 2013.

business in India. "Domestic OSP" are the OSP providing the Applications Services within national boundaries. International OSP is the OSP providing "Application Services" beyond national boundaries.

Part I. Regulation of the ICT Market

Chapter 1. Regulatory Framework of the Telecommunications Sector

§1. Background

26. To start with, the Indian Telegraph Act 1885 was the first attempt by the British to broaden the horizon of the telegraphic activities in the simpler and less-developed India at that time. The Act gives more power to the Government and the licensed Companies to conveniently use private and public land for placing telegraphic lines. The path was open for moving ahead in this field without hurdles. A number of policy reforms, legislations[8] and rules since have formed the legal framework of the country in this field. Regulation on Telegraph is a Central Government mandate which is empowered by the Constitution of India (Union List-Entry 31) to the exclusion of State or local governments. There is a plethora of legislations, rules, policies, guidelines and orders which go together to regulate the entire telecommunication world in India.

8. Indian Telegraphs (Presidency Towns) Act, 1888 (11 of 1888)
– Indian Telegraph (Amendment) Act 1914 (7 of 1914)
– Indian Post Office and Telegraph (Amendment) Act1914 (14 of 1914
– Indian Telegraph (Amendment) Act 1930 (27 of 1930)
– The Government of India (Adaptation of Indian Laws) Orders 1937.
– Indian Telegraph (Amendment) Act 1948 (45 of 1948)
– The Adaptation of Laws Order 1950.
– The Part B States (Laws) Act 1951 (3 of 1951)
– The Indian Telegraph (Amendment) Act 1957 (47 of 1957) (w.e.f. 1-7-1957).
– The Telegraph Laws (Amendment Act 1961 (15 of 1961) (w.e.f. 2-5-1961).
– The Indian Telegraph (Amendment) 1971 (33 of 1971) (w.e.f. 10-8-1971).
– The Indian Telegraph (Amendment) Act 1972 (38 of 1972) (w.e.f. 21-8-1972).
– The Indian Telegraph (Amendment) Act 1974(48 of 1974) (w.e.f. 1-6-75). The Indian telegraph (Amendment) Act 2003 (8 of 2004) w.e.f. 1-4-2002.) CHECK.
– The Indian Telegraph (Amendment) Act 2006 (57 of 2006) (w.e.f. 3-10-2006).

§2. Scope of the Law

27. The TRAI Act 1997 as amended in 2000 has a new segment – the Telecom Disputes Settlement and Appellate Tribunal (TDSAT). While on the one hand, the TRAI takes care of recommendatory and regulatory functions, the Tribunal, on other hand, takes care of disputes settlement. Under the term "telecommunications" and due to the wide definitions of certain terms under the TRAI Act 1997 the Indian legal framework takes into its scope certain services like Internet, radio paging, voice mail, V-Sat communications, E-commerce, broadcasting services, etc. As telecommunications falls under List I or Union list of the GOI, the Central Government has an upper hand in this field and has greater legislative competence. Thus, the entire legal framework in telecommunication sector consists of: the Indian Telegraph Act 1885 and the rules made thereunder; the Wireless Telegraphy Act 1933 and rules made thereunder; the Telegraph Wires (Unlawful Possession) Act 1950 and the rules made thereunder; the Cable Television Network (Regulation) Act 1996 and the rules made thereunder; the TRAI Act 1997 and rules made thereunder. This legal framework however deals with specialized form of telecommunication services under one single law like the Telegraph Act of 1885 and hence often financial and other legal issues result from it.

Recommendatory Functions

The recommendatory functions of TRAI are either done on its own or on the request of the licensor and include; the requirement and timing of the new service provider, terms and conditions of the license, revocation of license, measures to promote efficiency and facilitate the competition, technological improvements in the services of the service provider, type of equipment to be used by the service provider, etc.

Regulatory Functions

These include ensuring compliance of the license which is done by either issuing directions in this respect or by termination of license for non-compliance; fixing the terms and conditions of the interconnectivity between the service providers; ensuring technical compatibility and useful connection between difference service providers; regulate sharing of revenues among the service providers; lay down the standards of quality of services provided by the service providers, fix time for providing local and long-distance circuits of telecommunication between different service providers; maintain registers of interconnection agreements; ensure effective compliance of universal service obligation; levy fees and charges as determined by regulations; notify rates in the Official Gazette from time to time regarding rates of the telecommunication services provided within and outside India.

The TRAI Amendment Act 2000 has established a new body called the TDSAT. The Tribunal resolves disputes between licensor and licensee, between service providers or between service providers and consumers. It is also empowered to hear and dispose of appeal against any order, direction of the TRAI. The important feature of the amended Act is that earlier the tribunal had no jurisdiction over the disputes between government as a licensor and the licensee but now it is covered by the amended act. . The Tribunal however has no jurisdiction over disputes falling under the Monopolies and Restrictive Trade Practices Act 1969, over the complaints under the Consumer Protection Act 1986 and for certain disputes falling under section 7B of the Telegraph Act 1885.

However, from an order of the Tribunal an appeal can be taken before the Supreme Court of India.

The TRAI with its effective legal framework is able to create USD 5 billion foreign direct investment in the telecom sector. (June 2015). The TRAI Act procures many advantages for the stakeholders. It not only reduces the capital expenditure for constructing dedicated infrastructure by the individual operator but it also saves on operation cost. Cost reduction but at the same time maintenance of quality for the consumer has been the ultimate achievement of TRAI.

§3. Policy Objectives and Regulatory Principles

28. The telecom and broadband services are indispensable in today's common man's life. For sustained development of telecom and broadband infrastructure, India followed a defined policy. Thus, the key policies published are:

- National Telecom Policy 1994.
- New Telecom Policy 1999.
- Broadband Policy 2004.

29. The Objectives of the New Telecom Policy were:

- Access to telecommunications is indispensable to achieve the social and economic goals; the core of the vision is to provide affordable means of communications to the common citizen.
- Strive to provide a balance between service in uncovered areas and the economy.
- To cover telecommunications in remote, hilly and tribal areas of the country.
- Convergence of IT, media, telecom and consumer electronics and thereby guide the country towards the goal of IT Superpower.
- To convert Public Call Offices (PCOs), into Public Teleinfo Centers having multimedia capability like the ISDN services, remote database access, government and community information systems, etc.
- To encourage competition in the telecom sector.
- To encourage research and development efforts in the country and provide an impetus to build world-class manufacturing capabilities.
- To achieve efficiency and transparency in spectrum management.
- To protect defense and security interest of the country.
- To expand the area of telecommunications services to the rural area and at the same time to take rural density from 0.4 to 4 by the year 2010 and provide reliable transmission media in all rural areas.
- Provide Internet access to all District Head Quarters by 2000.
- To provide high speed data and multimedia capability using technologies including ISDN to all towns.

30. There was separately formulated a new Broadband Policy 2004 especially for the rollout of the Internet in India. An "always-on" data connection which is able to support interactive services including Internet access a download speed of 256 kilo bits per second (kbps) to an individual subscriber from the Point of Presence (POP) of the service provider. Overall, these Policies have gone a long way in laying down a road map for the private sector, establishing IT Parks in some major cities and speeding up the pace of telecom progress in the country.

§4. The National Regulatory Authorities

31. The TRAI established in 1997 by the Telecom and Regulatory Authority Act 1997 is the highest governing body in the area of telecommunications. It supersedes the Indian Telegraph Act 1885 (13 of 1885) in many respects and has a major role to play in issuing license to various telecommunication functionaries in the country. The TRAI Act was amended in 2000 by which recommendatory functions were separated from enforcement functions. A separate telecom tribunal – TDSAT was set up with both original and appellate jurisdiction. It was made mandatory for the Central Government to get prior recommendations of the TRAI before introduction of new services. TRAI's power to issue directions was restricted only to its enforcement functions. There could be taken a direct appeal from the decisions of the TRAI to the Supreme Court of India. Thus, neutrality of the Indian telecom regulatory regime was ensured through reliance on multiple agencies for conflict resolution.[9]

32. The main functions of TRAI encompass the following:

(a) Make request either *suo moto* or on the request of the licensor regarding the need and timing of the introduction of a new service provider, setting terms and conditions for issuance of a license and having power to revoke it in case of default by the license holder, encourage healthy competition and promote efficiency, make technological improvements, recommending the type of equipment to be used by service providers, finding measures for development of telecommunication technology and management of available spectrum.
(b) To fix the terms and conditions of compliance of the license notwithstanding the terms and conditions set before the passing of the Telecom and Regulatory Authority (Amendment) Act 2000, ensure technical compatibility and effective interconnection, regulate the sharing of revenue among service providers, laying down standard of quality of service of service providers, laying down time and ensuring the time period for providing the local and long-distance circuits, maintain register of interconnect services, and to keep it open for inspection, etc.
(c) Levying fees and other charges according to rates as approved by law.
(d) Perform such administrative and financial functions as entrusted to it by the Central Government.

9. Galal Ahmed & Bharat Nauriyal, *Regulation of Telecom in Developing Countries: Outcomes, Incentives and Commitment*, The World Bank, August 1995.

§5. Provision of Electronic Communications: Requirements and Conditions

I. General Authorization of Electronic Communications Networks and Services

33. The modern communications world in India is surprisingly guided and authorized by the century old main Act, the India Telegraph Act 1885. The entire world of ICT in the country is authorized by a patchwork of important legislations apart from the Telegraph Act. These are the Cable Networks Act 1995, The TRAI Act 1997 and the Prasar Bharti Act 1990. The GOI remains the highest authorizing body and has full control over the entire telecommunication system. However, the other governmental agencies include the Department of Telecommunication (DoT), the TRAI, the TDSAT and the Ministry of Information and Broadcasting. Each agency has a specialized field in the area of ICT like issuing licenses, making policies, resolving disputes and representing India at international communications forum. Government's market-friendly economic reforms which commenced in 1991 transformed the telecom, broadcasting and cable markets in the country.

34. Government's Exclusive Privilege: The Indian Telegraph Act 1885 gives exclusive privilege to the Government for establishing, maintaining and working telegraphs within India. (section 4(1)). The Telegraph Act stands as the time-tested pillar not only from the view point of its age but also from the viewpoint of its applicability in the modern communication world. This owes to the import of the term "telegraph" which means – any appliance, instrument, material or apparatus used or capable of use for transmission or reception of signs, signals, writing, images and sounds or intelligence of any nature by wire, visual or other electromagnetic emissions, radio waves or Hertzian waves, galvanic, electric or magnetic waves.[10] The Government may part with its privilege by issuing a license on certain terms and conditions. The Government by issuing a license to the service provider (the licensee) authorizes him to offer the services as agreed under the license. Thus, telecom and broadcast services are illegal if they are offered without a telegraph license.[11] The TRAI Act enlarges the legal concept of a telegraph, although somewhat indirectly. As a textual matter, the TRAI does not actually define a telegraph instead it defines the term "telecommunication service" to include service of any description (including electronic mail, voice mail, data services, audio tex services, radio paging and cellular mobile services, which is transmitted though signs, signals, writing images, and sounds or intelligence of any nature by wire, radio, visual or other electromagnetic means and also includes broadcasting and cable services. (section 2(1) (k) as expanded in January 2004).

---

10. An explanation to this section states that "radio waves" or "Hertzian waves" mean electromagnetic waves of frequencies lower than 3000 giga-cycles per second propagated in space without artificial guide section 3(IAA)/The Telegraph Act.
11. It is an offense to establish, maintain or work a telegraph in contravention of the Telegraph Act and makes it a crime for any person, with knowledge or belief about an illegally operated telegraph, to use that telegraph for messaging. [Sections 20, 21 of the Telegraph Act 1988].

II. Rights and Obligations Attached to the General Authorization

A. Establishment of Rights and Obligations

35. The rights of service providers and network operators have not been listed in the legal provisions in the country. The proposed Communication Convergence Bill 2001 however contains some rights. A "service provider" includes any person who provides a communication service.[12] However, the service provider shall not have any other right other than the right of a user for the purpose of only of laying cables or erecting posts.[13] After being authorized by the TRAI, he shall have the following rights:

- Such service provider shall have right to lay and establish cables and erect posts upon any immovable property belonging to a public authority (section 59;(1) proposed Communication Convergence Bill 2001).
- To place and maintain underground cables or posts (section 59; 2(a) proposed Communication Convergence Bill 2001).
- To enter upon such property for the purpose of checking, repairing, etc. (section 59; 2(b) proposed Communication Convergence Bill 2001).
- A service provider can make use of any private land for laying cables or erecting posts if allowed by the owner of such land (section 63 proposed Communication Convergence Bill 2001).
- In the latest regulations, the TRAI also gave right to the operators that "all access spectrums shall be shareable by two licensees having spectrum in the same band." Can be shared by MVNO (Guidelines of TRAI July 22, 2014).
- TRAI recommendations say that the mobile virtual network operators (MNVO) who do not possess spectrum have the right to tie up with existing operators without buying the spectrum (Regulation Order Dated 12 April 2011).

36. The network operators have following obligations under the Cable Television Networks (Regulation) Act 1995:

- No one can operate a telegraph without authorization or getting a license from the Government.[14]
- The Central Government can put an obligation on every cable operator to transmit or retransmit a program of any channel in public interest through addressable system.
- The Central Government can also "specify one or more free-to-air channels to be included in the package of channels" (basic service tier).
- In public interest, the Central Government can also specify the maximum rates to be charged by the operator. The Operators are under obligation to inform the subscribers about the current rates at regular intervals.
- All Cable operators must be in conformity with the advertisement Code and the Program Code (sections 5 and 6).

---

12. Section 2(29) - The Telecommunication Convergence Bill 2001.
13. Section 65 (proposed Communication Convergence Bill 2001).
14. Section 3- The Communication Convergence Bill 2001 (89 of 2001).

- The Cable operators are under obligation to maintain a register (section 7).
- The Cable operators are under obligation to use the “standard equipments” in cable television network (section 9).
- The operators are also obliged to make sure that they do not interfere with the authorized telecommunication systems.

Some of the other obligations are:

- Licenses typically include extensive network rollout obligations. These obligations required licensees to install sufficient network capacity and equipment within certain deadlines.[15]
- Licenses also contain financial and audit covenants that require licensees to maintain adequate accounts and prepare audited financial statements to reflect their operations including testing and certification requirements for the technology and equipment that licensees can use in their operations.[16]
- The licenses must provide the licensor with details regarding location of their switching centers, transmission centers and routing arrangements. The location of switches cannot be changed without the approval of the licensor.[17]
- Licensees are under obligation to cooperate with the Government in emergencies and for law enforcement and national security purposes.

B. Modification of the Obligations Attached to the General Authorization

37. It is under the general principle of the Law of Contract (The Indian Contract Act 1872) that the parties to the contract can consent for modification and amendments to an agreement. However, the agreement itself can have the clause regarding unilateral right to modify. For instance, the licensor reserves the right to modify terms and conditions on account of public interest and State security after notifying the licensee.[18] Such modifications do not require counter-signing or acknowledgement by the licensee. The notification regarding the modification can be made through a public circular. However, if the licensor reserves his unilateral right to modify then it must use this right sparingly and only for some good reason. It is emerging as a norm that the licensor (the government)/ must consult TRAI before making any modification but the government is not following this trend strictly especially when such modification is in the interest of the licensee.[19]

38. There were numerous complaints regarding arbitrary price hikes by the cable operators and hence the conditional Access system (CAS) was introduced by adding section 4A to the Cable Network (Regulation) Act 1995 in 2003.

39. The TRAI is authorized to lay down the standards of quality of service and to conduct the periodical survey of such service in the interest of general public and

15. Unified Access Service License Guidelines at para. 25.
16. Model Cellular License, Schedule II para. 24.
17. Id. at para. 42
18. *Guidelines for Issue of license for International Long-Distance Service* December 14, 2005.
19. Inter-circle Connectivity Circular at para. 5.

in the interest of consumers. Thus, the TRAI issued Direction[20] to the entire multi system operator providing cable TV services through Digital Addressable TV systems to ensure delivery of bill through post or e-mail, to provide online payment option to send electronic acknowledgment of payment of bill on the registered number of the consumer.

§6. Access and Interconnection

I. The New Concepts of Access and Interconnection

40. India experienced the first Internet access on August 15, 1995 when the indigenous VSNL launched its first services. It was opened for private participation in 1998 with a view to encourage growth of Internet penetration.

41. Interconnection: Interconnection has been defined under a number of Acts and Regulations[21] passed by the TRAI. It denoted sort of commercial and technical arrangements under which service providers connect their equipment networks in such a manner so as to enable their customer to have access to the customers, services and networks of other service providers. In India telecommunication since its inception has been interplay of the VSNL, the BSNL and the MTNL, all indigenous State authorities to manage it. However, the GOI and TRAI have always encouraged competition, the proliferation of ICTs among its masses and the cost-effective reforms. India too joined the League of Nations who encouraged maximizing of public interest and improving the quality of service and liberalization in the area of telecom thereby

---

20. Direction dated May 27, 2014. under s. 13 read with sub-clauses (i) and (v) of clause (b) of subsec (1) of s. 11 of the TRAI Act 1997 and Regulation 24 of the Standards of Quality of Service (Digital Addressable Cable TV Systems) Regulations 2012.No 6/4/2013-B & CS.
21. Section 2(g) The Intelligent Network Services in Multi Operators and Multi Network Scenario Regulations 2006.

– "Interconnections means the technical arrangements under which service providers connect, including through electromagnetic signals, their networks and services to enable their customers to have access to the customers, services and/or networks of other service providers. Section 2 ((xii) – The Register of Interconnect Agreements (Broadcasting and Cable Services) Regulations 2004."

– "Interconnection means the commercial and technical arrangements under which service providers connect their equipment, networks and services to enable their customers to have access to the customers, services and networks of other service providers." Section 2(viii) – The Telecommunication Interconnection Usage Charges Regulation 2003.

– "Interconnection means the commercial and technical arrangements under which service providers connect their equipment, networks and services to enable their customers to have access to the customers, services and networks of other service providers." Section 2(viii) - The Telecommunication Interconnect (Charges and Revenue Sharing) Regulation 2001.

– Interconnection means the commercial and technical arrangements under which service providers connect their equipment, networks and services to enable their customers to have access to the customers, services and networks of other services providers." Section 2 (iv) The Register of Interconnect Agreements Regulations 1999. Substituted by Register of Interconnect Agreements (Second Amendment) Regulations 2004 (14 of 2004) (w.e.f. 17.1.2005).

regulating interconnection with a number of regulations issued by the TRAI periodically. It aimed at multi-operator and multi-service scenario. TRAI initiated a number of consultative proceedings that collectively cover many regulatory issues addressing the needs of the new multi-carrier environment.

42. Telecom Interconnection Regulation: TRAI's Interconnection Regulation is the cornerstone of its regulatory scheme for interconnection in telecom services.[22] The regulation is a set of guidelines that apply to interconnection arrangements involving service providers with "significant market power".[23] The central feature of the regulation is a document called the Reference Interconnect Offer (RIO) which is basically an offering document in which a licensee describes its technical and commercial conditions for other licensees to interconnect with its networks. The regulation requires every licensee with "significant market power" to publish a RIO after obtaining TRAI's approval. A service provider is deemed to have "significant market power" if it controls more than 30% of the "total activity" in a licensed service area. There are four types of telecom services covered by this requirement: (1) basic or fixed line services (2) cellular services (3) national long-distance services (4) international long-distance services.[24] Individual RIOs must be consistent with the regulation's guidelines and must be based on the model RIO appended to the regulation. Once a service provider publishes its RIO, the RIO forms the basis for subsequent interconnection agreements between the service provider and other licensees and service providers. Although the RIO provides the basic elements for a licensee's interconnection arrangements, the licensees offering interconnection (the interconnection provider) and the party seeking interconnection (interconnection seeker) are free to modify and embellish RIO's provisions when formulating individual interconnection agreements.[25] An interconnection seeker may accept the interconnection provider's RIO conditions entirely and execute an agreement incorporating these conditions or it can use the RIO as the starting point to negotiate a customized interconnection agreement with the interconnection provider.

II. General Framework for Access and Interconnection

43. With the start of the Internet, India showed tremendous speed in catching up with the technological changes. Unified Access License (UAL) regime was introduced in November 2003. The license was issued on non-exclusive basis for twenty years, extendable by ten years at a time. In 2004, the Government came up with Broadband Policy 2004. The Policy lays stress on the creation of infrastructure through various technologies that contribute to the growth of broadband services. These technologies include optical fiber, Asymmetric Digital Lines (ASDL), cable TV network and Direct

22. Telecommunication Interconnection (Reference Interconnect Offer) Regulation (No. 2 of 2002) (the 'Telecom Interconnection Regulation).
23. *BSNL v. TRAI (*BSNL-III) Appeal No. 11 of 2002, (2005) 5 Comp LJ 292 (TDSAT, 27 April 2005).
24. According to the regulation's explanatory memorandum, it is an accepted regulatory principle in several countries that telecom companies with significant market power must publish reference offers regarding interconnection arrangements that affect their networks.
25. Telecom Interconnection Regulation cl.3.2

to Home (DTH). To encourage broadband connectivity both outdoor and indoor usage of low power Wi-Fi and WiMax systems in 2.4 GHz-2.4835 GHz band has been deli censed. The use of low power indoor systems in 5.15–5.35 GHz and 5.725–5.875 GHz bands has also been deli censed in January 2005. The SACFA/WPC clearance has been simplified. The setting up of National Internet Exchange of India (NIXI) would be helpful in bringing down international bandwidth cost considerably making broadband connectivity more affordable.

44. International Access: The International Telecommunication Cable Landing Stations Access Facilitation Charges And Colocation Charges Regulations 2012 (27 of 2012) defines "access facilitation" as essential facilities (including facilities for submarine cable) at cable landing station and "access facilitation Charges "means charges payable by the Indian International Telecommunication Entity to the owner of the cable landing station to interconnect or access the capacity acquired on indefeasible "Right of Use" basis or on short-term basis from an owner of the submarine cable capacity or a member of consortium owing submarine cable capacity. For every unit capacity provided on or after the first day of January 2013, the owner of cable landing station shall charge the Access Facilitation Charges as specified in the Schedule I of The International Telecommunication Cable Landing Stations Access Facilitation Charges And Colocation Charges Regulations 2012. (section 3)

45. Next-generation networks (NGN): The role of telecommunications have become not only vast but varied too with Value-Added Services (VAS). The increasing demand for VAS is compelling the service providers to plan convergence of the parallel networks into a single core network with service layers separated from network layers.[26] The NGN is a packet-based network in which service-related functions are independent from underlying transport-related technologies. It offers unrestricted access by users to different service providers and supports generalized mobility which will allow consistent and ubiquitous provision of services to users.

Access network: The user can connect to the IP-core of NGN in various ways using standard Internet Protocol (IP). Devices like mobile phones, personal digital assistants (PDAs) and computers too can register directly on NGN-core and it will not be barred by roaming even in other countries. The only requirement is that they can use IP and Session Initiation Protocol (SIP). Fixed access (like Digital Subscriber Line (DSL), cable modems, Ethernet), mobile access (like W-CDMA, CDMA2000, GSM, GPRS) and wireless access (like WLAN, WiMAX) are all supported. Other phone systems like the old telephone service and non-compatible VoIP systems are supported through gateways. With the deployment of the NGN, users may subscribe to many simultaneous access providers providing telephony, Internet or entertainment services. This may provide end users with virtually unlimited options to choose between service providers for these services in NGN environment.[27] The UAS caused hyper-competition in the telecom market in India and it became much tougher with the introduction of 3G and 4G competitive auction. According to one report some 670,000 route km (419,000 mile) of optical fibers have been laid down by major operators. Thus, to provide services in the rural areas the GOI took a proactive role to promote the NGN implementation in the country.

---

26. Consultation Paper on NGN; *Telecommunications Authority of India*. TRAI.
27. *Ibid.*

46. Interconnection: The global practice has been to have a central regulatory framework and also a number of regional groups[28] are striving to lay down a general framework as the incumbents are a big hurdle in the way of new entrants. Some countries have made the dominant operator responsible for cost-based principles to new entrants to interconnect with the other carriers such as access providers based on a regulator-approved Reference Interconnection Offer. (RIO).

47. The TRAI Through the Telecommunication Interconnection (Charges and revenue sharing) Regulation 2001 lays down the following general framework for interconnection:

- The interconnection charges shall be cost-based. For determining cost-based interconnection charges, the main basis shall be "incremental or additional" costs directly attributable to the provision of interconnection by the interconnection provider.
- No service provider shall discriminate between service providers in the matter of levying of charges for interconnection. However, a different charge shall be levied if justified on the basis of a substantial difference in costs incurred for providing that particular interconnection.
- No service provider shall be charged for any interconnection facility it does not seek or require. In case of any dispute arising between the interconnection seeker and provider of interconnection in the first case it will be mutually resolved. If it fails then it may be reported to the Authority (TRAI).
- In case of absence of a mutual agreement between the interconnection seeker and interconnection provider the charges will be as specified by the Authority when such Authority is approached.

48. The Telecommunication (Broadcasting and Cable Services) Interconnection (Digital Addressable Cable Television Systems) Regulations 2012 (No. 9 of 2012) passed by the TRAI also is the latest law which regulates interconnection in the country.

III. Conditions Applicable to Access and Interconnection

49. TRAI has come up with a number of regulations and their corresponding amendments updating it to set certain conditions before an interconnection seeker can have the interconnection facility. This results from the parent telegraph Act which is updated by TRAI Act and its amendments. A unified Access Service Provider means a Unified Access Service Provider who has been granted a license under section 4 of the Indian Telegraph Act 1885 (13 of 1885). UASP in respect of an area is one who provides unified access service according to the terms and conditions of the license.[29] The payments for the grant of the license shall include such sum attributable to the

28. The European Union (EU), the Asia Pacific Economic Cooperation (APEC), the Telecommunications Regulators Association of Southern Africa (TRASA) and Inter-American Telecommunication Commission (CITEL) and Malaysian Regulator have also issued a general framework for interconnection.
29. Explanation- Section 4- The Indian Telegraph Act 1885 (13 of 1885).

Universal Service Obligation (USO) as may be determined by the Central Government after considering the recommendation made in this behalf by the TRAI.

By virtue of section 4 of the Indian Telegraph Act 1885 (13 of 1885) the Central Government (GOI)[30] has formulated the following conditions in respect of grant of license to any person willing to enter into an agreement to provide services under the Act. The licensor reserves the right to modify the terms and conditions in public interest, in the interest of the State and for proper conduct of the Telegraphs. The conditions are:

- *General Conditions:* The general conditions include that the licensee shall ensure that total foreign equity in the paid up of the Licensee Company does not exceed 74% of the total equity (except for services for which different FDI cap has been prescribed). It will remain subject to all direct and indirect foreign investment and such investment shall be counted for the FDI ceiling. Foreign Investment shall include investment by Foreign Institutional Investors (FIIs), Non-resident Indians (NRIs), Foreign Currency Convertible Bonds (FCCBs), American Depository Receipts (ADRs), Global Depository Receipts (GDRs) and convertible, preference shares held by foreign entity. The Indian share holding shall not in any case be less than 26%.

FDI up to 49% shall be through direct route and it will be subject to the laws of India and not to foreign laws, and it will also follow the FDI policy of the GOI. The licensee is also under obligation to declare the Indian and foreign equity structure, direct and indirect in the license company. Any changes in the shareholding shall be consequently subject to the Indian laws.

The licensee shall have a minimum paid up equity capital equal to the sum of the paid up equity capital required for each service opted by the Licensee. The requirement under the license for the total minimum paid up equity capital shall be limited to INR 25 crores only. The total sum shall be in Indian Rupees. The net worth of promoters/equity shareholders shall not be counted for determining the net worth of the company. Additional service authorization shall mean fulfillment of required criteria. The license so granted shall give authority to the license holder in respect of the Services in the National Level, Telecom Circle/Metro Area Level and Secondary Switching Area (SSA) as listed in various Annexures II, V and VI of the said Order. The GOI reserves its right to operate in any area including the area for which license has been granted.

The licensee shall be free to establish, operate and maintain Telecommunication Networks and telecommunications services using any technology as per rules. In case of the license for the Access Spectrum the terms and conditions for allotment of spectrum shall apply.

The licensee shall use product and equipment that meet TEC standards. In the absence of these standards the licensee can use the equipment and products which meet the International Standardization bodies like the ITU, ETSI, IEEE, ISO, IEC,

30. Government of India – Ministry of Communications and of Telecommunications, Sanchar Bhawan, 20, Ashoka Road, New Delhi–110 001 India.

etc. or by International For a such as 3GPP, 3GPP-2, IET, MEF, WiMAX, Wi-Fi, IPTV, IPv6, etc.

The Licensee shall not provide any service for which separate authorization is required and for broadcasting services for which a separate license/registration is required as for Cable TV Networks (Regulation Act 1995 and guidelines for DTH License or any other broadcasting service issued by Ministry of Information and Broadcasting. However, there is a possibility to provide IPTV under the service authorization of Access Service/Internet service. It shall be the duty of the Licensee to make its own arrangements for all infrastructures and shall be solely responsible for installation, networking, operation and commissioning of necessary infrastructure, equipment and systems, treatment of subscriber complaints, issuance of bills, etc.

Transfer of License: The licensee is not authorized to transfer the license without the written consent of the licensor to any third party, or to sub-lease, etc. However, for the provision of the service by the licensee, he can employ franchisees, agents, distributors and employees. The licensor can control the activities of the agents or distributors through the licenses if they are found detrimental to the security of the nation. During the entire period of the license, the licensee shall follow the guidelines of the licensor issued from time to time. For the merger/demerger/acquisitions of license results from the verdict of the High Court or the Tribunal under sections 391–394 of the Companies Act 1956 will be effective only after the written approval of the Licensor.

Provision of Service: The Licensee shall be responsible for and is authorized to own, install, test and commission all the applicable systems for providing the service. The information regarding the start of the service in the Service Area will be provided by the licensee to the licensor and the licensor shall within ninety days of its presentation give the approval for it. Within fifteen days of the commencement of the service, the licensee shall intimate the licensor/TRAI about the commencement.

Duty to furnish information: The licensee is duty bound to furnish information to the licensor, to provide the licensor with such documents, accounts, estimates, returns, reports, etc., as required by the Licensor.

Penalty/Suspension/Revocation /Surrender/Termination of License: The licensor may impose a penalty not exceeding the amount as given in Annexure VI, for violation of the terms and conditions of the license agreement.

Termination of License: The licensor may through a written notice to the licensee revoke the license if: (1) licensee fails to perform his duties as prescribed; (2) fails to rectify any defect or deficiency in the equipment; (3) there is non-compliance of the terms and conditions of the license; (4) fails to comply with the FDI norms; (5) has furnished false information:

- *Commercial Conditions-Tariffs:* The Licensee shall charge the tariffs for the service provided according to the directions and orders issued by the TRAI from time to time.
- *Financial Conditions: Payment of Entry Fee and the payment of License fee is the first condition in this category. The Licensee will have to pay this as per the instructions of the TRAI and according to the standard set by it. An annual License fee as a percentage of Adjusted Gross Revenue (AGR) will have to be paid. For*

access Spectrum the a "presumptive AGR" for that authorized service and service area shall be arrived at in accordance with the relevant provision of the Notice Inviting Application(NIA) document of the auction of spectrum or conditions of spectrum allotment. In case the licensees obtain the spectrum then the licensees shall pay spectrum-related charges.

Performance Bank Guarantee (PBG) to cover the violations of the agreement and other conditions, the Licensee shall in prescribed format submit the PBG and shall maintain and keep it valid during the entire continuance of the license agreement.

Financial Bank Guarantee (FBG) – The Licensee shall submit separate FBG for the different areas. The Bank guarantee shall be valid for a period of one year. The Licensees shall extend the validity period at least one month prior to its expiry of validity. Failure to do so will amount to the violation of the conditions and the Licensor shall have power to encash it partially. It will be the duty of the Licensee to restore the encashed guarantees to the full amount failing which it will again amount to the violation of condition of license:

- *Technical Conditions*-The Licensee is under obligation to provide the details of the technology used by the licensee and which will have to be up to the standards of TEC. Where TEC standards are not possible the Licensee shall utilize only those equipment and products which are up to the international standards set by bodies such as ITU, ETSI, IEEE, ISO, IEC etc., or set by international for a such as 3GPP, 3GPP-2, IETF, MEF, Wi-Fi, WiMAX, IPTV, IPv6, etc.

The Licensee must also comply with the directions and follow the norms on electromagnetic field exposure by BTS (Base Stations). The Licensee must adopt Renewable Energy Technologies (RET) for powering the Telecom Network and must deploy energy efficient equipment.

Network Interconnection: The interconnection among networks of the Licensee shall take place if so authorized by the Licensee. In such a case, the Licensee shall conform to the TEC standards and the standards or Interface Requirements (IR) and the various Licensees must also conform to the national standards of CCS No. 7 as amended by the Telecom Engineering Center (TEC). The licensee shall interconnect with other Telecom Service Providers at the Points of Interconnection (POI). The Licensee shall operate and maintain the licensed Network conforming to Quality of Service (QoS) standards to be mutually agreed with other TSPs in respect of Network-Network Interface subject to the conditions and directions of the TRAI. The Licensee must also maintain the QoS and inform the Licensor about it periodically:

- *Operating Conditions:* The Licensee also has to follow a number of conditions in respect of its relation with the subscribers. The Licensee must without discrimination provide service to the subscribers on the same commercial principle and must maintain a transparent waiting list open to inspection. The Licensees must register the subscriber, must widely publicize the provision of service and shall not refuse registration of demand unless for any technical reason. The Licensee can suspend its services by giving sixty days' notice to the Licensor and to the subscriber. Licensee must issue bills to the subscriber and must maintain record of the entire billing, etc. For satellite-based services, the Licensee must take necessary clearances from INSAT Network Operations Control Center (NOCC) on payment of prescribed charges.

The Licensee must not provide service to Telecom Service Provider who do not require license under section 4 of the Indian Telegraph Act 1885 or whose license has been revoked or suspended.

During the entire period of the license, the Licensee shall be subject to the relevant provisions of the Indian Telegraph Act 1885 (13 of 1885), The Indian Wireless Telegraphy Act 1933, The Telecom and Regulatory Authority of India Act 1997 and the Information Technology Act 2000:

– *Security Conditions:* The Licensee shall have to take special care of security-related instructions of the Licensor. Must provide full access to the switching centers, transmission centers, routers and other network elements including equipment installed. All the foreign personnel deployed by the Licensee must get security clearance from the GOI. The Licensee shall be fully responsible for the security of the entire networks and shall have organizational policy on security and security management of their networks including Network Forensics, Network hardening, Network penetration test, etc., and must also follow the ISO standards as applicable at the relevant time. The licensee must also take care that the Telecom Infrastructure and installations do not become a safety or health hazard.

Calling Line Identification (CLI) shall be provided by the licensee and the network should also support Malicious Call Identification and Centralized Automatic Message Accounting (CAMA) and similar safety measures maintaining at the same time privacy of communication.

Any violation of the safety measures would if amounting to an offense be dealt with the Indian Penal Code 1860.

§7. Numbering

I. General Statement

50. Like the rest of the world, India too has witnessed a paradigm shift in the telecom sector as the telecommunication, information technology and broadcasting industries converge. The Government showed a longer vision and is continuously coming up with futuristic plans to take maximum mileage out of the present ICT scenario. The thrust area for the Government has been; coming up with measures for optimal utilization of numbers, short codes and INSCP Codes, pricing of numbers, taking note of the worldwide expansion of the Internet Protocol (IP) long-lasting suitability of numbering plan, impact of Mobile Number Portability (MNP) and carrier selection on the numbering plan and review of the SDCA-based Numbering Scheme.

Thus, numbering plan is a "Fundamental Plan" which is updated to meet the challenges of the ever growing telecommunications. On the one hand, the progress has opened wide doors for revenue streams for the operators it also opens new possibilities of better, faster and cheaper services for the consumer.

The area and time of service is growing continuously. To achieve this ubiquity the main resource the number resource is used to identify and differentiate among the end users. Numbering and Electronic Addressing are concerns not only for the telecommunications service providers but also they are equally important for ISPs, broadcasters and IT companies, Content Providers, governments, regulators and the end users. The availability of numbering resource for telecommunications services akin to spectrum for wireless services is finite and scarce. Substantial revision of the numbering plan is complex, time consuming and expensive and thus it becomes all the more important to use these resources in a sensible and planned manner.

II. National Numbering Plans

51. India has promptly responded to the speeding ICT industry both in planning and in practice. The National Numbering Plan (NNP) provides a set of rules and guidelines for the use and assignment of numbers to telephone services delivered over the public Networks. The Plan includes assignment of numbers to international services, trunk service, emergency services and special services such as voice mail and intelligent Network (IN). The structure of the national number complies with the International Telecommunication Union Standard Sector (ITU-T) Recommendations.

52. From 1993 when the first number plan was done, India has revised it several times, the last time in 2008. The National Fundamental Plan 1993 was done at a time when the country was not fully aware of the Internet idea and the basic telecommunication services were at a very rudimentary and simpler stage. The cellular mobile services had just begun, paging services were coming through and the main operator was the Government or the public sector undertakings. Number allocation was thus a simple job.

53. National numbering Plan 2003: About a decade later the telecommunications scenario in the country underwent a big change, the introduction of the Internet, privatization in the telecom sector all necessitated a new plan which is futuristic and flexible and which could be affecting the telecommunications activities for the next thirty years. The NNP 2003 was formulated with a projected forecast of 50% tele-density by the year 2030. This made numbering space available for 750 million telephone connections in the country comprising the anticipated number of 300 million basic and 450 million cellular mobile connections. The NNP 2003 was intended to conform with International Telecommunications Union (ITU) standards, meet the new challenges, reserve numbering capacity to meet the undefined future needs, support effective competition by fair access to numbering resources, standardize number length wherever possible and to keep the changes in the existing scheme to a minimum.

54. Modifications to NNP 2003: Taking into consideration the evolving needs in the telecommunication sector the TRAI recommended two changes in it in March and April of 2006. These were -permitting usage of strings containing #, $, £, etc., for accessing High Speed Data Services in Wireless Networks and second, permitting use of * and # provisioning of value-added intra-network services like USSD (Unstructured Supplementary Service Data) by Access Providers.

55. The Inevitable Changes: Though a time frame of thirty years was thought for the viability of the NNP2003 but unprecedented growth of the mobile segment, gradual migration from circuit switching to packet switching, increase in number of connections and the telecommunication subscriber-based density reached 384.79 million and overall tele-density reached 33.23% in December 2008. The new technologies like VoIP, (Voice over Internet Protocol), Third Generation Networks (3G), Next Generation Network (NGN), General Packet Radio Service(GPRS), Wireless Fidelity (Wi-Fi), Wireless Interoperability for Micro wave Access (WiMAX), etc., created new pressure on numbering resources. Thus, on March 20, 2008 Amendment to National Numbering Plan 2003 was made[31] with following changes: (i) Level "90" is earmarked as access code for Cellular Mobile Services and can be allocated for the same; (ii) Level "91" earmarked as access code for Cellular Mobile Services can also be allocated for the same; (iii) IN services allocated in level"090" is to be shifted to IN service level "1800" and suitable allocation shall be made; iv) paging services shall be allocated an access code in level"8" if required.

III. Numbering Management and Allocation

56. Numbers have played a crucial role in telecommunication and a well-designed numbering plan ensures a structured approach to allocation and assignment of numbers which is in accordance with the international standards. Numbering plan must take into account the effect which developments like convergent services, smart services, machine-to-machine communication and premium services are likely to make in the numbering resources. In India, the last major review of the numbering plan was made through the Numbering Plan 2003 having space for 750 million telephone connections, 450 million cellular mobile and 300 million basic connections. With the mammoth expansion of the telecommunication services, presence of large number of competitive service providers, and massive growth in number of connection especially in the mobile segment the TRAI in 2010 felt need for revision of the allocation system.

Allocation Criteria – The Consultation Paper of TRAI also considered the allocation criteria in which the larger and quicker allocation of numbers as demanded by the service providers was given importance. The proper management of the numbering resources through a numbering returns that would not only include parameters to see how the numbers have been used but also some future management is also done also gained importance.

57. Department of Telecommunications (DoT): DoT is the central authority in the country for number planning and allocation of numbers. India follows ITU-T E.164 recommendations with open numbering plan 450 million mobile and 300 million fixed numbers.

---

31. Office Memorandum No. 16 -3/2003-BSII/Vol.VIII dated Mar. 20, 2008; DoT, Ministry of Communications & Information Technology Government of India. New Delhi.

Presently, ten-digit numbering scheme excluding "0" has been adopted both for the fixed and mobile telephones.[32] For fixed line, the STD code of the Short Distance Charging Area (SDCA) is included in ten digits. For local dialing, the number of digits to be dialed varies with the capacity of the SDCA. And for mobile, it is ten digits for local dialing. Number allocation is as follows:

- *Fixed Line Services*—The Service Providers have been given pre-defined levels that decide the amount of numbering resources they have. The level allocated to different service providers is as follows:

  (1) BSNL/MTNL – Complete Level 2.
  (2) Reliance Communications – Complete Level 3.
  (3) Bharti Airtel – Complete Level 4.
  (4) Shyam/HFCL – Sublevels of Level 5.
  (5) Tata Tele Services – Complete Level 6.
  (6) M's Data com – Sublevels of Level 7.

  For two- and, three-digit SDCA code exchanges, a block of 1, 00,000 numbers and for four-digit SDCA code exchanges, a block of 10,000 numbers are allocated. The service providers are also allowed to use these allocated numbers in more than one circle. If the service providers after they demonstrate 80% utilization of numbers already allocated to them make a request then additional numbers are allocated to them.
- For Mobile Services: Level 9 is earmarked for mobile services. Mobile service providers are allocated 1 million numbers in an area as a start and additional numbers are allocated without any charge, on request after 60% utilization. M/s BSNL has been allotted complete level"94" for their mobile services. M/s Reliance Communication Ltd. And M/s Tata Teleservices Ltd were initially allotted some sub-levels of "93" and "92" respectively for migration from limited mobility to full mobility in CDMA network. Later complete "93" level has been allotted to M/s Reliance Communications Ltd and "92" level to M/s Tata Teleservices Ltd.

58. The anticipated scenario and a package planning ahead for about thirty years by the NNP 2003 were saturated in 2009. The gross underestimation is evident from the fact that the fixed lines slipped down from 42 million in April 2009 to 36.83 million in April 2010. The anticipated figure of 450 million connections by 2030 was easily achieved in 2009 and it is expected that the 1 billion mark would exceed by the end of 2014. The NNP 2003 no longer matched with this exponential speed and there arose

32. There was a survey in which the stakeholders were asked about the adoption of 11-digit number or to continue with the 10digit one. The majority of stake holders rejected the 11 digit proposal saying that it is avoidable at present (2010) as it is inconvenient from the view point of the subscribers and time consuming and challenging from the view point of the subscribers. Recommendations on Efficient Utilization of Numbering Resources- ***Telecommunications Regulatory Authority of India*** –August 20, 2010.

an emergent situation to review it.[33] Thus, inclusion of allocation criteria concentrated on larger and quicker allocation of numbers that some service providers had raised from time to time. There was also plan for management of the numbering resources through a numbering return that would not only include parameters to see how the numbers have been used but also forecast of requirement that would help the Numbering Plan in advance.

IV. Number Portability

59. The Government sanctioned Mobile Number Portability (MNP) which allows a mobile phone user to retain their original numbers and switching off to another mobile network operator. It is a subscriber-friendly option at the same time it promises improvement in the quality of service (QoS). The government has announced guidelines for MNP License in the country on August 1, 2008 and has issued a separate License for MNP on March 20, 2009.It has identified two MNP operators for two zones in the country and issued licenses to them and decided to implement it from December 31, 2009 in Metros and category "A" service areas and by March 20, 2010 in rest of India. The Department of Telecommunication (DoT) has already issued licenses to two global Syniverse Technologies Pvt. Ltd. And M/s MNP Interconnection Telecom Solutions India Pvt. Ltd. And MNP is implemented in the whole country in one go from October 31, 2010.

60. The Regulatory Framework: *The Telecommunications Number Portability Regulations 2009* has been passed by TRAI after consulting all the stakeholders. The Regulations provide a framework for governing relevant aspects of MNP by:

- laying down clear eligibility conditions for porting of mobile telephone numbers;
- defining rights and obligations of various stakeholders i.e., the Donor Operator, the Recipient Operator and the MNP service provider;
- laying down procedure to be followed by each player in the chain in processing number porting request;
- Specifying clear time limits for completion of various steps by each player in the chain i.e., the Donor Operator, the Recipient Operator and the MNP service provider; and
- providing for least disruption of service to the consumer.

The Telecommunications Number Portability Regulations 2009 has been amended by the formulation of the – The Telecommunications Number Portability (Second

33. The TRAI managed to have a Consultation Paper entitled ***"Efficient Utilization of Number Resources"*** with all the stakeholders and the last date was Feb. 19, 2010. The discussion focused mainly on three areas; long-term suitability of the numbering plan, allocation criteria for numbers for fixed line and mobile services and annual numbering return and pricing of numbers.

Amendment) Regulations 2010 by TRAI by which certain amendments[34] have been made in the 2009 Regulations.

61. Salient features of The Telecommunications Number Portability Regulations 2009 – These Regulations have the following salient features:

(1) MNP facility is allowed only within a given licensed service area.
(2) A subscriber can make a request of porting only after ninety days of its connection and for reporting his number yet another ninety days' period must pass.
(3) The subscriber wishing to port must approach the Recipient Operator[35] and must also pay the required charges to him.
(4) The subscriber is also required to clear all the dues of the Donor Operator[36] and he must assure the Recipient Operator that in the event of his not paying all the dues to the Donor Operator his ported mobile number is liable to be disconnected by the Recipient Operator.
(5) A subscriber can withdraw his porting request within twenty-four hours of his request and in which case the porting charges are non-refundable. The Regulation envisages four days for the porting process to be completed.
(6) Access Providers are required by the Regulation to implement all Call Query method.
(7) The Originating Operator shall be responsible to route the call to correct terminating network.

62. The Telecommunication Mobile Number Portability Per Port Transaction Charge and Dipping Charge Regulations 2009.[37]Although the MNP is subscriber-friendly and also improves the quality of service, yet it was felt that the service providers do not benefit from it and are required to carry extra burden as explained below:

– Compensation for network up gradation: The MNP requires modification both in the hardware and software of the service providers making it compliant to the required MNP. This necessitates compensation and reimbursement of the service providers.

---

34. In sub-regulation (2) of Regulation 1 of the Telecommunications Number Portability Regulations 2009 for Clause (b), following clause has been substituted which says;

"(b) Regulations 6, 7, 8, 9, 10, 11, 12 and 13 of these regulations shall come into force in Haryana service areas on the Nov. 25, 2010

Provided that Regulations 6, 7, 8, 9, 10, 11, 12 and 13 of these regulations shall come into force in different service areas as may be specified by direction issued by the authority from time to time.

– In Regulation 10 of the 2009 Regulations for the words "twenty-hours", wherever appearing, the words "four working days" shall be substituted.

35. Means an Access Provider who will be providing mobile telecommunication service to the subscriber after porting and includes his agent (s. 2(q)).

36. Means a Cellular Telecom Service provider or Unified Access Service Provider, to whose network the mobile number belongs at the time the subscriber makes a request for porting (s. 2(e)).

37. Notification No. 116-5/2009-MN,dated Nov. 20, 2009. Published in the Gazette of India. Extra, Part III, s. 4, dated Nov. 20, 2009.

- Compensation for Donor Operator: Extra cost is incurred in processing the porting as well as loss of recurring revenue due to switch over of the subscriber to a competing provider.
- Although the Authority (TRAI) did not agree with all of the above arguments, the Telecommunication Mobile Number Portability per Port Transaction Charge and Dipping Charge Regulations 2009 are formulated fixing the Per Port Transaction Charge at INR 19 (section 3). As for the Dipping Charge, mutual agreement has been struck between the Mobile Number Portability Service Provider and the Access Provider or International Long Distance Operator.

§8. Radio Spectrum

I. Introduction

63. Radio frequency is a limited natural resource and the word "Spectrum" actually denotes a collection of various types of electromagnetic radiations of different wavelengths. In India, radio frequencies are used for multiple services like space communication, mobile communication, broadcasting, radio navigation, mobile satellite services and aeronautical satellite services and for defense communications. There are about 650 million subscribers on date (2010). Thus, it is one of the most crowded spectrums thereby resulting in poor voice quality, call drop, undelivered messages and such other minor complaints.

With the expansion of telecommunication, made possible by the ICTs, the spectrum has become indispensable for easy flow of information. Thus, international cooperation in this area has become important never as before; sharing of the electromagnetic spectrum is for the benefit of each country hence The ITU at the World Radio Communication Conferences allocates spectrum frequencies to various countries. Allocation of spectrum on common bands has also become necessary for international facility on phones. As the mobile handsets are aligned to the GSM 900/1800 bands hence common bands would facilitate international services.

II. Management of the Radio-Electric Public Domain

64. The Wireless Planning and Coordination (WPC) wing of the Ministry of Communications established in 1952 is the National Radio Regulatory Authority responsible for Frequency Spectrum Management including licensing and it entertains all the wireless users in the country. WPC is divided into major sections like the Licensing and Regulation (LR), New Technology Group (NTG), and Standing Advisory Committee on Radio Frequency Allocation (SACFA). SACFA is responsible for taking care of major frequency issues, making of the frequency allocation plan, making recommendations on the various issues related to ITU and to sort out problems referred to the committee by various wireless users.

65. The TRAI is the independent regulator of telecommunication business in India. Apart from other objectives to enhance telecommunication business the TRAI also recommends and regulates the timing and need for the introduction of the new service provider, ensures successful interconnection and technical compatibility between various service providers. It also lays down terms and conditions for the issuance of license to a service provider.

66. In India the policy document on spectrum is the National Frequency Allocation Plan – 2008 which was made effective from April 1, 2009. National Frequency Allocation Plan (NFAP) also manages the radio frequency spectrum in general. It forms the basis for the development and manufacturing of wireless equipment and spectrum utilization in the country. Although spectrum allocations are available from 9 kHz to 1000 GHz in the radio regulations, the usable part of spectrum is much less due to availability of equipment and economy of scale. Thus, spectrum review is basically for the frequency band below 100GHz. The radio frequency spectrum is shared by various radio communication services for variety of applications including public telecom services, aeronautical and maritime safety communications, radars, seismic surveys, rocket and satellite launching, earth exploration, natural calamities forecasting, etc.

67. The government of India attaches great importance to spectrum management and the radio regulatory process. With the rapid expansion of the telecommunication services, spectrum management has become not only intricate but also challenging. As per New Telecom Policy -99, the NFAP is to be revised in line with the decisions of the World Radio communication Conferences. In the aftermath of the World Radio communication Conference held in 2007,the NFAP-2008 has been revised according to its decisions in line with the outcome of WRC-07 to meet the spectrum requirements amidst fast growing wireless technologies. Thus, India came up with National Frequency Allocation Plan -2011 to encourage and promote indigenous technologies by provisioning of small chunk of the spectrum in certain frequency bands, sub-bands in small limited geographical areas. The Salient Features of the NFAP-2011 are:

- It is in the spirit of the decisions of the World Radio communication Conference 2007 of the International Telecommunication Union contained in Radio Regulation (ed. 2008).
- It is developed to cater to newly emerging technologies such as Ultra Wide Band (UWB), Intelligent Transport System (ITS), Short Range Devices, etc.
- Efforts are made to ensure equitable and optimum utilization of the scarce and limited natural resource of radio frequency spectrum.
- It has enabled provisions in few frequency bands for indigenous development and manufacturing.
- Due care is taken to ensure protection of existing services.

68. National Telecom Policy 2012: With the expansion of wireless technologies in delivery of services in ICT, Sector NTP-2012 incorporates framework for increasing the availability of spectrum for telecom services including triple play services (voice, video and data) for which broadband is the key driver. This will be facilitated by deployment of services through appropriate instrumentalities at the same time safeguarding national interest.

III. Rights of Use for the Radio-Electric Public Domain

A. General Statement

69. Globally speaking, spectrum is a scarce resource. It is thus subject to strict government regulation, which entails identifying and fencing off specific frequency bands for the exclusive use of designated persons or entities. The future growth in telecom services would be wireless centric. Even at present spectrum management is very vital and with the entry of multiple operators offering various telecom services using different kinds of wireless technologies and with the trends of convergence the task of spectrum management is becoming more complex. Thus, keeping in mind the scarcity principle, there are two principal concepts associated with spectrum regulation: (1) allocation and (2) assignment. Allocation implies the designation or earmarking of a range of radio frequencies for users within a specific country. The ITU is usually responsible for making international allocations of frequencies among countries. The ITU is required to be strict in such allocation so as to respect each nation and its geographical boundaries. Allocation also denotes the domestic classification of various types of spectrum uses within a country. Thus, the total amount of spectrum allocated to a country by the ITU is re-allocated within that country among different categories of needs and services in accordance with national priorities and strategies. Assignment refers to specific allotment of frequencies among individual users and it may impose conditions and restrictions.

70. In the beginning spectral efficiency was limited in India due to the limited availability of spectrum. With the expansion of spectrum the number of subscribers were given preference over use of efficiently using other inputs like the Base Transceiver Stations (BTS). Thus, technical efficiency resulted in high reuse of spectrum hence more BTS and cell towers. In some areas the inter-site distance between cell towers is less than 100 meters which is one of the lowest in the world leading to iron clad structures clogging some of the cities. This results in the decline of the unit costs and an increase in the scale of the operation in respect of the range of subscriber minutes observed in the industry to date. In this respect the policy makers allow accumulation of spectrum where such accumulation leads to lower costs without increased threat of cartelization. This would allow operators to integrate operations and aggregate spectrum holdings to take advantage of economies of scale.

B. The Rights of Use for the Radio-Electric Public Domain

71. Right to use the spectrum: This License Agreement does not confer any right to allotment and use of spectrum for which separate specific Frequency Allotment and Wireless Operating License (WOL) shall be required from WPC Wing. The National Telecom Policy 2012 ensures availability of adequate spectrum to meet current and future demand for microwave access/backhaul in appropriate frequency bands. It also proposes to delink spectrum in respect of all future licenses. Spectrum shall be made available at a price determined through market-related process. This is further assured by the spectrum management goals that it will move at the earliest towards liberalization of spectrum to enable use of spectrum in any band to provide any service in any technology as well as to permit spectrum pooling, sharing and later trading to enable optimal utilization of spectrum through appropriate regulatory framework.

C. Procedure for Limiting the Number of Rights of Use

72. The mobile subscribers have added to the use of spectrum requiring more base stations or a large amount of spectrum. The utilization of spectrum for commercial purposes began in the country in 1995. There is no specific provision in the archaic laws namely: The Indian Telegraph Act 1885; The Indian Wireless Telegraphy Act 1933; The Information Technology Act 2000 or in the National Frequency Plan 2011 regarding the procedure for limiting the number of rights of use of the spectrum. To overcome this lacuna the National Telecom Policy of India 1999 and NTP 2012 also slightly touch upon it. The Communication Convergence Bill 2001 however when enacted will make India one of the few countries of the world to have such legislation. It contains some provisions regarding it which are as follows: (1) no one is allowed to use any part of the spectrum without assignment from the Central Government or the Commission when established under the present Act; (2) all the public service broadcasters must have license and registration to own or provide any network infrastructure facility or networking service or any value-added network application. The Bill also proposes the establishment of a Spectrum management Committee with the Spectrum Manager; (3). the Spectrum manager shall assign frequencies, allocate frequencies, monitor the utilization of the spectrum all users. The Communication Commission of India is made responsible for assignment of the non-strategic and commercial spectrum.

73. The National Telecommunication Policy 2012: The NTP has made valuable proposals regarding spectrum management as follows: (a) to make effort for liberalization of spectrum to enable use of spectrum in any band to provide any service; (b) to make periodic audit of spectrum utilization; (c) to make spectrum available for new technologies; (d) prepare a roadmap for availability of additional spectrum every five years; (e) to make available adequate globally harmonized IMT spectrum in the 450 MHz,700 MHz, 1800 MHz, 2.1 GHz, 2.3GHz, 2.5GHz, 3.5GHz bands and other bands to be identified by ITU for commercial mobile services; (f) to identify additional frequency bands periodically for exempting them from licensing requirements for operation of low power devices for public use; (g) to encourage indigenous development of technologies; (h) to review the existing geographical unit of allocation of spectrum with a view to identifying scope for optimization; (i) to promote use of white spaces with low power devices without causing harmful interference to the licensed applications in specific frequency bands by deployment of Software Defined Radios (SDRs), Cognitive Radios (CRs).

D. Conditions Attached to the Rights of Use and Procedure for its Modification

There is no specific provision for this in the telecommunication Law of India

E. The Transfer of Rights to Use the Radio-Electric Public Domain

There is no specific provision for this in the telecommunication Law of India

§9. Public Service Obligations and Other Public Rights and Obligations

I. General Statement

74. National Task Force on Information Technology and Software Development (IT Task force) was constituted in 1998 by the GOI with the objective of establishing an enabling environment to promote the usage of ICT in School education area and for availability of access devices, connectivity to the Internet and promotion of ICT literacy.

II. Public Service Obligations

A. Introduction

75. The Telecom connectivity in India has been dense and ever increasing. The deep penetration into rural India of mobile telephony has been made possible in 2006 with the amendment of the Indian Telegraph Act 1885 to support mobile and broadband facility in the Universal Service Obligation Fund (USOF). It has covered the area of Individual Access, the Public Access, etc. The provision of public access facilities by way of Village Public Telephones (VPTs) and Rural Community Phones (RCPs) have been provided. Economic benefits like Stimulation of Rural Economic Growth, Rural BPOs and KPOs, Positive Externalities by connecting more and more people to the benefits of ICT and social benefits like Social Development, Government Services and Main Streamlining Rural India have been achieved with the expansion of ICT to the remote areas.

B. Universal Service

1. Concept and Scope

76. India is basically an agricultural country and majority of the population lives in rural India. As such the need of a greater chunk of the population to avail of and benefit from ICTs is more significant in the country. However, the high capital cost and a lower revenue generation in these areas comes as a hurdle in extending the fruits of ICT to these remote and rural areas. Normal market forces cannot be the incentive for the telecom sector to serve these backward areas. To balance the inadequate market mechanism and the communicational and other needs of these inaccessible areas, for providing the vital telecom connectivity to them a global drive to provide Universal Access and Universal Service to ICT has also been shared by India. "Universal Service Obligation" means "the obligation to provide access to telegraph services to people in the rural and remote areas at affordable and reasonable prices."[38] The New Telecom Policy-1999 provided that the resources for meeting the USO would be raised through a "Universal Access Levy" ("UAL") which would be a percentage of the revenue earned by the operators under various licenses. The Universal Service Support Policy came into effect from 0104-2002. The Indian Telegraph (Amendment) Act 2003 gives a statutory status to the USOF. The Indian Telegraph (Amendment) Rules 2004 lays down the administrative framework for the said USOF. The Indian Telegraph Act 1885 as amended in 2003, 2006, 2008 provides for the exclusive utilization of the Fund for the Universal Service Obligation.

2. Designation of Operators

77. The implementation of USO-related activities is carried out by the "eligible operators" as the Indian Telegraph (amendment) Rules covering Basic Service Operators, Cellular Mobile service Providers, Unified Access Services Licensees and Infrastructure Providers (IP-I). These providers are both public and private sector companies

3. Costing and Financing of Universal Service Obligations

78. The Indian Telegraph (amendment) Act 2003 added Part IIA to the Indian Telegraph Act 1885 (13 of 1885) for the establishment of the USOF (Section 9-A). The Fund is kept under the Control of the GOI and all the moneys shall be credited to the Fund as follows:

- The sums of money received towards the USO under section 4[39] shall first be credited to the Consolidated Fund of India and if by virtue of law the Parliament of India approves then such sum shall be credited to the Fund for being utilized exclusively for meeting the USO (section 9B).
- If the Parliament by law authorizes then the GOI shall by way of Grants and loans credit necessary sums of money in the Fund (section 9C).

---

38. Section 3(1A) Inserted by Act 8 of 2004. The Indian telegraph Act 1885 (13 of 1885).
39. Power of the Government of India to grant license can be on certain payments. The explanation to Section 4 thus reads - *Explanation-* The payments made for the grant of a license under this sub-section shall include such sum attributable to the USO as may be determined by the Central Government(Government of India) after considering the recommendation made in his behalf by the Telecom and Regulatory Authority of India established under subs. (1) of s. 3 of the Telecom and Regulatory Authority Act 1997 (24 of 1997).- The Indian Telegraph Act 1885 (13 of 1885).

- The balance to the credit of the Fund shall not lapse at the end of the financial years.

79. Administration and Utilization of Fund: The GOI is the ultimate authority in matter of administration and utilization of the Fund. The Government is authorized to use the fund according to the rules so made from time to time. The Fund shall be exclusively used for meeting the USO and the Government shall be responsible for the coordination and timely utilization and release of sums in accordance with the criteria set by the Rules made (section 9D).

80. Resources: The resources for implementation of USO are raised through a Universal Service Levy (USL) presently fixed at 5% of the Adjusted Gross Revenue (AGR) of all Telecom Service Providers except the pure value-added service providers like Internet, Voice Mail, E-Mail service providers, etc. The GOI is also authorized to give grants and loans. (section 9-C; The Indian Telegraph Act 1885 as amended 2003). The annual revenue share license fee shall be reduced to the extent of reduction in contribution towards USOF levy if the license in the service area meets the prescribed qualification. The balance to the credit of the Fund shall not lapse at the end of the financial year. (section 9-A (2) (c) (The Indian Telegraph Act 1885, as amended 2003). Credits to the Fund shall be subject to approval by the Parliament.

81. The Rules: The Rules for administration of the Fund known as Indian Telegraph (Amendment) Rules were originally published on March 26, 2004. The Rules were later amended in order to enable support for mobile services and broadband connectivity in rural and remote areas of the country as Indian Telegraph (amendment) Rules 2006 and the same were published on November 17, 2006. The Rules were again amended to provide subsidy support to eligible operators for operational sustainability of Rural Wireline Household DELs installed prior to April 01, 2002, for a period of three years subject to a ceiling of INR 2000 crores (20 Billion) per annum for the country. The latest are the Indian Telegraph (Amendment) Rules 2008 published on July 18, 2008.

C. Other Public Service Obligations

82. The Central Government and the various State Governments, various autonomous bodies and Public Sector Undertakings have made prolific use of ICT. For almost all the departments, public or private it has become the mainstay of carrying out their functions. The initiatives are many and have come up in varied environments to address different needs of citizens, businesses, governance, organizations, etc. Major means for service delivery has been through e-governance initiatives. The major thrust for use of ICT in the governments has been through the National e-Governance Plan (NeGP) which is steered by the Department of Information Technology under the Ministry of Communications and Information Technology, GOI.

83. According to the United Nations Public Administration Programme, Public Service Obligations include the following:

- Bhoomi: The online delivery of land titles. Though made on August 20, 2008 in the Department of Revenue in the State of Karnataka it has now become popular with most of the States in the country.
- The E-District: The Tiruvarur District of the State of Tamil Nadu had accomplished near total automation of Government functioning at the grass root level in Taluk office District Rural Agency DRDA, Collectroate Block offices, Town Panchayat office and Regional Transport office, Land Record administration, etc. (Created August 20, 2008).
- FRIENDS: The online Citizen Payment –FRIENDS Fast Reliable Instant Efficient Network for Disbursement of Services centers offers a one-stop front end IT enabled payment corner.
- Central Vigilance Commission Website: To propagate the idea of zero tolerance for corruption the website was created in 2008.
- Gyandoot: Community – Owned Rural Intranet Kiosks – launched in January 2000 is recognized as a breakthrough in e-government demonstrating a paradigm shift. It is a low cost rural Intranet.
- Tender Notice Information System: The Department of administrative Reforms published details of tender notices on the Internet via the Tender Notice information system of the Government of Delhi.
- Public Distribution Management System: Through this project the preparation of below-poverty –level and above-poverty level ration cards was computerized.
- Management Information System for Education: It serves mainly as a means of adding, editing details about schools/employees searching for schools/employees online transferring relieving and joining of employees and generating various reports.
- Computerized Bus Pass System: The Delhi Transport Corporation launched the computerization of bus passes through which passes and ID Cards could be issued.
- Web-Based Blood Bank Management System: This System of the department of Health and Family welfare provides stock of blood for different groups in the various blood banks.

84. Many telecom and cable companies rely on physical connections such as wires and cables to connect their customers to their networks, switches and exchanges. Most of the service providers usually find it convenient to place their wires and cables along major highways and roads using rights of way. The National Highway Authority of India (NHAI) is the major government authority in respect of highways and a right-of-way clearance is required from it. The Border Roads Organization is also involved in it.[40] In states also the licensees are required to approach the local PWDs (Public Works Department) state highway agencies, etc. Clearance of right-of-way applications takes ample time. However, states like Tamil Nadu have streamlined procedures for processing right-of-way applications from telecom licensees and IUT Companies.

40. *See* , Ministry of Road Transport and Highways "Laying of Optical Fibre Cables and Telecom Ducts on National Highway Land" ,No. R-W/NH-33044/17/2000-S&R July 23, 2003.

D. *Colocation and Facility Sharing*

85. Currently, there are ninety-seven colocation centers from nineteen areas in India. The country offers a wide range of units and companies that give facility to the customers to locate their servers at minimum cost and complexity. The shared infrastructure of a data center gives security to the customer at competitive rates. Such centers are equipped with secure hosting area, air-conditioning, fire system, power backups security and round-the-clock technical support. The Software Technology Park of India STPI is one of the first ISP license with operational jurisdiction covering all of India. It provides leased line services to the premium segment where quality is of utmost concern. The national service delivery and management infrastructure includes fifty-one independent gateways, huge quantities of international bandwidth on international fiber and satellites a NOC, comprehensive Network Management Systems (NMS), a data center and a disaster recovery (DR) site.

E. *User's Rights*

1. Generally

86. We are living in a networked society. The ICTs have made digital communication more Pan earth, affordable, speedy and accessible as never before. ICTs have become a harbinger of knowledge sharing, information exchange, and of boosting the quality of life. It also enhances many fundamental human rights such as the right to health, education, freedom of assembly, freedom to move, to travel. It is estimated that by 2017, 90% of the world's population will have 3G coverage, 50% shall have 4G coverage and by 2018 Smartphone subscriptions will exceed 3 billion. In June 2011, the "Report of the special Rapporteur on the promotion and protection of the right to freedom of opinion and expression" presented to the seventeenth session of the United Nations Human Rights Council" appealed to all the states to provide maximum facilitates to the users and citizens regarding universal access to the Internet.

§10. Administrative Charges

87. The TRAI revises the spectrum allocation charges and spectrum fee. It is the main body which makes recommendations and advises the Ministry to revise/amend/increase the charges. It is a constantly changing phenomenon and also depends much on the fiscal policy of the government. The Department of Telecommunication (DOT) has recently (January 2014) considered a middle ground to resolve that stalemate over introducing a uniform spectrum usage charge regime. Under the existing rules, operators are required to pay a fee for using spectrum. This fee ranging between 1% and 8% of annual revenue is determined on the quantum of spectrum an operator holds. TRAI proposed to change this. Thus, in the new plan the usage fee for incumbent mobile operators will be brought down to 3% of the annual revenues compared with a maximum charge of 8% at present. The TRAI suggested increasing the license fee from the existing 6%–8% which will help the government to plug loss of revenues as some ISPs and BWA (Broadband Wireless Access) spectrum holders did not roll out services despite obtaining the spectrum in 2010. TRAI suggested a new definition of revenue for ISPs on which the government should levy 8% annual fee.

88. India expects to raise INR 45,471.02 crores in the current financial year through March 31, 2015 from communication services including proceeds from spectrum auction and one-time charges as against INR 40,847.06 crores estimated to have been raised in 2013–2014.

Chapter 2. Regulation of Competition in the ICT Market

§1. General Statement

89. India has become a global leader in the ICT sector, capitalizing on its talent pool, innovative entrepreneurs, lower cost of operation, online retailing, cloud computing, e-commerce and the innovative remote delivery model and has become one of the fastest growing ICT markets in the world. The market size of information technology in India is expected to touch USD 44.8 billion in 2014 as compared to USD 35.1 billion in 2012 as per International Data Corporation. (IDC). The IT infrastructure market (comprising servers, storage and networking equipment) is projected to grow to USD 2.1 billion in 2013, an increase of 9.7% as compared to 2012 (Gartner).The market is driven by hardware refresh, optimization and consolidation efforts. The construction of new data centers gives added impetus to a market primarily driven by service providers. The telecom sector showing phenomenal growth in the few decades has become the second largest telephone network in the world after China. As per Gartner the mobile services market in India is expected to grow to INR 1.2 lakh crores (USD 19.97 billion) in 2013 an increase of 8% from 1.1 lakh crores (USD 18.28 billion) in 2012.

90. Regulation and Competition are antagonists but they are also indispensable. To achieve the goal of competition regulatory measures must focus at competitive environment. With its more attractive investor-friendly policies and foreign direct investment (FDI) policies India has become a promising ICT market. Chart A below shows the length and breadth of the ICT market in India and its upward graph. Liberalization started in 1981 when India signed contracts with Alcatel of France to merge with the State-owned Telecom Company the ITI to set up 5 million lines per year. In 1994, the Indian Government introduced a National Telecommunications Policy that changed ownership, business management and regulation of ITI. Complete ownership of facilities was restricted only to the government organizations. After 1995, with the passing of the Telecommunications Regulatory Authority of India Act 1997 the Telecommunications Regulatory Authority of India (TRAI) was established which reduced government interference in deciding tariffs and policy making in the telecom sector. At this juncture, the World Bank and ITU advised the Indian Government to liberalize long-distance services to relax the monopoly of the State-owned companies and to facilitate competition in the long-distance carrier business which would help reduce tariffs. The Government, however, liberalized the local services postponing foreign investment in the long-distance business after five years. For cellular service, the Government allowed two service providers and gave a fifteen years license to each. In 1999, there was more liberalization with functional separation of the Ministry into two; one the policy maker and the other service provider; the Department of Telecommunication Services (DTS) which later came to be known as the VSNL. In April 2002, the Government decided to cut its stake from 53% to 26% and to throw it open for sale to private enterprises. After March 2000, more liberalization took place when licenses were issued to private operators. The license fee for cellular service providers was cut down and increased the allowable stake to 74% for foreign companies. This automatically brought down the service fees, reduction in tariffs taking the mobile to the palm of every common Indian.

91. The Competition Scenario: The rise of the ICT graph in India (see below Chart "A").The State-owned incumbent VSNL is the seventh largest telecom company in the world in terms of its numbers of subscribers. In the landline services, apart from State-owned BSNL/MTNL there are several private players like Bharti Airtel, Tata Indicom, Reliance Telecommunications, Tata Teleservices although facing hard competition from mobile telephones. The competition has forced the landline services to become more efficient and its demand is now easily met even in urban areas. The mobile network graph has shown sharp steep and it was as early as September 2004 that the number of mobile phone connections crossed fixed line connections. And currently there are estimated 875.48 million mobile phone users as compared to 29.08 million fixed line subscribers. India follows the GSM mobile system, in the 900 MHz band. Recent operators also operate in the 1800MHz band. 3G operations are carried out in 2100 MHz band. The dominant operators are Airtel, Vodafone, Idea Cellular, Tata DoCoMo, Reliance Communications and State-run BSNL/MTNL. There are also some other operators with comparatively lesser area coverage like Aircel, Loop Mobile, Videocon, MTS, Uninor, etc. International roaming agreements also exist between many operators and foreign carriers. Though the Broadband connections in India are more expensive compared to other Western Europe and U.K. and U.S. though they are comparable with other parts of Asia but mobile phone industry is on continuous rise due to price falling.

COMMUNICATIONS IN INDIA- Up to APRIL 2016	
TELEPHONY	
Telephone subscribers (Wireless and landline)	1.059 billion (April 2016)
Mobile subscribers	1.034 billion (April 2016)
Fixed line subscribers	25.04 million
Monthly telephone additions	0.43 million (April 2016)
TELEDENSITY 83.32% (April 2016)	
URBAN	153.14% (April 2016)
RURAL	51.67% (April 2016)
INTERNET ACCESS	
Internet users	462.12 million (January 2016)
Broadband Internet users	151.09 million (April 2016)
Internet penetration	**34.8% (January 2016)**

Share of world Internet users	13.5% (January 2016)
Country Code (Top-level Domain)	.in
BROADCASTING	
Television channels	869 (February 2016)
Radio stations	345 (March 2016)

CHART "A"

92. India thus became a model in following the line advanced by the World Bank and other international institutions in matter of *corporatization and progressive liberalization*. Liberalization helped service expansion, greater coverage, quality service, cost reductions and outsourcing of the management of networks to professional easement managers and network operators. Corporatization by the Government and the bifurcation of the policy making and regulatory organs, making it free from political influence went a step further in privatization and also made a beneficial effect on making the telecom sector more open to new approaches. Thus, with the need to expand the ICT services to the masses the private sector in India proved to be very innovative in infrastructure sharing and economizing on investment. Outsourcing to professional asset managers has had an effect of allowing companies to provide maximum service with minimum investment, augmenting revenues and profits in the process.[41]

§2. Market Definition Procedure

93. The benefits of a competitive communications market is public interest and social good. With India becoming a telecommunication hub and a contestable market for IT products and ITES, the Competition Act 2002[42] was formulated right at the time when ICTs were gaining momentum in the country. The Competition Act 2002 seeks to ensure fair competition and by combating anti-competitive malpractices. The Act establishes the Competition Commission of India (CCI) which is at the apex of the entire anti-competition drive and which is responsible for looking into the complaints, grievances, practices having adverse effect on competition and also the power to punish the defaulters. For determining whether a market constitutes a "relevant market" for the purposes of the Act, the Commission shall have due regard to the "relevant geographic market" and "relevant product market". For the "relevant geographic market" the Competition Commission of India shall have regard to the following factors:[43]

41. Source; ESCAP Statistical Yearbook 2009- ESSCAP data on ICT for 2009 CIA Fact Book.
42. It is successor the Monopoly and Restrictive Trade Practices Act 1969 which has now been repealed.
43. Section 19(6) the Competition Act 2002.

(a) Regulatory trade barrier.
(b) Local specification requirements.
(c) National procurement policies.
(d) Adequate distribution facilities.
(e) Transport costs.
(f) Language.
(g) Consumer preferences.
(h) Need for secure or regular supplies or rapid after-sales service.

While determining the "relevant product market", having regard to all or any of the following factors:[44]

(a) Physical characteristics or end use of goods.
(b) Price of goods or services.
(c) Consumer preferences.
(d) Exclusion of in-house production.
(e) existence of specialized producers; classifications of industrial products.

§3. Market Analysis Procedure

94. The Competition Commission of India 2002 for the purpose of determining whether a combination would have or likely to have an appreciable adverse effect on competition in the relevant market, the Commission has to have regard to the following[45] factors:

(1) actual and potential level of competition through importers in the market;
(2) extent of barriers to entry into the market;
(3) level of combination in the market;
(4) degree of countervailing power in the market;
(5) likelihood that the combination would result in the parties to the combination being able to significantly and sustainably increase prices or profit margins;
(6) extent of effective competition likely to sustain in the market;
(7) extent to which substitutes are available \or are likely to be available in the market;
(8) market share, in the relevant market, of the persons or enterprise in a combination individually and as a combination;
(9) likelihood that the combination would result in the removal of a vigorous and effective competitor or competitors in the market;
(10) nature and extent of vertical integration in the market;
(11) possibility of falling business;
(12) nature and extent of innovation;
(13) relative advantage of any combination by way of its contribution to economic development;

44. Section 19(7) the Competition Act 2002.
45. Section 20(4) the Competition Act 2002.

(14) whether the benefits of the combination outweigh the adverse impact of the combination if any.

§4. Operators with Significant Market Power

I. Identification of Operators with Significant Market Power

95. The CCI can inquire into any contravention of section 3(1)[46] or section 4(1).[47] It can do so on its own motion or on receipt of any information from any person, consumer or trade association, etc. To consider whether an agreement has an appreciable adverse effect on competition the Commission has to have regard to the following[48] factors:

(1) Creation of barriers to the new entrants in the market.
(2) Driving existing competitors out of the market.
(3) Foreclosure of competition be hindering entry into the market;
(4) Accrual of benefits to consumers.
(5) Improvements in production or distribution of goods or services.
(6) Promotion of technical, scientific and economic development by means of production or distribution of goods or provision of services.

96. In considering whether an enterprise enjoys a dominant position, the Commission has to have regard to all or any of the following factors:

(1) Market share of the enterprise.
(2) Size and resources of the enterprise.
(3) Size and importance of competitors.
(4) Economic power of the enterprise including commercial advantage over competitors.
(5) Vertical integration of the enterprises or sale or service network of such enterprises.
(6) Dependence of consumers on the enterprise.
(7) Monopoly or dominant position whether acquired as a result of any statute or by virtue of being a Government company or a public sector undertaking or otherwise.
(8) Entry barriers such as regulatory barriers, financial risk, high capital cost of substitutable goods, or service for consumers.
(9) Countervailing buying power.
(10) Market structure and size of market.
(11) Social obligations and social costs.

---

46. Section 3(1) the Competition Act 2002 relates to anti-competitive agreements. It prohibits agreement by enterprise or person or association in respect of production, supply, distribution, storage, acquisition or control of goods or provision of services which is likely to have appreciable adverse effect on competition.
47. Section 4(1) the Competition Act 2002 relates to abuse of dominant position.
48. Section 19(3) the Competition Act 2002.

(12) Relative advantages, by way of contribution to economic development by the enterprise enjoying a dominant position having or likely to have appreciable adverse effect on competition.
(13) Any other factor that the Commission may consider necessary for the inquiry.

II. Legal Status of Operators with Significant Market Power

A. Introduction

97. There is intense competition in the mobile service segment. The TRAI published the guidelines dated May 20, 2003 which clarified that differential tariffs for calls terminated within same network would amount to discrimination. There was opposition to this from stakeholders. Thus, in the Guidelines of May 24, 2004, the TRAI decided to forbear in the matter of non-discrimination with respect to tariffs and this was conveyed to all service providers. The service providers thus could offer differential tariffs for off-net and on-net calls. But these tariffs had the potential to discriminate in favor of a particular operator with adverse effect on competition in the relevant market. Thus, the differential tariff structure in the nature of anti-competitive conduct continues to be an issue of regulatory concern. An operator with significant market power may adopt Vertical Price Squeeze providing service in both upstream and downstream markets in any particular service area. The operator controls certain services that are key inputs for competitors in downstream markets and where those same key inputs are used by the operator or its affiliates to compete in the same downstream market. Thus, in telecommunication markets, the operator with significant market power can increase the prince to competitors for the upstream input i.e., dedicated to local circuit while leaving behind the downstream prices the same i.e., price for its dedicated Internet access services. The result would be a reduction of profits of competitors. Thus, an operator with significant market power can often squeeze the margins of competitors by raising whole sale prices (upstream market) paid by competitors at the same time lowering retail prices (downstream markets) in competitive services. Thus, such squeezing of the margins of competitors imposed by pricing strategy of the operator with significant market power could materially affect competition. Toughening vital operating conditions on the market unfairly limits competition hence the TRAI intervened by passing an order[49] in which it laid down guidelines for strict compliance by the service providers. The order *inter alia* laid down that differential discount structure in the provision of leased circuits by an operator with significant market power in any service area in the nature of vertical price squeeze will not be allowed.

49. No. 301-31/2004-Eco. Telecom regulatory Authority of India – New Delhi dated Dec. 8, 2004.

B. Obligations with Regard to Access and Interconnection

1. General Statement

98. Efficient Interconnection is a prerequisite for sustainable competition. Agreements between the Service Providers interconnecting with each other form the backbone of the entire activity. Interconnections issues are not uncommon thus regulatory guidelines are a must for the effective and expeditious and trouble free interconnection in the telecom sector. An accepted Regulatory principle is to ensure that the Service Provider with Significant Market Power (SMP)[50] publishes a Reference Interconnect Offer (RIO) stipulating the various technical and commercial conditions including a basis for Interconnect Usage Charges for Origination, Transit and Termination. The TRAI in consultation with the service providers has prepared a Model RIO.[51] The Service Providers with Significant Market Power shall submit their proposed RIO to the TRAI for approval which shall be published after it is approved. Such RIO can be modified as per service requirements, mutually agreed charges and other items. The obligations regarding the RIO are as follows:

- The service provider with SMP must detail out the commercial and technical conditions in the RIO.
- It shall then be published. Interconnection Agreements shall be based on such RIO.
- Any change or modification in the RIO can be done only with the approval of the TRAI.
- The Interconnection Provider and the Interconnection Seeker both with mutual agreement can bring a change in the interconnection Agreement to enter into an individualized Agreement.
- The RIO shall also contain certain conditions to meet the requirements of the public networks operators giving due consideration to the rights and obligations of the service provider as entered into the Interconnection Agreement.

2. Carrier Selection and Pre-selection

99. Competition in the telecom market improves work quality and the convenience of the consumers. The vision of TRAI is that carrier selection shall not only improve the quality of service but it will bring the call charges down thus helping the subscribers and at the same time giving a boost to healthy competition in the telecom sector. Choice of long-distance carrier has been there since the telecom sector in India was opened to competition. License will contain technical conditions regarding use of equipment

---

50. A service Provider shall be deemed to have significant market power if it holds a share of 30% of total activity in a licensed telecommunication service area. These services are categorized as Basic Service, Cellular Mobile Service, National Long Distance Service and International Long Distance Service. Para. 3.3 The Telecommunication Interconnection (Reference Interconnect Offer) Regulation 2002 (2 of2002).No. 409-10-2002-TRAI (FN
51. The Telecommunication Interconnection (Reference Interconnect Offer) Regulation 2002 (2 of2002). No. 409-10-2002-TRAI (FN).

by the licensee which should be suitable enough to support selection facilities such as dynamic call-by-call selection, pre-selection, etc. On recommendations of TRAI Carrier Access Code (CAC) and Carrier Identification Codes (CIC) have been allocated by DOT. Directions were issued to implement carrier selection. A free choice to customers for selecting their long-distance carrier has been incorporated in the terms and conditions of various license agreements like:

- New Basic Service License (Clause 2.4,16.1,17.3).
- Cellular License (Fourth Operator) (Clause 27.5).
- Unified Access Service License(Clause 23.3,26.5).
- NLD License (Clause 17.1).
- ILD License (Clause 17.1).

100. The TRAI made recommendations to the Department of Telecommunication (DOT) on June 19, 2001 for Allotment of Codes to NLD Operators for introduction of Dynamic Call-by-Call Selection of NLD Carriers by subscribers. The TRAI recommended: adoption of "10" as the NLD Service Code, 20 Codes ("40" to "59") to identify NLD Carriers. Although the TRAI realized that the number of NLD operators will be less than twenty for the planning period of five years and mentioned that it will be reviewed later. On July 24, 2002, TRAI issued Direction to Access Providers (BSOs/CMSOs) and National/International Long-Distance Operators regarding the implementation of carrier selection in their respective networks. (available at trai.gov.in). As per the NNP 2003the carrier, identification codes are in the range of 00-99. If a subscriber dials "010" or "0010" followed by two-digit carrier code the national or international call will be carried by the selection carrier. In case the subscriber dials a national or international number without making such a choice then the call may be carried by the default NLD/ILD chosen by the access provider. The default carrier is usually the access provider if CPS has not been implemented. TRAI direction dated July 24, 2002 envisaged that in all cases of long-distance calling in which the subscriber has not pre-selected his carrier and has also failed to dial the four-digit fix, i.e., Carrier Access Code (CAC), the calls will be routed by the Access Providers (BSOs/CMSOs) to a recorded announcement. The announcement shall make the subscriber to choose either the Call-by-Call or Pre-selection and as a result of the full implementation of the carrier selection there will be no default traffic. Recently it is observed that default carrier is in the interest of the subscriber and he should not be forced to dial extra digits on every long-distance call. If default carrier is not followed then the subscriber will be forced to dial additional digits on all NLD/ILD calls which may provoke adverse public reaction, dialing errors and other complexities. Thus, CS is less expensive, easier to implement and is supported by most existing exchanges.

101. Pre-selection: Pre-selection of carrier is usually made offline by the consumer and the access network provider programs it into the subscriber data. The choice of this carrier applies to each call and the carrier selection prefix is not needed. The Department of Telecommunication (DOT) vide letter dated August 24, 2000 requested TRAI to issue regulations in the areas covering carrier pre-selection (CPS) or Carrier Access Code (CAC) to be dialed by the subscriber for dynamic selection of NLDO in accordance with guidelines for issue of NLD licenses. In CPS, the subscriber makes a choice of preferred carrier in advance and all calls are routed through this carrier. This method would involve up gradation of hardware and software of most of the switches especially in the incumbent's network. The advantage is that no extra digits are to be dialed. If only one pre-selected carrier is allowed then there would almost be two bills. In the July 24, 2002 Direction the subscriber was having the facility to pre-select separately national and international carrier. However, selection of both NLD and ILD carriers for any international call was not mandated. The authority's decision was based on appreciation of the fact that giving simultaneous choice of NLDO and ILDO to the subscriber will require major system modifications in the Access Provider's network and the absence of simultaneous pre-selection will not be a disadvantage. Another problem would be dialing of two more digits if both NLDO and ILDO are selected which will be very confusing for the subscriber and would give rise to billing issues. In the absence of simultaneous selection of national as well as international carrier default carrier needs to be decided. For specifying default carrier, following options are available for consideration of stakeholders:

(1) If the codes are not dialed or subscriber has not pre-selected the national/international long-distance carrier, default carrier selection may be left to the discretion of Access Provider.
(2) As the tariff for ILD calls is being offered by the ILDO to the subscriber directly, there instead of allowing pre-selection of NLDO also it would be better to leave the choice of NLDO on the ILDO.

Chapter 3. Regulation of Cryptography and Other Dual-Use Goods

§1. Regulation of Cryptography

102. Cryptography is an ancient art, but in the digital context it has undergone a revolution to match with the Internet environment. The computer revolution even revolutionized the cryptographic means and the most genius quality of computers to calculate monstrous numbers with lightning speed and comfort gives new definition to the art of cryptography.[52] The classical cryptography mainly resting on language and words is supplanted by computers using cipher design and cryptanalysis and are characterized by their operation on binary bit sequences. The 1970s saw the increase in use of computers in the West, encryption of computer data to give secrecy and confidentiality to it progressed further but together with it the means and methods to challenge cryptography grew with the defaulters and the vandals. Thus, the mathematical approach, the computer processing power and the cryptographic algorithm led to counter the problem of code breaking in an effective manner. Thus, the United States' Data Encryption Standard (DES) designed by the International Business Machines; the key agreement algorithm published by Whitfield Diffie and Martin Hellman and the Rivest, Shamir & Adelman (RSA) algorithm published in Martin Gardner's Scientific American column unleashed an era of modern cryptography.[53]

103. Need to Regulate: The proliferation of computers and the widening horizons of telecommunication systems expanded the use of high quality cryptography. The users, the criminals and the law enforcers were equally attracted by it and concepts like, privacy, civil rights and the authentication problems raised their heads. Although the encoded message promised reliability of the data yet after being transmitted it "cannot itself provide conclusive evidence that it did originate from the alleged sender."[54] Consequently, to make cryptography more reliable and less vulnerable there originated the idea of "Trusted Third Parties."(TTP). This system soon became popular with governments as it allowed the State to play a role in the online dealings but to regulate them. In US, the Escrowed Encryption Standard (EES) also known as "clipper chip" was approved though it was criticized by the liberals. The security of the cryptographic approach became a crucial problem both with the parties and the State. The aim of crypto analysis is to find some weakness or insecurity in a cryptographic scheme. State efforts to regulate cryptography were speeded up and in March 1997, the Council of

52. Fatima Talat, ch. 6- *Electronic Signatures and Crime-*; Cyber crimes Eastern Book company- 1st ed., 2011 at 292.
53. *Ibid* at 293.
54. Ian Lloyd, ch. 8 "*Legal Barriers to Electronic Contracts: Formal requirements and Digital signatures*" in Lilian Edwards & Charlotte Waelde (eds), *Law and the Internet: Regulating Cyberspace* (Hart Publishing, Oxford 1997) 144.

the OECD adopted Guidelines for Cryptography Policy including directions to enable countries to include it in their national laws. These are:

- Cryptography methods must be such that they inculcate trust and confidence in the prolific use of modern communication systems.
- Cryptographic methods must give "right to choose" to countries to meet suitability to their national laws.
- Cryptographic methods must equally suit the needs of governments, businesses and individuals.
- There must be technical criteria to suit national and international needs.
- Right to privacy must be respected.
- Parties must have a well-defined policy regarding lawful access to plaintext or cryptographic keys of encrypted data.
- Organizations and individuals must have fixed liabilities under law. There must be coordination among governments to have unified policy on cryptography.
- Not only from the viewpoint of national security but also from the view point of criminal and law enforcer's cryptography cannot be left unregulated. Regulation started U.K. and in 1999. In France use of cryptography was restricted In countries like Belarus, Kazakhstan, Mongolia, Pakistan, Russia, Singapore, Tunisia and Vietnam restrictions were imposed.

104. Case of India: In India there are few companies involved in the development of cryptography. For quite a long time cryptography remained a defense subject and it was in 1995 that India introduced a list of items that required licensing before export and encryption software for telemetry systems in specific was on the list and it did not relate to encryption in general.[55] In 1997. the Council of OECD issued Guidelines for Cryptography Policy urging nations to adopt methods to inculcate trust and confidence in the online communication systems. India was a signatory to the United Nations Commission on International Trade Law (UNCITRAL) which adopted the Model Law on electronic Commerce in 1996. Thus, in conformity to the said Model Law 2001 India came up with its first cyber – legislation namely the Information Technology Act 2000 (21 of 2000) which recognized digital signatures based on asymmetric

55. "Cryptography and Liberty 1999; an International survey of Encryption Policy," at http://www.gilc.org/crypto-survey-99.html.

cryptosystems bringing them at par with manual signatures. For regulating cryptography India adopted the PKI system.[56]

105. PKI Scenario in India -The IT (Amendment) Act 2008 has now substituted the term "electronic signature" for the term "digital signature". The Act provides for the Controller of Certifying authorities (CCA) who are entrusted with the responsibility of regulating the working of certification authorities who intern is given the responsibility to issue the Digital Signature Certificates (DSCs) for electronic authentication of users. The CCA certifies the public keys of Certifying Authorities using its own private key, which enables users in the cyber space to verify that a given certificate is issued by a licensed Certifying Authority. For this it operates the Root Certifying Authority of India (RCAI). The CCA by virtue of section 20 of the IT Act 2000 maintained repositories which have now been deleted under the Amendment Act of 2008.[57]

The RCAI is operated using the SmartTrust software. Certification Practice statement of the RCAI guides the CCA personnel to perform Root Certifying Authority functions. The Term "root" signifies the entire Certifying Authority matrix including the software and its operations The National Root Certifying Authority uses a 2048 bit RSA key pair and the Certifying authority entity uses a 1024 bit RSA key pair.[58]

Regulatory Provisions; The main regulatory provisions are limited and the earlier law[59] has been replaced by a new one. Under the new section 69 of the IT (Amendment) Act 2008 violation of the Directions to intercept, monitor or decrypt information is made a punishable offense with imprisonment up to seven years and with fine.

---

56. The PKI-Infrastructure There arose a need to keep an intermediary which could act as an agency between contracting parties so as to avoid doubts regarding the authenticity of electronic signatures. The public-key cryptography is highly mathematical hence, "all users must have confidence in the skill, knowledge and security arrangements of the parties issuing the public and private keys." If the users themselves issue such public and private key there may be lack of trust in the certifiers of the public keys."(ch.1,"Introduction to the Model Law: Purpose and Origin of the Model Law: Purpose" in UNCITRAL *Model Law on Electronic Signatures with Guide to Enactment* 2001, 25. Thus though the certification of the public key could be given by involvement of third party who could act as a reliable mediator "to associate an identified signatory or the signatory's name with a specific public key" became a practical and legal necessity. In the Model Law 2001 the terms "Certifying Authority," "Certification Authority" and "supplier of certification services" are used for such third party.
57. Formerly under the IT act 2000, the Controller had the job maintaining a repository of all the Certifying Authorities in the country. The National repository of Digital Certificates (NRDC) maintained it under Section 20.
58. Sandeep Oberoi, "*India PKI Forum*", Presentation made at PKI Consortium Seminar, Nov. 08, 2007.
59. Section 69- IT Act 2000 (21 of 2000). ***Directions of Controller to subscriber to extend facilities to decrypt information-*** Such directions could be issued on the grounds of: (1) interest of the sovereignty and integrity of India; (2) the security of the state; (3) for friendly relations with foreign states; (4) public order or for (5) preventing incitement to the commission of any cognizable offense. Such subscriber or in charge of the computer is kept under obligation to provide technical assistance to decrypt the information failing which a punishment of imprisonment up to seven years is provided.

§2. Regulation of Dual-Use Goods

I. General Statement

106. India's recent non-proliferation policies have impacted upon companies that trade in goods and technologies with potential applications to weapons of mass destruction (WMD), missiles and conventional arms collectively called "strategic items". To facilitate greater access to advanced technology products (ATP), India is currently seeking membership in the four main multilateral export control regimes (MECRs)); the Nuclear Suppliers Groups (NSG), AustraliaGroup (AG), Missile Technology Control Regime (MTCR) and Wassenaar Arrangement (WA). Thus, India is following the guidelines and practices of these regimes.

107. Dual-use goods and technologies are those items, goods, software or technology which are beneficial both for the defense and the civilians. It is the prerogative of the State to control the goods and investments which are used by the defense department from being misused by the general public. This is not only in the interest of the defense department but also in the interest of the country. The Internet, infra-red and many other technologies exist today because of the increasing technology dependence of war. A greater part of these restrictions take the form of "end user" licenses and laws that prevent export to certain "end users" or nations. The Foreign Trade Development and Regulation) Act No. 22 of 1992 (FTDR) (amended 2010)[60] is the principal legal document for India's strategic control system which empowers the GOI (GOI) to "make provisions for prohibiting, restricting or otherwise regulating" all or specified classes of exports or imports upon public notification in the Official Gazette. It also authorizes the GOI to formulate and amend India's foreign trade policy, which the GOI issues in five-year increments and updates annually. In India the export and import of dual-use items is regulated by the Directorate General of Foreign Trade (DGFT) situated within the Department of Commerce and Industry (DCI). The DGFT regularly issues the "Exim Policy" which regulates and governs the terms and conditions of export and import of such dual-use items. Such dual-use items are classified as *Special Chemicals, Organisms, Materials, Equipment and Technologies*. (SCOMET).

The DGFT is empowered to license the export and import of Items on the India Tariff Classification (Harmonized System) or ITC (HS) list.

108. The Exim Policy: As per the present policy it is mandatory for all the entities. whether public or private. to obtain permission from the DGFT before entering into any arrangement regarding export or import of any SCOMET items when such arrangements involves an obligation to facilitate or undertake site-visits, on-site verification or access to records/documents of the foreign States, or foreign third parties, The DGFT before granting such permission must take into consideration the bilateral or multilateral agreements to which India is also party. The regulation of export or import of such dual-use items depends on the prohibition or permission of such items under a license. Grant of license depends on many factors like the end use \/end user. The export or import of such items must be in conformity with the Indian

60. *The Foreign Trade Development and Regulation Act No. 22 of 1992 (FTDR),* ch. II, s. 3(2) available at Director General Of Foreign Trade homepage http://dgft.delchi.nic.in/.

Laws but export from a country outside India also requires compliance with the laws of that country. Thus, where such items are not allowed under the laws of a foreign country then it will be considered as an offense in India. .The GOI has the power to make rules to prohibit the export of certain goods, technologies, equipments and prohibit unlawful activities in respect of Weapons of Mass Destruction (WMD) Delivery systems (Prohibition of Unlawful Activities) Act 2005.

II. The List of Dual-Use Items and Technology

109. The government of India has made changes to its national export lists that could have impacted on companies that trade in dual-use and munitions goods and technologies from India. Thus, India follows the path set by other countries in this matter.[61] The WMD Act authorizes the GOI to regulate the export, re-transfer, re-export, transit and transshipment of any items related to the development, production, handling, operation, maintenance, storage or dissemination of a WMD or missile delivery device. The DGFT as empowered[62] announces Indian Trade Classification (Harmonized System) of Export and Import Items 2012.[63] The list harmonizes with both HS 2012 of World Customs Organization and Tariff Schedule of Customs. The ITC (HS) 2012 contains "Schedule 1 Import Policy" and "Schedule 2 Export Policy".

110. Imports: New ITC (HS) Import Schedule 1.Import Policy 2012. The import licensing system is substantially less developed than its controls on exports items found on ITC(HS); Schedule I

- Section I – Live Animals and Animal Products.
- Section II – Vegetable Products.
- Section III – Animals or Vegetable Fats and Oils and their Cleavage Products Prepared Edible Fats; animal or Vegetable Waxes.
- Section IV – Prepared foodstuffs; Beverages, Spirits and Vinegar. Tobacco and Manufactured Tobacco Substituted.
- Section V – Mineral Products.
- Section VI – Products of the Chemical and Allied Industries.
- Section VII – Plastics and Articles thereof; Rubber and Articles thereof.
- Section VIII – Raw Hides and Skins, Leather, fur skins and Articles thereof; Saddlery and Harness; Travel Goods, Handbags and Similar Containers. Articles of Animal Guts (other than Silkworm Guts).

---

61. January 2012- Canada's Foreign Affairs International Trade's Export Controls Division (ECD) announced a number of changes in the Canadian Export Control List which included dual-use items; in February 2012 at the 6th European Forum on Export Controls there was much discussion on Art. 22 of the European Control Regulations which focuses on dual-use goods and the US Bureau of Industry and Security (BIS) also implemented changes to the Export Administration Regulations which focuses in the dual-use goods.
62. In exercise of powers conferred by s. 5 of the Foreign Trade (Development & Regulation) Act 1992 (22 of 1992) read with para 2.1 of the Foreign Trade Policy of the Government of India.
63. Notification No. 111/RE (2010) /2009–2014 dated Apr. 18, 2012. File No. 01/89/180/66/AM-12/PC.2A.: *Government of India, Ministry of Commerce and Industry, New Delhi.*

- Section IX – Wood and Articles of Wood, Wood Charcoal Cork and Articles of Cork; Manufacturers of Straw of Esparto or other Plaiting Materials Basket ware and Wicker ware.
- Section X – Pulp of Wood or of other Fibrous Cellulosic Material; Waste or Scrap of Paper or Paperboard; Paper and Paperboard and Articles thereof.
- Section XI – Textile and Textile Articles.
- Section XII – Footwear, Headgear, Umbrellas, Sun umbrellas, Walking Sticks, Seat-Sticks, Whips, Riding-Crops and Parts thereof; Prepared feathers and Articles made thereof; Artificial Flowers; Articles of Human Hair.
- Section XIII – Articles of Stone, Plaster, Cement, Asbestos, Mica or Similar Materials; Ceramic Products; Glass and Glassware.
- Section XIV – Natural or Colored Pearls, Precious or Semi-Precious Stones, Precious Metals, Metals Clad with Precious Metal and articles thereof; Imitation Jewelry Coin.
- Section XV – Base Metals and Articles of Base Metals.
- Section XVI – Machinery and Mechanical Appliances; Electrical Equipment; Parts thereof; Sound Recorders and Reproducers, Television Image and Sound Recorders and Reproducers, and Parts and Accessories of such Articles.
- Section XVII – Vehicles, Aircraft, Vessels and Associated Transport Equipment.
- Section XVIII – Optical, Photographic, Cinematographic, Measuring, Checking, Precision, Medical or Surgical Instruments and Apparatus; Clocks and Watches; Musical instruments; Parts and accessories thereof.
- Section XIX – Arms and Ammunitions; Parts and Accessories thereof.
- Section XX – Miscellaneous Manufacturers.
- Section XXI – Works of Art, Collectors' Pieces and Antiques.

111. ***Exports***-Export of dual-use items and technology under India's Foreign Trade Policy is regulated. The FTDR defines an export as "taking out of India any goods, technologies or services by land, sea or air." Goods and technologies and services subject to export licensing requirements are listed in India's national export product control list known as the Special Chemicals, Organisms, Materials Equipment and Technologies (SCOMET) list. The list is periodically amended by the GOI.[64] The SCOMET list is located in Appendix 3 of Schedule 2 of the ITC(HS) divided into eight distinct categories (Categories 0–7). The DGFT is the primary licensing agency for most items on the SCOMET list (Categories 1 through 7)[65] while the DAE issues licenses for all the nuclear and nuclear dual-use commodities found in SCOMET Category 0.[66] The categories are as follows:

- Category 0 – Nuclear materials, nuclear-related other materials, equipment and technology.

---

64. FTDR-s. 5 and Foreign Trade Policy (2009-2014) para. 2.1
65. The export of items in Category 2 of the SCOMET list (microorganisms, toxins, pathogens, etc.) may also be controlled by other applicable guidelines. Foreign Trade Handbook of Procedures.Vol 1 (2010-2011 supplement), para. 2.48, Note 3.
66. India's System of Controls over Exports of Strategic Goods and Technologies," Ministry of External Affairs website.

- Category 1 – Toxic chemical agents and other agents.
- Category 2 – Microorganisms, toxins.
- Category 3 – Materials, Materials Processing Equipment and related technologies.
- Category 4 – Nuclear-related other equipment, assemblies and components; test and production equipment; and related technology not controlled under Category-0.
- Category 5 – Aerospace systems, equipment including production and test equipment, related technology and specially designed components and accessories thereof.
- Category 6 – (Reserved).
- Category 7 – Electronics, computers and information technology including information security. Each category contains exhaustive listing of items covered under that category. Special conditions applicable to items under different categories are mentioned under each category.

III. Transfer of Dual-Use Goods from the EU

112. Common Rules for Export: The Regulation lays down the Rules that the exports of items from European Union to non-EU countries are free from non-quantitative restrictions.[67] The Regulation lays down important protective measures and procedures for unusual developments in the market. Consultation with other EU countries within an Advisory Committee chaired by a member of the Commission and having other representatives from the EU countries must take place, where the trends and export conditions are discussed and the countries are asked to send the statistical data for assessing the economic and commercial conditions. The Commission may also ask the countries to exercise surveillance over the products as according to their national legislations.

113. Protective Measures: The EU in its own interest may require the adoption of appropriate measures to prevent or control a critical situation as follows:

- It may allow international commitments entered into by all the EU countries to be fulfilled.
- The Commission may also make export of a product subject to export authorization as per rules set by the Commission.
- These protective measures may be confined to exports to specific countries or exports from certain regions of the EU.
- The Commission may also implement certain measures for immediate action.
- There may also be consultation regarding the effect of these measures and the necessity for their continuation or revocation in certain area.
- The Regulation does not prevent the EU countries from applying quantitative restrictions on exports on the ground of public morality, welfare of people at large, animal welfare, in the interest of historical or things of artistic value, commercial importance, etc.

67. Council Regulation (EC) No.1061/2009 of Oct. 19, 2009 establishing common rules for exports.

IV. Intra-community Transfers

114. The Weapons of Mass Destruction and Their Delivery systems (Prohibition of Unlawful Activities) Act (No. 21 of 2005) (WMD Act) authorizes the GOI to regulate the export, re-transfer, re-export, transit and transshipment of any items related to the development, production, handling, operation, maintenance, storage or dissemination of a WMD or missile delivery device. It also established a catch-all control that restricts exports of non-listed items destined for a WMD end use and it provided a rudimentary legal basis to regulate technology transfers.

115. Technology Transfer: The DGFT is authorized to license and regulate electronic transmissions of strategic technologies designated on the SCOMET list. The WMD Act and the FTDR (as amended) define "technology" as "any information (including information embodied in software), other than information in the public domain, that is capable of being used in the development, production, or use of any goods or software; or the development of or the carrying out of an industrial or commercial activity or the provision of a service of any kind."[68]

116. Transfer of Sensitive Technologies: Such technologies listed or restricted under India's catch-all provision are subject to control in India under the following circumstances:

- A person located within India seeks to transfer restricted technologies to a person or place outside India.[69]
- An Indian located outside India wishes to transfer restricted technologies to a person who too is outside India.[70]
- An item is exhibited, sold, supplied or transferred to a foreign entity or foreigner who is resident, operating, visiting, studying or conducting research or business within Indian territory, airspace, or an Exclusive Economic Zone (EEZ).[71]

"Catch–All" Control: Restrictions are imposed on trade in non-listed items that appear to be for a WMD relevant end use by the WMD Act and FTDR.

Thus, if a trader "knows" that the item is "intended to be used in the design or manufacture of a biological weapon, chemical weapon, nuclear weapon or other nuclear explosive device or in their delivery systems"[72] but it does not appear on the national control list even then he will have to apply for the export license from the DGFT. The Indian catch-all control extends to individuals or entities facilitating the execution of a transaction (brokers and intermediaries), if they are aware that the transaction in question is related to a prohibited activity.[73]

---

68. When technology is described wholly or partly by reference to the uses to which it (or the goods to which it relates) may be put, it shall include services which are provided or used, or which are capable of being used, in the development, production or use of such technology or goods. FTDR Amendment Act 2010, s. 2(m).Also *see*, WMD Act, s. 4(I).
69. WMD Act, s. 13(3)(a)
70. WMD Act, s. 13(3)(b).
71. WMD Act, s. 13(4)
72. WMD Act, s. 11 and FTDR Amendment Act 2010, Art. 14C.
73. WMD Act, ss. 11 and 12, FTDR Amendment Act 2010, Art. 14C.

End User Controls: India prohibits transfers to non-State actors or terrorists of any material, equipment or technology that could contribute to the development of a WMD. India abides by UN Security Council (UNSC) Resolutions and has enacted export prohibitions against several sanctioned countries, entities and terrorists. India prohibits the "direct and indirect" import or export of designated arms and WMD-related goods and technologies to or from Iran, North Korea and Iraq.

India also maintains an Exporter Black List known as the Denied Entities List (DEL), which consists of parties who are previously refused or denied an export license though the DEL is not in public domain. GOI denies export license not only to the listed entities of DEL but also to anyone who controls such entities on the DEL are reportedly those who also appear on the list maintained by the U.S. Government(USG), the UN and other countries and also entities who are listed on Indian inputs. If a company submits an inquiry to DGFT concerning a particular end user, DGFT will provide a "yes" or "no" answer regarding the entity's status on the DEL. The exporters are bound to procure an End User Certificate (EUC) and assurances that the recipient will not re-export or re-transfer the item to anyone other than the end user of record.[74] For some items in Category 0 of the SCOMET list, the DAE may also require formal assurances from the recipient State to certify that adequate physical protection and International Atomic Energy Agency (IAEA) safeguards will mitigate the risk of diversion and ensure that the items will not be used in a nuclear explosive device.[75]

74. Chapter 2; *Handbook of Procedures* (Vol 1). Also available on the Government of Indiawebsite: http://dgftcnic.in/exim/2000/procedures/ftphbconnects0910.pdf.
75. *Foreign Trade Handbook of Procedures*, Vol.I (2009–2014), para. 2.49 (III) and Resolution No. AEA/27(1)/2005-ER, Guidelines for Nuclear Transfers (Exports), s. (3) (a) and (b).

Chapter 4. Legal Status of Standardization

§1. Standardization in the ICT Market

117. The Indian presence in international telecom standards is marginal. There is a need to have a Telecommunication's Standard Development Organization(TSDO)[76]as an autonomous body to consolidate various efforts in the country and to work towards influencing international standards to incorporate Indian requirements /IPR into Indian telecom standards. From time to time the DoT and TRAI have been striving for standardization to meet the international standardization model. For Next Generation Network (NGN) to ensure ubiquity, interoperability and a competitive marketplace NGN is to done on open and consensus based international standards. Government laid stress on the technical development and standardization for NGN revolution in the country.[77]

118. With the speeding up of the ICT expansion, a forum has been set up with private-public partnership comprising Government, industry, operators, academician and standardization bodies, called the Global ICT Standardization Forum for India (GISFI). The main objective of GISFI is to harmonize and pool together the standardization efforts within the Indian market and make use of all standardization bodies having the aim of making India a knowledge-based economy The GISFI will serve as a booster to competitiveness with companies and would also give an investor-friendly environment. The GISFI received full support from the Government. The GISFI not only meets the oncoming challenges but it also creates an atmosphere favorable for national and international investment. It is a national platform where all the minds to expand ICT activities will meet, discuss and decide points related to up gradation of the ICT in India. It will help India scientifically, financially and industrially to make it a Global Power in the field of ICT.

119. . The GISFI encompasses the following activities:

- Laying down provisions and requirements for the ICT Standardization process and to erect agreements that: (1) provide one or more solutions for a given problem ensuring a repeated use; (2) provide a basis for future research and product developments as per global standards; (3) weigh equally the interest of all involved parties.
- Provision for using well thought existing solutions.
- Providing India with a normal procedure in conformity with other nations of the world so that cooperation is simpler and purchasing is simpler.

---

76. 11.3.3 R & D, IPR and Standardization- Report on the Working Group of the Telecom Sector For the Twelfth Five-Year Plan (2012–2017). Government of India –DoT –Ministry of Communications and Information Technology. August 2011.
77. Recommendations on issues Pertaining to NGN- Telecom Regulatory Authority of India – March 2006.

120. The National Telecom Policy 2012-The NTP envisages the following objectives regarding standardization:

- To promote the ecosystem for design, Research and development, IPR creation, testing standardization and manufacturing i.e., complete value chain for domestic production of telecommunication equipment to meet India telecom sector demand to the extent of 60% and 80% with a minimum value addition of 45% and 65% by the year 2017 and 2020.
- Develop and establish standards to meet national requirement, generate IPRs and participate in international standardization bodies to contribute in formulation of global standards, thereby making India a leading nation in the area of international telecom standardization. This will be supported by establishing appropriate linkages with industry, R & D institutions, academia, telecom service providers and users.

§2. Conformity Assessment and Mutual Recognition

121. In the information society conformity assessment of IT products and services meeting accessibility requirements is the main issue. Public procurement is an important instrument for accessibility.

122. Mutual Recognition Agreement – India – as a progressive nation in the area of ICT – has signed Memorandum of understanding (MoU) with the following countries:

- India – South Korea – Digital signatures are being widely used in India and South Korea for various domestic applications relating to e-Governance-Trade-CCO(Certificate of Origin), e-Tendering /e-Procurement-IPO (Intellectual Property Office), e-Income Tax, e-Banking, e-Company Registration and Administration, e-mail signing, encryption, etc. Until the signing of the MoU ion January 18, 2014 the Certifying of such one country was not recognized in another country. Hence after signing of the MoU there has been MRA between the two countries thus facilitating trade, landmark commercial agreements between the two countries as they now mutually recognize the digital signature certificates.

Chapter 5. Legal Status of Out-of-Court Dispute Settlement In the ICT Sector

§1. General Statement

123. As India surges ahead in the ICT Sector and as the fruits of ICT reach the grassroots level, more and more people are in contact with the telecom services. Apart from benefitting from it, disputes are bound to arise thus the need arose to settle these disputes legally and at the same time protecting the interests of millions of consumers. This will ensure not only the safeguard of the commercial interests and telecommunication needs of the consumers but at the same time it will also serve as a guard to the services provided by the ever increasing stakeholders in the country. To minimize customer grievances and to provide an effective and uniform mechanism to deal with such grievances the GOI has established a two-way mechanism:

A. The Telecom and Regulatory Authority of India Act 1997

124. The Telecom and Regulatory Authority of India Act 1997. The objective of the said Act, apart from establishing a regulatory authority in the telecom sector, is also to establish a Telecom Disputes and Appellate Tribunal (TDSAT) "to regulate the telecommunication services, adjudicate disputes, dispose of appeals and to protect the interests of service providers and consumers of the telecom sector."[78] The Act (section 11) also does away with the provisions of the main act in the field; the Indian Telegraph Act 1885 (13 of 1885). The section 11 also ensures the standard and quality of service to be provided by the service providers and safeguards the interests of the consumers in the telecommunication sector.

B. The Consumer Protection Act 1986

125. The Consumer has received ample attention from the regulatory framework and from the legal perspective in the telecom sector. To see that the interests of the consumer are not jeopardized by the service providers and other players in the arena there are the following legal documents which provide redress to the consumer out-of-the-judicial courts:

(1) The Telecom Consumers Complaint Redress Regulations 2012.
(2) The Consumer Protection Act 1986.

78. Preamble- The Telecom and Regulatory Authority Act 1997.

§2. Out-of-Court Dispute Settlement with Regard to Access and/ or

Interconnection:

126. There has been provided as one of the functions of the TRAI to hold periodical surveys of the service provided by the various service providers in the interest of the consumer. (section 11). The TRAI Act establishes a mechanism as follows to hear the disputes of consumers in respect of access and interconnection.

The Dispute Solving Mechanism:

TDSAT-The Central Government establishes the TDSAT-The Act makes the TDSAT the main authority to hear the disputes and excludes totally the jurisdiction of civil courts in this respect. Thus, the Civil Courts are not empowered to hear, entertain, any suit or proceeding which lies before the TDSAT and also the civil courts do not have power to pass any injunction in respect of any action taken by the TDSAT (section 15).

Limits of the Jurisdiction of the TDSAT: While the TDSAT has power to hear and adjudicate upon disputes between the consumer and the service provider, the following matters are excluded from the jurisdiction of the Tribunal: (section 14)

- The monopolistic trade practice, the restrictive trade practice and the unfair trade practice which are subject to the jurisdiction of the Monopolies and restrictive Trade Practices Commission established under section 5(1) of the Monopolies and Restrictive Trade Practices Act 1969 (54 of 1969).
- The complaint of an individual consumer which is before the district forum /the state level forum/the national level forum established under the Consumer Protection Act 1986 (63of 1986).
- Dispute between the telegraph authority and any individual mentioned under section 7B (1) of the Indian Telegraph Act 1885(13of 1885).

127. Procedure before the TDSAT: The Central Government/State Government/ any individual may make an application before the Tribunal for settlement of dispute referred to:

- Between a licensor and a licensee.
- Between two or more service providers.
- Between a service provider and a group of consumers.

The judgment of the Tribunal shall contain concise statement of case, points of decisions, the reasons for such decisions and decision thereupon where the Tribunal had failed to assign sufficient or cogent reason in support of its findings. When anyone is aggrieved by the decision of the Tribunal can appeal before the Appellate Tribunal within thirty days of receiving the copy of the decision/order of the Tribunal. The Appellate tribunal can also entertain an appeal even after expiry of such thirty days if it is satisfied with the reasons so forwarded by the appellant. The Appellate Tribunal must dispose of the appeal expeditiously within ninety days of its receipt and if it fails to do so it must record reasons for it. (section 14-A (1), (2), (3) (4), etc.

Appeal Before the Supreme Court: Notwithstanding anything in the Code of Civil Procedure 1908 (5 of 1908), an appeal shall be brought under section 100 of the CPC before the Supreme Court of India within ninety days of passing of order or decision (not being an interlocutory order) of the Appellate Authority (Section18).

§3. Out-of-Court Dispute Settlement Involving Consumers and Other End Users

128. The consumers' interests has been provided with legal protection within the Consumer Protection Act 1986 and the Telecom Consumers Complaint Redress Regulations 2012.The TRAI has regarded consumers as important stakeholders in the development and regulation of the telecom industry. The Consumer Fora under the Consumer Protection Act 1986 may entertain individual applications for individual grievances but for matters affecting a large body of telecom consumers the matter is ought to be referred to the/TDSAT.

129. Mechanism and Procedure under the Consumer Protection Act 1986: The Act to protect the interest of the consumers and to provide them with speedy remedy does establish a three-tier Forum hierarchy; the District Forum, the State-level Consumer Redress Forum and the National Consumer Redress Forum. The aggrieved consumer makes an application before the District Forum with required amount of fee and thereafter the opposite party is issued notice to present its case within thirty or extension of fifteen days before the Forum. The Forum shall dispose of the application within five months of filing of the reply of the opposite party in technical matters and within three months in all other cases. (section 13). The District Forum and the State Level Forum and the National Commission have the power to order the defaulting party to replace/remove defect/restore price /pay compensation to the aggrieved. Anyone dissatisfied by the decision of the District Forum may appeal before the State Commission within thirty days of the decision with required fees and if he is again dissatisfied by the decision of the State Commission then within thirty days of its decision it can apply to the National Commission.

130. The Telecom Consumers Complaint Redress Regulations 2012-These Regulations are passed by TRAI[79] and are applicable to all the service providers including the BSNL and MTNL providing:

- Basic Telephone service.
- Unified Access Service.
- Cellular Mobile Telephone Service
- Internet Service.

79. TRAI Notification No. 305-20/2009-805, dated Jan. 5, 2012, passed in exercise of powers conferred by s. 36 of the TRAI Act 1997. The Regulations have been since amended thrice in 2012.

The Regulations will not apply to any Internet Service Provider ISP) whose total number of subscriber in any financial year does not exceed INR 5 crores or whose number of subscribers does not exceed ten thousand.

131. Mechanism of Complaints from Telecom Consumers- Establishment of Complaint Center- Every Service Provider is directed to establish a Complaint Center within forty-five days of its commencement. (Regulation 3). The Call Centers set up by the service provider in accordance with the Telecom Consumers Protection and Redress of Grievances Regulations 2007 (3 of 2007) dated May 04, 2007 shall continue to be the Complaint Center for such service providers. The working language of the Complaint Center shall include the regional language apart from Hindi and English. The Complaint Center shall be accessible through a Consumer Care Number[80] which shall be toll free.

Establishing of Complaint Monitoring System: Every service provider within forty five days of its commencement is under obligation to constitute a "Web Based Complaint Monitoring System" to enable the consumers to monitor the status of their complaints. The service provider must also inform the general public about the address of such Center through newspaper, etc. After receiving the complaint the Center must assign a docket number to such complaint which will be preserved by the service provider with the details of the complaint for about three months in its system. (Regulation 7(2)) The service provider shall inform the consumer through SMS the action taken by it in respect of the complaint. Every service provider shall ensure redress of the complaint within the time limit as fixed by the Quality of Service regulations issued by the Authority and where no such timeframe is given must dispose it off within three days. (Regulation 8).

132. Establishment and Composition of the Appellate Authority: Every service provider shall within forty five days of its commencement shall establish an Appellate Authority to entertain appeals from the Complaint Center. Such Appellate Authority shall be separate or common to licensed service areas and if he has a license for the whole of India then he shall establish such Appellate Authority either in any part of India or for the whole of India. (Regulation 10(1)). Along with the Appellate Authority the service provider shall also establish an Advisory Committee consisting of two members; one from the consumer organization and the other being the representative of the service provider.

Procedure for Appeal: If a consumer is dissatisfied with the redress of the Complaint Center or if he is not informed by the Center about the redress, etc. then the consumer may appeal through e-mail/facsimile/or by post within thirty days after the expiry of the time limit set under Regulation 8. After receipt of the appeal the Advisory Committee shall register it by assigning a unique Appeal Number to it, inform the appellant about it within three days of receipt of the appeal, intimate to the service provider about such appeal along with a copy of the said appeal asking him to respond within seven days. (Regulation 13). The Advisory Committee shall render its advice on the appeal within fifteen days and the Secretariat shall place it before the Appellate Authority within two days of receiving such advice. The Appellate Authority shall then conduct necessary inquiry and dispose of the appeal preferably in accordance

80. Customer Care Number means a telephone number earmarked by a service provider to access its complaints. Regulation 2 (j) *The Telecom Consumers Complaint Redress Regulations 2012*

with the advice given by the Advisory Committee. In case the Appellate Authority does not decide on the basis of the advice given by the Advisory Committee then it shall record reasons for it. It is optional for the appellant to be present before the Appellate Authority or not. (Regulation 14).

Part II. Protection of Intellectual Property in the ICT Sector

Chapter 1. Application of Copyright in the Area of ICT

133. The term "copyright" has added dimensions today because in the Internet environment the difference between the "original" and the "copy" seems to vanish completely: "it is the most widely breached and the least fully understood by anybody but intellectual property lawyers."[81] The *Berne Convention* says that "there will be a copyright infringement when an individual copy of a work held in electronic format without the authority of the copyright holder." (Article 9(1). The entire ICT mechanism and the communication chain[82] rest on the "copying" action: when transmitted the original data never reaches the recipient but it is only the last copy which reaches him. There is a lurking possibility that the ISPs may retain a copy of such information before transmitting it to the other router. Such "evanescent copies" though temporary in nature are sufficient infringement of copyright laws.[83] Like the traditional, real world inventions or innovations, software products can also be protected as intellectual property. A copyright gives legal protection to the creativity or expression of the creator. It protects his innovation from being copied or misused by others, from possible piracy and from someone else illegitimately taking credit of the fruits of his labor.

134. The Intellectual Property has protection under both the copyright laws and the patent laws. The patent laws give strong protection to IP as compared to the copyright covering. Cyberspace is a place where copyright infringements and acts of piracy flourish; computer program codes are easily copied.[84]Article 10(1) of the Agreement on Trade-Related Aspects of Intellectual Property Rights (TRIPS) provides copyright protection to computer programs. Article 4 of the WIPO Copyright Treaty (WCT) also provides protection to computer data as "literary works". The Indian legal protection of software copyright meets international standards partially. The Indian law does not prevent a properly registered software package from being copied for

81. Andrew Charlesworth & Chris Reed, *Computer Law: Problems of Policy and Jurisprudence in the Information Age* (Thomas West, US 2004) 250.
82. *Ibid.* 363
83. There exists a controversy that the "evanescent copies" in the RAM being of temporary nature cannot be the object of copyright infringement while is also advocated that the ISPs are always free to preserve a copy in the hard disk or may keep it in "cached" form. *Id.*
84. Karjala Dennis S, *Recent United States and International Developments in Software Protection-European Intellectual Property Review*, 16(1) (1994) 13.

use on multiple computers, and does not object to copying of the software for non-commercial use. Deterrence regarding copyright infringement is insufficient because of difficulty in procuring evidence and the simple punishment the law gives. Conviction rates in this field are law due to multiple reasons.

135. Indian Law: In India the Copyright Act 1957[85] is the major law governing copyrights in the country. It is believed that "copyright is national in nature"[86] as the protection is limited to the boundaries of a country but in the present scenario of the ICT proliferation and in the borderless world protection seems to be transnational.

136. Meaning of Copyright: Under the Copyright Act 1957[87] the term "copyright" encompasses the following acts:

(a) Regarding literary, dramatic or musical work not in the form of computer; to reproduce, issue copies, perform work in public or communicate to the public, to make film on it, to translate it, to make adaptation, etc.
(b) Regarding a Computer Program: to do any of the acts as specified in Clause A, to sell or give on commercial rental or offer for sale or for commercial rental any computer program provided that such commercial rental does not apply in respect of computer programs where the program itself is not the essential object of the rental.
(c) Regarding artistic work; to reproduce the work in any material form including depiction in three dimensions of a two-dimensional work or vice versa, to communicate the work to the public to include the work in any film to make any adaptation of the work, etc.
(d) Regarding Cinematograph film; to make a copy of the film, to sell or give on hire copy of the film, to communicate the film to the public
(e) Regarding Sound recording; to make any other sound recording of it, to sell or give on hire such work.

---

85. Amended in 1999, the Copyright Rules 1958 as amended in 1995 and the International Copyright Order 1999 as amended in 2000 Last amended 2013.
86. Raman Mittal, ch. 5 "*Copyright Law and the Internet*" in SK Verma & Raman Mittal (eds.), *Legal Dimensions of Cyberspace* (Indian Law Institute, New Delhi 2004) 115.
87. Section 14 Clauses (a) to (e).

Chapter 2. Legal Protection of Software

§1. General Statement

137. The software industry in India and all over the world are soft targets of pirates. Because of their intangible nature the software products are not only easy to copy and misuse but it is a tough job to contain the public tendency to piracy as well. Computer software is actually a set of mathematical representations, formula or algorithms or "a set of instructions expressed in words, codes, schemes or in any other form including a machine-readable medium capable of causing a computer to perform a particular task or to achieve a particular result."[88] According to the World Intellectual Property Indicators Report 2013 the IP filing trends globally are at an all-time high.[89] As an indicator of the fact that IT industry in India is gradually making a shift towards IP driven products and services the Annual Report of the Indian Patent office shows that there is five times increase in number of Indian patent applications between the years 2009-2012. The Indian IT-BPM firms which are growing speedily by offering the value and proposition of cost savings and efficiencies in delivering business processes the challenges are formidable and there is a need to move to an IP-led model. The IP in computer situation is tacit and peculiar by nature and the legal protection is not enough but protective measure within the organization is a better option.

138. Computer Software under Indian Law: Although to date no specific law has been formulated in India for the protection of computer software, IP laws have been amended timely and suitably and software is protected under the copyright and patent lass and also through trade secrets:

– *Software Protection under Copyright law:* Section 2(o) of the Copyright Act 1957 says that "literary work includes computer programs, tables and compilations including computer literary databases. "Literary work" means an expression in print or writing and no importance is given to its merit. Thus, the expression can be not only in understandable words but it can also be in the form of symbols or notations, visible representations, etc., a computer program is defined under the Act as "… a set of instructions expressed in words, codes, schemes or in any other form including a machine-readable medium, capable of causing a computer to perform a particular task or achieve a particular result." The Act however does not differentiate between the source code and the object code although they are covered under the Act as literal elements of computer program. Computer software in inclusive of program manuals, papers, printouts, punch cards containing information in a particular notation, magnetic tapes, discs required for operating computer or any perforated media and other data storage device. Even magnetic discs and tapes and floppy disc which are recorded by means of electronic impulses

88. Section 2(ffc) Copyright Act 1957. (India).
89. Pradeep Udhas (KPMG), Gary Matuszak, (KPMG) Chanrashekhar (NASSCOM); *Innovation Transforming the Growth Landscape*, 2.

are databases and are forms of literary work. However, the concept or idea of algorithms is not capable of copyright protection but programs which are operating computers are accepted to be within the ambit of artistic and literary work and thus protectable.[90]

- *Software Protection under Patent Law:* Patents can be used to protect the ideas in software to protect the functional aspects of the software and the law can be enforced against one who implements the patented feature by way of copying, reverse engineering or by developing it independently. The TRIPS Agreement (Article 27.1) can be used for including computer programs but in the Agreement there is no explicit direction to the Members regarding granting of patent protection to computer programs. The Patents Act 1970 did not expressly exclude the "computer programs" but under section 2(l) (j) a patentable invention was required to be non-living and tangible. Under this expression the software in the form of a mathematical algorithm could not be patented as it was something not in tangible form. However, software combined with a machine or computer under its influence becomes novel machine and thus could be regarded as "patentable". But again to fulfill the criteria of "patentability" it had to fulfill the condition of newness, inventive step and capability to be an industrial application under section 2(l) (j) of the Patents Act 1970. However, under the pre-Revised Act a software program on its own was not eligible for protection without hardware but the embedded system as a part of hardware was regarded patentable. Thus, under the pre-Revised Act the IBM was granted two patents.[91] The Patents (Amendment) Act 2002 excludes computer programs from patentability. Under section 2(k) "a mathematical or business method or a computer program per se or algorithms" are non-patentable. This section is in similarity with the European Patent Convention (EPC, section 52). However, although the EPO (1985), USPTO (1995) and JPO (1997) give guidelines there are no such guidelines by the Indian Patent Office. The question rests on the fact that what is the meaning and extent of the term "software program". The software patenting in India is thus hampered for the time being

§2. Subject Matter of Protection

139. Organizations in India have defined Intellectual Property on a wide spectrum of innovation ranging from reusable knowledge assets to high and software products. Based on the survey conducted by KPMG there is felt a widely circulated idea that there should exist a clear ownership for the asset to be considered as IP which could be achieved only through copyright and patent laws and regulations. It is realized that commercial value of an IP asset can be fully realized only through effective protection and monetization strategies. Apart from the commercial value of the software the literary or artistic work which it holds also has aesthetic and social value for the author. In the beginning software were sold as inseparable parts of the computer system but now software products have opened a new commercial counter where the computer

90. Stewart S M, *International Copyright and Neighbouring Rights*, Vol, I (Butterworths, USA) 1989.57.
91. One granted in February 1996 (Patent No. 176178) and another in 2001.

readable form like the diskettes, floppy disks, CD-ROM are separate from the computer hardware. The tangible forms of software namely the disks and diskettes, etc. are different from the software embedded in it.[92] The queer nature of the software puts them in altogether a different category. It is not the tangible disk which is the subject matter of transfer /sale in such cases but actually the owner passes certain rights in use the data therein. Computer software like biotechnology is subject to fierce competition[93] susceptible to easy mass copying with limited duration.

§3. CONDITIONS OF PROTECTION

140. The Indian Copyright law gives protection to all sorts of "literary work" including the computer programs. To qualify for protection the "literary work" must be original. The term "originality" has been interpreted by the Indian courts in consonance with the interpretation of the British courts.[94] To be eligible for legal protection the expression of thought is given importance and not the originality of ideas; the expression of thought in print or in writing is given importance for purposes of legal protection. The degree of originality is not given as much importance as the labor, skill judgment and the finances which are spend in a creation. To acquire a copyright, it has to be registered with the Copyright Office by making an application in the prescribed form along with prescribed fee to the Registrar of Copyrights. The registrar after holding inquiry may register the name of the author as owner of copyright in the Register of Copyrights.[95] In case of the computer programs the law does not require the mentioning of the source code and copyright software.

§4. OWNERSHIP

141. According to section 17 of the Copyright Act 1957 the author of a work shall be the first owner of the copyright so possessed. This is true in respect of the computer programs as well. The Act however differentiates between the "First Owners" in relation to a particular work or act done by the person concerned. Thus, the section 17:

(a) *Ownership under Course of Employment:* Whereas the author does any literary, dramatic or artistic work asked by the proprietor of a newspaper, magazine, etc. to be published in such newspaper/magazine under the contract or apprenticeship then in such a case the proprietor shall be the first owner if there is no contract which makes the author the owner and incase there is no such contract then the author shall be the first owner.

---

92. Matthan R., The Law Relating to Computers and the Internet. (Butterworths, India) 2000.276.
93. Verma SK, *IP Protection of software and Software Contracts in India- A Legal Quagmire*. Journal of Intellectual Property Rights.Vol.17. July 2012, 284–295.
94. *RG Anand v. Deluxe Films*, AIR 1978 SC 1613.
95. Sections 44, 45 -The Copyright Act 1957.

(b) *Creation for Consideration:* In such instance where a work such as a painting/portrait drawn, a photo taken, or an engraving or film made is done at the request of a paying customer, then – in the absence of a specific contract bestowing ownership on the creator – the person on whose request the work is made shall be the first owner.
(c) *Course of Employment:* Where in cases the clauses A and B do not apply and there is a contract of employment between the employer and the author of some work then the employer will be the first owner.
(d) *Public Speech:* Where a person asks another to deliver a speech in public or to address the public then the person who asks such another shall be the first owner of such speech or address and the fact that the person who delivers such speech is employed by any other person will not affect the ownership of the person who asks to make such speech, etc.
(e) *Government Work:* Whereas the government has asked a person to do some work then if there is no contract to contradict it, the Government shall be the first owner.
(f) *Public Undertaking Work:* Whereas any work is done on the direction of a public work undertaking then if there is no contract to the contrary then such public undertaking shall be the first owner.
(g) *Work of the International Organization:* Whereas any work of any international organization as per section 41 falls under any of these categories:

- work is first done by or under the direction of it;
- there is no copyright in that work in India at that time; or
- if the work is published as a result of an agreement between the organization and where no right is reserved to the author.

In any of the above case the international organization shall be the first owner. (section 17 (e)).

§5. Scope of Exclusive Rights

142. Under the Copyright Act 1957 copyright means the exclusive right to do or authorize the doing of any of the following acts in respect of a work or any substantial part thereof;[96] The Copyright Act 1957 also protects the author's economic rights in the copyrighted work (section 14 and 57) which also includes the rights in computer programs. The owner of a copyright thus has the following rights:

(1) All the copyrights: The Owner shall enjoy the following rights in respect of the computer programs to the exclusion of all others:

- The right to reproduce the work and to publicize it, to make any film or sound recording of his work; to make translation or adaptation of the work, etc. (section 14)

96. Section 17 -The Copyright Act 1957.

(2) *Assignment of Copyright:* The owner of a copyright has the right to assign his copyright to another person in respect of some present work or some future work, partially or fully. The assignor of rights shall be the owner in respect of rights not assigned and the assignee shall be the owner in respect of rights so assigned. The representatives of the assignee shall be treated as assignee. (section 18).
(3) Special Rights: Apart from the copyrights the author shall have the right to claim authorship of the work; to restrain or claim for damages in respect of any harm, distortion, mutilation modification, etc., is done to his copyrighted work during the term of copyright and which at the same time harms his reputation. Such rights can also be exercised by the representatives of the author. (section 57).
(4) *Rights of Owner in respect of infringed copies:* The owner of a copyright shall have a right to retake or claim possession of the infringed copies from the person who makes such copies of the copyrighted work un author singly. However, if the maker of such copies claims innocence as regarding author's rights and pleads "no knowledge" of author's rights or denies any ground for having reason to believe that the copies are infringed ones then the owner cannot claim his rights. (section 58).

143. Exclusion of owner's rights: In respect of computer programs certain acts have been excluded from the copyright area of the owner: the making of copies and adaptation of a computer program; to make backup copies of the work for security purposes; any act to obtain information necessary for the interoperability of any program if such information is not otherwise readily available; the observation, study or testing of any computer program to determine the ideas and principles which under line any elements of the program and where such acts are necessary for the functions for which the computer program was supplied; the making of copies from those copies which were made for non-commercial personal use. (section 52(aa) (ab), (ac), (ac).

§6. Limitations on the Scope of Protection

144. Although the Copyright Act 1957 has included computer programs within the term "literary work" for the purposes of according copyright protection to it yet it has not simplified as to what in computer context is the literal part. The scope of infringement is connected with the act of infringement. The infringement of a non-literal part or the copying of computer design will constitute copyright infringement. The question in computer software cases has been with regard to the limits of substantial copying, and as to what are the portions which come under the copyright protection. [97]In India the Copyright Act does not recognize the idea-expression dichotomy as expressed by TRIPS (Article 9(2)). In *RG Anand v. Deluxe Films*, the Supreme Court of India apart from "look and feel" test also discussed the "abstraction test" as laid down by the US Supreme Court.[98] The Court concluded that it was not proved that the similarities in the defendant's work were the result of copying but held that there was

97. *Microsoft Corporation v. Vijay Kaushik and Another*, 2011 (48) PTC 127 (Del)
98. *Nichols v. Universal Pictures*, 45F.2d 119.

a common theme.[99] Thus, there is no precise test laid down by the Indian Courts to determine the area of infringement of copyright in computer programs. The "abstraction test" of "abstraction-filtration-comparison" (AFC) also has not been followed in India.[100] In computer programs as the nature of the work is extremely technical hence an ordinary test is not suitable. Generally speaking the copyright laws in software protect everything except when the expression is in an industry standard or if the expression is functional necessary to accomplish a functional task such as compatibility. Thus, icons by themselves are not protectable. Object code and source Code are the literal portions of the program and are protected under the Copyright Act 1957.

§7. Duration of the Protection

145. In India the Copyright Act 1957 gives equal status to the computer software and other artistic and literary works – section 2(o) of the Copyright Act 1957 says that "literary work includes computer programs, tables and compilations including computer literary databases. A "computer program" under the Act is defined as a set of instructions expressed in words, codes, schemes or in any other form including a machine-readable medium capable of causing a computer to perform a particular task or achieve a particular result"(section 2 (ffc)). Thus, the logical result is that the various provisions of the act *ipso facto* apply to all types of computer software. Copyright not being a perennial right has a fixed duration under law within which it is beneficial. The Duration of software protection is thus as follows: (sections 22–29)

- *Duration in literary, dramatic. artistic, and musical work* – When published during the lifetime of the author then the protection extends up to sixty years after his death and if it is joint-authorship then for sixty years after the death of the last author (section 22).
- *Duration in Anonymous and Pseudonymous Work:* In case of a literary, dramatic, artistic and musical work not being a photograph then in case of a publication the duration shall start from the next calendar year in which it is published up to sixty years and if the identity of the author is declared then the rule regarding a known author namely sixty years from the death of the author will be the period of protection (section 23).
- *Duration in regard to a Photograph*–When the photograph is first published then from the beginning of the next calendar year up to sixty years next (section25).
- *Duration in respect of other Works:* The duration rule under The Copyright Act 1957 takes sixty years as the longest time for according protection to the work of an author or creator. The basic rule followed under the Act is that the year of publication of the work in some matters and the year of death of the author is taken as the year of counting the period of protection of sixty years which varies slightly. Thus, the duration in cinematograph films, the sound recordings, works

99. This was followed in *Barbara Taylor Bradford v. Sahara Media Limited* (2003) 47 SCL 445(Cal); *Raja Pocket Books v. Radha Pocket Books*, 1997(40) DRJ 791 (Delhi); *Zee Telefilms v Sundial Communications*, 2003 (27) PTC 457 (Bom).
100. *Computer Associates v Altai*, 982F.2d 693 (1992).

of Government, public undertakings and international work is sixty years from the next calendar year of its publication (sections 26–29).

§8. Complementary Provisions

146. The Copyright Act 1957 is an elaborate law which circumscribes all the relevant matters connected with copyright in India. The entire Act by itself extends to even the software protection in the country. The holder of a copyright has inherent in it the right to allow any other person to make use of his work or creation. For this he is required to issue a license to such other person as per the provisions of the rules under Chapter IV of the Act read with Copyright Rules 2013.[101]

License by the Owner: The owner of a copyright, either by himself or by his agent can grant a right to another person in writing. This he can do for his existing or future work. The agreement must declare the duration, territorial extent, royalty, and other important matters relevant thereto. (section 19, 19-A). Where no duration is specified or where no territorial extent is specified then it shall deem to be five years from the date of assignment and India respectively. The assignment usually provides for possession of software for a specified period of time.[102] The assignor or the owner can retain his moral rights even after the assignment.[103] Section 57 of the Act also says that moral rights cannot be taken away by way of a license assignment. section 52 however does not declare as to the assignment of "fair use" rights in the license agreement. The licensee cannot rent or lease the software for any direct or indirect profits as right to rental; lease or lending, etc., is granted to the owner of copyright in software. (section 14(b) (ii)).

Compulsory License-Where there comes a question regarding license for publication of work for public good and an application is made to the Copyright Board[104] for grant of it then it must be accompanied with sufficient evidence to show that the owner has refused or allowed such republication and the reasons forwarded by it. The Board after hearing the applicant and the owner of the copyright shall if satisfied direct the Registrar of Copyright to issue the compulsory license to the applicant.[105]

147. Relinquishment of Copyright – The owner of a copyright on his own volition may give up or relinquish his right/rights in any copyrighted work. (section 21). Such act of the owner shall not affect the rights of other persons connected with it. The owner can relinquish his right in any one or more or all of his work which he will do

101. The Copyright Rules 2013, Notification. G.S.R. 172(E)- Gazette of India – Ministry of Human Resources,(Department of Higher Education), Government of India. New Delhi. Dated the Mar. 14, 2013.
102. Verma SK, *IP Protection of Software and Software Contracts in India- A Legal Quagmire.* Journal of Intellectual Property Rights.Vol.17. July 2012, 288.
103. *Srimangal & Co. v. Books (India) Ltd.* AIR1973Mad.
104. Established under s. 11 of the Copyright Act 1957.
105. Rule 7(3), The Copyright Rules 2013, Notification. G.S.R. 172(E)- Gazette of India – Ministry of Human Resources,(Department of Higher Education), Government of India. New Delhi. Dated the Mar. 14, 2013.

by sending a notice to the Registrar of Copyrights. Such notice shall contain among other things the name, identity nationality of the owner, title of his work, its language, the rights he wishes to relinquish, the details of the publisher, the registration number, the date and time, etc. The Registrar of Copyright shall within fourteen days of publication of the notification in the official gazette shall post it on the Copyright website which will remain in public domain for three years.[106] The rights of the owner shall cease to exist in the owner from the date of notice. (section 21(1)).

106. Rule 4 & 5 – The Copyright Rules 2013.

Chapter 3. Legal Protection of Databases

§1. INTRODUCTION

148. Databases are the offsprings of technological advancements in machine readable or other form which by reason of selection or other digitization of colossal data results into databases. Data which is already available is methodically collected at one place and is in an accessible condition. For purposes of copyright law a database has been defined as a compilation of data arrangement of the contents constitute intellectual creations.[107] Data can also be originally produced in digital forms which are readable as visuals, statements, texts, pictures, images, charts and tables and spreadsheets and in the form of other visible representations. Digitization helps easy storage and easy accessibility of huge computer datasets. Databases such as a telephone directory are "compiled out of necessity in the ordinary course of business the originators of many electronic databases take on the risks and tasks of gathering raw data" and organizing it through an efficient search engine for easy access to data.[108] Databases may be "original" or "non-original". The copyright protection of compilations continues in case of databases as well. One theory known as the "sweat of the brow" or "industrious collection" propounds that databases and compilations receive protection per se i.e., without showing any authority or original authorship and that creativity is a concept that is alien to the requirements of "originality". If lots of money, labor and time are invested into the creation of databases then such investment shall be sufficient to get copyright protection even if it lacks creativity. This theory advocates that it will give incentive to the compilers to develop new databases. The hard work which goes in compiling the huge yet structured datasets necessitates protection.[109] However, the advocates of the "modicum of creativity rule" interpret "original" as including a minimum level of creativity. The level of creativity, though minimal, requires that the work is original and not imitated and thus worthy of copyright protection. Note that an innovative character is not required.

149. Before 1996 the European Union countries had different levels of protection of databases and compilations while the U.K. recognized the "sweat of the brow" doctrine,[110] Germany required a higher level of creativity in order for works to qualify for copyright protection.[111] In 1996 The Directive unified the copyright criteria in the

107. Article 10.2, TRIPS; Art. 5 WCT.

108. Smith Graham J H,*Internet Law & Regulation*, 3rd ed. (Sweet & Maxwell, London), 2002, 246.

109. Nelson, Russell G., "*Seeking Refuge from a Technology Storm: The Current Status of Database Protection Legislation* ", Journal of Intellectual Property Law, Vol 6, 1999, 453.

110. *BBC v. Wireless League Gazette Publishing Co.*,(1926) ch 433: *Independent Television Publications v. Time Out*, (1984) FSR64; *Waterloo v. Reed*,(1992),FSR 409: *Dun & Bradstreet Ltd. v. Typesetting Facilities Ltd.* (1992) FSR 320.

111. Fromm Nordemann,*et. al* Urheberrecht (Copyuright Law), Commentary to secs 2 and 4 of Copyright Act, 8th ed.,1994.

European Community and adopted the "modicum of creativity rule" in granting copyright protection.[112] With expanding ICTs India is becoming more capable in the database field which is opening commercialization possibilities for it.

§2. Legal Protection of Original Databases

I. Subject Matter and Conditions of Protection

150. The copyright law is subject to the requirements of "originality" and has protected collections of data as "literary works." In India databases are protected under the generic category of compilations.[113] India being a member of the Berne Convention and TRIPS Agreement, the condition of "originality" is a special condition to accord copyright protection.[114] The Copyright Act 1957 does not define "originality" but to obtain copyright protection or the compilation it must have some sort of creativity in it; the Act insists on original work of authors or creators. The Indian Courts have also not been explicit on the concept of "originality" and each case is decided on the special "facts and circumstances" which it exhibits. Some of the verdicts have depicted the "sweat of the brow theory" and have rules that skill, labor and judgment test are applied in copyright infringement of databases. In cases like *McMillan v. Suresh Chander Deb,*[115] *Govindan v. Gopalkrishna*[116] and in a number of other cases[117] the courts have held that a compilation developed through investment of time, money, labor and expertise rises to the standard of literary work through it must have been retrieved from a common source. The underlying idea in all such decisions was that no one can make ill use of another's skill and labor and even a small amount of creativity attracts protection. A recent judgment in *Diljeet Titus, Advocate & Others v. Alfred A. Adebare & Ors.*[118] the Delhi High Court has ruled that the copyright in a database prepared by an advocate in another employer's resources, expertise and investment belongs to the employer-advocate. Referring to section 17(1)(c) of the Copyright Act 1957 the Court held that a work done during the course of employment or apprenticeship shall be the copyright of the employer provided there is no contract to the contrary. Again in *Eastern*

112. Article 3.1, Directive 96/9/EC of the European Parliament of databases
113. Section 2(1)(o) read with s. 13(1) Copyright Act 1957.The term "literary works" include compilations. India being a member of the Berne Convention and TRIPS Agreement, the condition of "originality" is a special condition to accord copyright protection
114. Article 10(2), Agreement on Trade-Related Aspects of Intellectual Property Rights (Annex IC, Marrakesh Agreement Establishing the World Trade Organization) (Apr. 15, 1994), 33I.L.M. 81 (1994); Article 2(5), Berne Convention for the Protection of Literary and Artistic Works (July 24, 1971), (amend. Sep. 28, 1979).
115. I.L.R.17(Cal),951, 961.
116. AIR 19565 Mad. 42.
117. *ShyamlalPaharia v. Gaya Prasad Gupta Rasal*, AIR 1971 All. 58; *Ganga Vishnu Shrikisondas v. Morishwar Bapuji Hegishte I.L.R.13*(Bom),358, 363 (1889); *Burlington Home Shopping Pvt. Ltd.v. Rajanish Chibber*, (1995) 6 Entertainment Law Review 159 (Delhi).
118. 2006(32) PTC 609 (Del).

Book Company v. Desai[119] the court held that in the case of compilations there can be a similar compilation prepared by another person but he cannot violate/infringe upon the "fruits" of the labor of previous compiler. The Court rejected the protection for "Head notes" prepared by the plaintiff holding that "protection of copyright must inhere in a creative, original selection of facts and not in the creative means used to discover the facts". Referring to the US Court's decision in *Feist Publications, Inc. v. Rural Telephone Service Co.,*[120] the court said that there should be a modicum of creativity in the selection, arrangement or coordination of the contents of a database to attract copyright protection.

II. Ownership

151. As an original database is given the same protection under the Copyright Act 1957 as a "literary work" in India, its rights of ownership are also on the same footing as the literary work.

III. Scope of Exclusive Rights

152. There is no specific law addressing the databases in India. As the databases and compilations come under the phrase "literary work", by analogy the exclusive rights of the owner in respect of original databases is the same as the one of the owner of a copyright of a "literary work". It thus falls under the category as described under the Copyright law as follows:

- The owner has the exclusive right to: (i) reproduce the work or storing it in electronic form; (ii) to issue copies of the work to the public; (iii) to use the work publicly; (iv) to make any cinematograph film, etc., with it; (v) to translate it; (vi) to make adaptation of the work.
- To sell/give on rent such databases. [section 14(b) (i) (ii) The Copyright Act 1957.].

153. However, the following acts shall not amount to copyright infringement in respect of databases (which are treated the same as computer programs):

(a) The making of copies or adaptation of the computer program for utilization of it for the purpose for which it was created.
(b) To make backup copies of it.
(c) The doing of an act necessary to obtain information essential for operating interoperability of an independently created computer program.
(d) The observation, study or test of the computer program.
(e) The making of copy from a legally obtained copy for non-commercial personal use.

119. AIR 2001 Delhi 185.
120. 499 U.S. 340 (1991)

[section 52(1) (11), (ab), (ac), (ad). The Copyright Act 1957].

IV. Duration of the Protection

154. Duration of protection in the case of original databases: As the databases or compilations are included in the term "literary work" hence the protection given to such literary work logically applies to the original databases. Thus, if published during the lifetime of the author then the protection extends up to sixty years from his death and if it is joint-authorship then for sixty years from the death of the last author. (section 22; The Copyright Act 1957).

§3. Legal Protection of Non-original Databases

I. Subject Matter and Conditions of Protection

155. The digital environment has called for a vast reform of the existing law regarding many subjects touching copyright. One of these being the need for a legal regime for non-original databases. Non-original databases involving substantial investment and effort denote databases that lack the prerequisite of originality or creativity to qualify for legal protection. It largely depends on the database industry in India to understand that whether the developing countries including India do need a *sui generis* protection of non-original databases. Eighty percent of the databases in India still emanate from the domain of the Government out of which only 40% is available to the public. Only a small portion of the above data (about 40%) is available to the general public. The remaining 60% of data is either internal data that is department specific and therefore holds no relevance for the general public or "classified," as it includes sensitive information pertaining to atomic research, space research, defense research, etc. The types of database companies active in India are similar to those found in other parts of the world, e.g., databases containing legal information, medical and commercial information, traveling and tourist information, educational institutions information and other compilations covering almost all the areas of public life. The potential for data creation in India and data wealth is mainly in the following areas:[121]

- *Traditional knowledge Data:* The Government has established Traditional Knowledge Digital library (TKDL). It contains all useful information connected with the traditional medicinal (Ayurvedic) knowledge, cultural knowledge concerning folklore.
- *Genomic Data* – The genomic industry in India is regarded as one of the "biodiversity" center treasuring potential rich source of animal /plant/microbial genomic data. It can fetch substantial revenue for the country.

121. *Standing Committee on Copyright and Related Rights*-Seventh Session, Geneva-May 13–17 2002.-WIPO- Study Prepared by Mr. PhirozVandrevala, Chairman-National Association of Software and Service Companies. (NASSCOM)- New Delhi – SC CR/7/5/

- *Information Technology:* India has emerged as the strong IT superpower and consequently the IT industry and the ICT together give a big boost to the revenue collection of the country. Thus, the Government has recognized this and has taken up the "database creation" as one of its top most priorities.

156. To date the country lacks a non-original (or even original) database specific legislation. The decision of the Delhi High Court in *Himalaya Drug Co. v. Sumit*[122] the Court preferred to follow the Fiest standard of "a modicum of creativity" and denied protection to copy-edited judgments. Thus, the said judgment indicates that the Indian copyright regime does not protect "unoriginal" database and it is not even regarded as a separate tort under the unfair competition and thus this common law right may not be available to protect the efforts of the Indian database industry.

II. Ownership

157. There is no legislation on the subject in India.

III. Scope of Exclusive Rights

158. There is no legislation on the subject in India.

IV. Duration of the Protection

159. There is no legislation on the subject in India.

122. Suit No. 1719 of 2000.

Chapter 4. Legal Protection of Computer Chips

§1. General Statement

160. Chips, often referred to as "the crude oil of the information age",[123] are the store house of massive information and data which can be easily and instantaneously be transmitted world over. The Export-Import Bank of India (Exim Bank) in its recent study has estimated the size of the electronics industry in India to exceed USD 150 billion by 2015. Since the 2005 emergence of an IP regime in the country, India has come a long way in the field of establishing a viable patent system for its electronics industry. With the entry of international players like *Flextronics, Elcoteq, Intel, Motorola, Texas Instruments, Nokia and Samsung* the electronics industry has gained considerable importance. Innovations are continuing at an overwhelming pace and thus the GOI policy has been relaxed so that the electronics manufacturing industry covers the entire spectrum starting from components to sub-assemblies and – as the most important element – the integrated chips. Thus, the electronic hardware production in the country is expected to rise from USD 20 billion in 2009 to USD 100 billion by 2014 and USD 400 billion by 2020 which includes exports of USD 4 billion in 2009 growing to USD 15 billion by 2014 and USD 80 billion by 2020. The semiconductor industry in India is also instrumental for these developments and is rightly called the "sunrise industry". India has proven its expertise in chip design and where the activities used to center around mere testing and support, they then moved to product upgrading and have now matured into a full-fledged product development industry. This expansion into innovation oriented industries, highlights the crucial rule Intellectual Property now has to play. Of the seven Intellectual Property Rights (IPRs): (1) copyright and related rights; (2) trademarks; (3) patents; (4) industrial designs; (5) layout designs of integrated circuits; (6) geographical indications; (7) Undisclosed Information apart from geographical indications and plant varieties, all others provide a fine interplay of protection in electronics industry. IP can take many forms such as employment, contracts, non confidentiality agreements, firmware, software, IC designs, electronic ASIC, IC, MCM, board and systems designs and embedded components, core device components, company's brand, etc. A Report of the Indian Trade and Patent Office indicated that out of every top ten foreign filers of patents nine are from the electronics industry. About 8000 applications were filed from within the electronics industry alone, which shows about 35% increase in the last four years. Consequently the protection of IPR in the field of Layout Design or the semiconductor integrated circuits drew the attention of law makers. Thus, India being a signatory to the TRIPS Agreement and to the World Trade Organization (WTO) passed the Semiconductor Integrated Circuits Layout Design Act 2000 which fulfills the obligation of TRIPS agreement (Articles 35–38) regarding the protection of semiconductor integrated circuits layout designs.

123. A. J. W. Van de Gevel, *From Confrontation to Competition in the Globalized Semiconductor Industry*, May 29, 2000.

§2. Subject Matter of Protection

161. Protection under Patent or IP Laws: Integrated circuits consists of a number of building blocks each block being patentable. as an integrated circuit contains hundreds and thousands of semiconductor devices a claim to an integrated circuit would require including hundreds or thousands of individual elements resulting into hundreds of pages thus such a narrow claim shall provide almost no protection. A claim inclusive of thousands of elements would be not only extremely complex, cumbersome but also expensive. The prolonged procedure to file application and compared to the short life span of the integrated circuit makes the law insufficient. As design patents protect the ornamental and not the functional aspects of a manufactured article in its drawings and as circuit layout is more functional than ornamental design patent protection is practically inapplicable to integrated circuits. The layout of transistors on the semiconductor integrated circuit or topography of transistors on the integrated circuit determines the integrated circuits as well as its processing power hence layout design of transistors comes as a form of IP basically distinct from the other forms of IP like the copyrights, trademarks, patents or industrial designs.

162. The Indian Law on Semiconductor Chips: Since the early 1970s chip piracy became prevalent as its copying is easier and cheaper. A *sui generis* protection was thus badly required. Chip pirates without effort made considerable gains while the legitimate companies spending so much on Research and Development were not gaining accordingly. Thus, the *Semiconductor Integrated Circuits Layout Design Act 2000* (SICLD) protects the layout design expressed in any manner which is original and which has also not been commercially exploited for two years from the date of application for registration and which is inherently distinctive and capable of being distinguishable from any other registered layout design is protected. [section 7].The Act defines the following as:

- *"Semiconductor integrated circuit"* means a product having transistors or other circuitry elements, which are inseparably on a semiconductor material or an insulating material or inside the semiconductor material and design to perform an electronic circuitry function (section 2 (r)).
- *"Layout Design"* means a layout of transistors and other circuitry elements and includes lead wires connecting such element expressed in any manner in a semiconductor integrated circuit (section 2(h)).
- *"Commercial exploitation*" in relation to SICLD means to sell, lease, offer or exhibit for sale or otherwise distribute semiconductor integrated circuit for any commercial purpose. (section 2(e)).

163. Under the Act protection is given to the layout design itself which will be different from protection in a chip product.[124] The Act in India however follows the

124. The US law follows a different pattern whereas a mask work is not eligible for protection unless it is fixed in a semiconductor chip product. Thus according to s. 901(a)(3) of the SCPA a mask work is "fixed" in a semiconductor chip product "when its embodiment in the product is sufficiently permanent or stable to permit the mask work to be perceived or reproduced from the product for a period more than transitory duration."

IPIC Treaty's definition of "layout design" [125] as it requires strict adherence to the terms of the Treaty. (Article 2 through 7). Explanation to section 17 of the SICLD Act lays down that the right conferred by the registration of a layout design shall be available to the registered proprietor notwithstanding the fact that the layout design is incorporated in an article or not. Layout design can be registered if they are: (1) original; (2) inherently distinctive; (3) distinguishable from other registered layout designs; (4) not already commercially exploited for more than two years before date of application for registration. Thus, not "novelty" but distinctiveness is the condition for registration under the Act. A layout design if it is the result of the creator's own intellectual efforts would be considered "original" for the purposes of registration. The Act recognizes that layout design will usually contain design elements already existing or protected in the semiconductor industry which is an important issue for semiconductor layout designs as they are in the vast majority of cases new compilations of well-known elements. Not only that "creator's own effort" is a condition but the Act also requires that such design should not be commonplace among the creators of layout designs and manufacturers. This can be evident by original combination of elements of design that are not themselves original. Thus, a new topography can be the result of a combination of commonplace elements, which have not been combined in precisely the same way as before. There may also be chance that any newly designed layout design will have at least some features or combination of features which are dissimilar to features which are already well known in respect of semiconductor products. In a U.K. case[126] the term "commonplace" Justice Laddie who liked Counsel's submission that any design which is "trite, trivial, common-or-garden, hackneyed or of the type which would excite no particular attention in those in the relevant art is likely to be commonplace".

As for the second requirement under the Act that it must be inherently distinctive or inherently capable of being distinguished from any other registered layout design although the terms appear in the Trade Marks Act 1999 have different meanings. "Inherent distinctiveness" can be tested as follows:

- Even though well-known designs elements may be there but in fact the functions performed by it must be not only new but different from that performed by other layout designs.
- The elements and substances used in the manufacture of the layout –design should be novel in the industry.

This requirement of "distinctiveness" is peculiar about the Indian law only.

164. The third requirement is with respect to commercial exploitation; thus any act of leasing, selling, offering, exhibiting for sale in respect of a layout design is its commercial exploitation. The main test is to see if there is anything done for commercial purpose like distributing a layout design though not for money may also amount to commercial purpose.

125. The IPIC Treaty defines it as "the three-dimensional disposition, however expressed, of the elements, at least one of which is an active element, and of some or all of the interconnections or an integrated circuit, or such a three –dimensional disposition prepared for an integrated circuit intended for manufacture". Art. 2(ii).

126. Ocular Sciences Ltd. Aspect Vision Care Limited [1997] RPC 289.

§3. Conditions of Protection

165. In India like any other developed country law extends protection to the distinctive layout designs which are not previously commercially exploited and registration is the way to extend protection to it. There are elaborate provisions under the Semiconductor Integrated Circuits Layout Design Act 2000 (37 of 2000). The GOI is empowered under the Act to appoint a person as Registrar of Semiconductor Integrated Circuits Layout Design.[127] The GOI is also empowered to establish a Registry having a head office and several branches as the Government fixes to carry out the functions under the Act. There shall for the purposes of registration be a register maintained by the Registry Office. Thus, the registration of a layout design will be done only if it fulfills the following conditions:

- It is original.
- It is not commercially exploited anywhere in India or in a convention country. If a layout design has been commercially exploited for less than two years from the date of filing an application for registration in India or in any convention country then it will be regarded as not being commercially exploited for purposes of this Act.(Proviso to section 7 (1)).
- It is inherently distinctive.
- It is inherently capable of being distinguishable from any other registered layout design.

166. A layout design shall be considered to be original if it is the result of creator's own intellectual efforts and is not commonly known to the creators of layout designs and manufacturers of semiconductor integrated circuits at the time of its creation. The Proviso to section 7(2) says that a layou -design consisting of such combination of elements and interconnections that are commonly known among creators of designs and manufacturers of semiconductor integrated circuits shall be considered as "original" if such combination taken as a whole is the result of creator's own intellectual efforts.

§4. Ownership

167. The SICLID Act prohibits registration of two or more persons who claim to be the creator of a layout design. This basic rule has an exception that when two or more persons claiming to be the creator of a layout design are so related with each other that; a) both of them have put combined intellectual effort in creating the design or b) both of them are connected in such manner that their effort in creating the layout design becomes indistinguishable then both of them shall be registered as the joint – owner (joint proprietor) of the registered layout – design. [128] A registered proprietor in relation to a layout design is the person who is for the time being registered as the proprietor of the layout design. [section 2 (o)].A registered proprietor has the power

---

127. Section 3- ch.. II *Semiconductor Integrated Circuits Layout Design Act 2000 (37 of 2000).*
128. Sections 14–17 The *Semiconductor Integrated Circuits Layout Design Act 2000*(37 of 2000).

to assign the layout design and to give effectual receipts for any consideration for such assignment. [section 20].

§5. Content of Exclusive Right

168. The registration of the layout design gives to the registered proprietor of the layout design the exclusive right to the use of the layout and to obtain relief in respect of infringement. The right shall be available to the registered proprietor of that layout design irrespective of the fact as to whether the layout design is incorporated in an article or not.[129] The Act provides comprehensive protection to the layout designs of semiconductor integrated circuits as a recognized IP and also gives the proprietor a bundle of rights under it. There is one significant exception to this exclusive right; any person may reproduce the layout design "for the purposes of scientific evaluation, analysis research or teaching…"[130] This is in consonance with the fair dealing exception in copyright law. The Act also allows "reverse-engineer" layout designs for the purpose of analyzing the layout designs and incorporating the insights of their analysis into an original layout design of their own. Thus, for the sake of development of creativity and also to follow the spirit of the IPIC (section 6(2) (b)) and the TRIPS Agreement this provision is made. This will also support the successful entry of the integrated circuit market segment with a new product which is compatible with established products The registered proprietor also has the exclusive right to import, sell or distribute for commercial purpose any semiconductor chip products in which the registered layout – design is embodied.[131]

169. Enforcement of Exclusive Rights –The infringement of the layout design is regarded as an offense punishable with imprisonment up to three years or with a fine which should not be less than INR 50,000 and which may extend to INR 10 lakh or with both.[132] Although the Act does not provide for civil remedies but it also does not expressly rule out the application of civil remedies which means that resorting to remedies like an injunction, accounts of profits and damages to enforce rights regarding integrated circuit layout designs is possible. Section 16 explicitly says that "no person shall be entitled to institute any proceeding to prevent, or recover damages for the infringement of unregistered layout design" and it can be interpreted to mean that such remedies are available in respect of registered layout designs. The Act however exempts the innocent purchaser of infringing chip products who had no knowledge or any reasonable ground to know that such product is an incorporated or registered layout design. However, if after coming to know about it if the innocent purchaser continues with his acts in respect of such layout design then he will have to pay royalty to the registered proprietor of the amount as settled between the two.[133]

---

129. Section 17 The *Semiconductor Integrated Circuits Layout Design Act 2000* (37 of 2000).
130. *Ibid* at s. 18
131. *Id.* at s. 18(1)(b) and Art. 6(1)(ii) of the IPIC Treaty and the TRIPS Agreement.
132. *Id.* at s. 56. In respect of infringement of a layout design the registered proprietor can file a written complaint before the Magistrate Class I who is competent to take cognizance. The Court can order forfeiture of such goods and may also order its destruction in case of conviction.
133. *Id.* s. 18(6).

§6. Duration of the Protection

170. Protection under the Act extends for ten years which is in conformity with Article 38(1) of the TRIPS Agreement. While the TRIPS Agreement and the IPIC Treaty are silent on the date of commencement of protection the Indian law regards it as the date of first commercial exploitation anywhere in India or anywhere in the world whichever earlier. Such protection shall extend up to a period of ten years from the date of filing an application for registration or from the date of first commercial exploitation as given above. (section 15).

Chapter 5. Other Intellectual Property Rights in the ICT Sector

§1. Generally

171. IP protection boosts innovation. The electronics industry of India is estimated to exceed USD 150 billion by 2015. The electronics industry makes a phenomenal contribution to India's GDP. This formidable progress of the industry calls for a strong protection for their product lines. It provides many technological innovations. To recapitulate, there are seven forms of recognized IPRs in India: Copyright and Related Rights, Trade Marks, Patents, Industrial Designs, Layout Designs of and Integrated Circuits, Geographical Indications, Undisclosed Information. Out of these seven, around five provide a fine interplay of protection in electronics industry. IPRs can be incorporated in many different instruments, such as employment contracts, non-disclosure agreements, firmware, software, IC designs, electronic ASIC, IC, embedded components, core device components, company's brand, etc.

172. The fact that patenting of software is becoming more important globally is not lost on Indian policy makers. The pirated software is a national risk and the companies also become deterrent apprehending great loss as a result of the pirated software. It is estimated that in India about 64% software is pirated and as a result great revenue loss is suffered by the government. A strong regime on the protection of IPRs in the area of ICT is long overdue in the country.

§2. Legal Protection of Multimedia Works

173. Multimedia is also a form of expression with the help of various technological works; it is an amalgamation of varied technologies and can be called a creature of the computer age. It can be defined as interactive software stored and transmitted in digital form which incorporates multiple forms of audio, video, graphics, text, animation, photography and special effects for display and performance on the monitor which is computer controlled. It is a form of interpretative system providing a broader range of information. Thus, multimedia works have opened a new area of legal issues as such creations are also placed for *en masse* publicity and is a ultimately a big source of profit. As it is also a kind of IP hence multimedia licenses are issued involving different types of IP rights and most licenses which involve photographs, film, video, audio, graphics, text and animation raise legal issues regarding copyright and the rights of publicity. Trademarks, service marks trade dress, trade secrets and moral rights are also raised in multimedia projects. The issues which were common in respect of earlier technologies like the VCR and disk recordings would also help the claimants of the IP rights in respect of multimedia works although the earlier technologies were no so useful unless found in the new technological format. The multimedia developer needs to know the types of IP rights it will get from the licensor. Generally speaking, the developer of multimedia who gets the license once, is expected to have it worldwide or "universal publication" rights.

§3. Legal Protection of Web Pages

174. Creation of a web page is the offspring of the Internet. The entire data trove on the Internet is available in the form of web pages; and a web page is the creation of the website creator and owner, having its own expressions, exclusive designing and special effects which are the result of website owner's own creativity. The question therefore arises to the exclusive claim of the creator over the designing of the web page adding a new category of IP on the Internet.

Thus, the creation of a website may raise concerns like the; copyright concerns, trade mark concerns, domain name concerns, defamation and linking and framing. [134] In India the Copyright Act 1957 (14 of 1957) is a comprehensive law which protects all forms of IP on the net as all forms of "literary work" fall under such creations. Various clauses of section 14 of the Act define the scope of the term "copyright." The Copyright (Amendment) Act 2012 broadens the scope of the copyright in respect of literary works and other creativities with the help of electronic medium. Thus, the protection of the web page owner' rights also fall under the following clauses whereas the term "web page" has not been specifically mentioned in the Act:

- Incase of a computer program the copyright owner has the exclusive right to reproduce the work; issue copies; perform the work in public; make any cinematograph film or sound recording, make any translation of the work; to make any adaptation of the work; (section 14 Clause (b)(i) and (a).).
- To sell or give on commercial rental or offer for sale or for commercial rental (section 14(b) (ii)).
- In case of an artistic work the owner of copyright shall have the right to reproduce the work in any material form including storing of it in any electronic medium; depiction of it in three dimensions of a two-dimensional work, or depiction of a two dimensions of a three-dimensional work? (section 14 (c) (i) as Amended 2012).

175. Thus, the creation of website is included in the above clauses of the Copyright Act 1957 (14 of 1957) and the issues are covered not only under the copyright law but also under the domain name provisions as well as under the law of defamation depending on the nature of the issue.

134. *Website Legal Issues*- By Brad Bolin, an Intern working for Daniel A. Tysver. (Beck & Tysver) (1998–2013) Bitlaw.

Chapter 6. Internet Domain Name Registration

§1. Background

176. To establish one's presence on the Internet one has to have an address, a locating indicator. A domain name is the virtual equivalent of a postal address in the real world, i.e., a locator. Internet Protocols (IPs) are long numerical expressions to locate an organization or an individual on the Internet which has its drawback in being legible only by the machine. To overcome this the linguistic version of the IP was established known as the "Domain Name System" (DNS).

177. The emergence of powerful search engines coupled with browsers which require only the identification of a part of a Uniform Resource Locator (URL) to locate the required site urged businesses to resort to domain names to reassert their presence on the Internet. Consequently the domain names became an exclusive identity of an organization ultimately becoming the online counterpart of classical trademarks. Today domain names reflect the goodwill, reputation and high recall value in respect of a business. As it gave an identity to the business houses and corporate giants hence apprehensions regarding their piracy or misuse came up as the main issues. Legislators therefore started treating domain names at par with trademarks and legal protection to the same came as a necessity. This was done by the Internet Corporation for Assigned Names and Numbers. (ICANN).[135] The ICANN adopted the Uniform Domain Name Dispute resolution Policy (UDRP) on October 24, 1999. The policy offers an expedited administrative proceeding for trade mark holders to contest "abusive registrations of domain names" and it gives to the registrar the power to cancel, transfer or suspend a domain name in case of a dispute.

178. The Indian Domain Name Policy: India has liberalized its domain name policy as in its previous policy only the commercial entity which was registered in India could apply for it. With the expansion of the commercial world there came repeated demands to allow the foreign corporate to have a domain name in the country as it was not feasible for the foreign corporate to incorporate a local entity only for the purpose of holding a domain name registration in India. The highlights of the liberalized policy are as follows:

- New categories of the sub-domains like gen.in., firm.in and ind.in have been added.
- For a foreign entity to register a domain name in India the sub-domains would be co.in, gen.in and firm.in.

135. It is a non-profit corporation that was established with the aim of allocating IP address for the assignment of protocol parameter and for root server system management functions. The registration process is done by the administrator of a Top-level Domain (TLD). The TLD gives unique number or address to the applicant so as to differentiate between various applicants and to maintain their identity.

- The co.in requirement to have a mandatory local presence in India has been done away with to some extent.
- The gen.in category has been added to facilitate foreign corporate who were unable to meet the local presence requirement.
- The previous condition that he name server should have physical presence in India and that the domain name applicant should have permanent Internet connectivity through an ISP has also been removed.

§2. The Assigning Authority and the Registrars

179. The domain name regulatory authority or the ICANN adopted the Uniform Domain Name Dispute Resolution Policy (UDRP). The policy provides for incorporation of terms and conditions into the registration agreement concerning disputes between the registrant and any party other than the registrar over registration and the use of a registered domain name. According to this policy the registration of a domain name is considered abusive if the following conditions are fulfilled:

- The domain name is identical or closely similar to a trade or service mark in which the complainant has rights.
- The holder of the domain name has no rights or legitimate interests in respect of the domain name.
- The domain name has been registered in bad faith.

180. In India registration of.IN domain name has been allowed since 2005. Registration has been tremendously liberalized, has become cheaper and is allowed to citizens and foreigners equally. This has paved the way for so-called cyber squatters. And thus there has been steady rise in cybersquatting cases after the expiry of the sunrise period in January 2005. "IN" is India's top-level domain on the Internet like. COM. IN can be used for e-mail, web sites and other applications. Unlike other domains "IN" is the unique symbol of India in the world. IN Registry is the official.IN Registry appointed by the GOI to operate under the authority of the NIXI. The Department of Information Technology (DIT) in association with the Internet Service Providers Association of India (ISPAI) has promoted the NIXI as a not-for-profit company under section 25 of the Indian Companies Act 1956 with the aim of facilitating improved Internet services in the country. NIXI aims at regulating Internet traffic originating and having a destination within India and assuring its security. The Ministry of Communications and Information Technology through the Department of Information Technology has implemented the "New Policy for.IN Internet Domain Name registration & National Internet Exchange with effect from January 1, 2005. This policy basically governs the registration and administration of .IN domain names in India. This policy is based on the internationally accepted UDRP as prescribed by ICANN and sets out the terms and conditions to resolve a dispute between the registrant and the complainant arising out of the registration and use of the.in Internet Domain Name.

181. Registrars – A Registrar provides direct services to Domain Name Registrants. The database of the Registry contains customer information and other valuable information regarding domain name registration. ERNET is India's exclusive Registrar for ac.in, edu.cin, & res.in. The Registrars first process the name registrations for Internet end users and then sends the necessary DNS information to a Registry for entry into the centralized Registry database and ultimate propagation over the Internet.

§3. The Legal Status of Domain Names

182. With proliferation of the Internet all the things associated with it increased; namely the domain name by itself became a soft target of cyber criminals. Ultimately many legal issues raised their heads. In India the sole cyber law the Information Technology Act 2000 (Amended 2008) does not address domain names. As domain names became identical with trademarks of the paper world in India the protection is accorded under the Trademarks Act 1999 though it has no extraterritorial jurisdiction. However, various judicial pronouncements in India regarding the domain name issues and the legal protection accorded to it have become a good source of law on the subject. The time Internet started getting a hold over the commercial and social world in India the domain name disputes reached the doors of justice.

183. Case Law in India: In the case *Satyam Info way Ltd. v. Sifynet Solutions Pvt. Ltd.*[136] The Supreme Court of India ruled that Internet domain names are subject to the same legal norms as applicable to other IP such as Trade Marks. The Court held that "the use of the same or similar domain name may lead to a diversion of users which could result from such user mistakenly accessing one domain name instead of another. This may occur in e-commerce with its rapid progress and instant (and theoretical limitless) accessibility to users and potential customers and particularly so in areas of specific overlap." The Court further said that the ordinary consumers/users seeking to locate the functions available less than one domain name may get perplexed if they arrive at a different but similar looking website which offers no such services. In such a situation the user could well conclude that the first domain name owner had misrepresented its goods and services through its promotional activities and the first domain owner would thereby lose their customer. In this case the Supreme Court itself declared that there is no legislation in India which explicitly refers to dispute resolution in connection with domain names. The Trade Marks Act 1999 is not extraterritorial and is insufficient for the protection of domain names in the country.

In the case *Yahoo! Inc. v. Akash Arora & Another*[137] the Delhi High Court awarded relief to *Yahoo! Inc.'s* petition against the defendants who were attempting to use the domain name <yahooindia.com> for Internet-related services. *Yahoo! Inc.,* who was the owner of the trademark *"Yahoo"* as well as the domain name <yahoo.com>, contended that by adopting the deceptively similar domain name <yahooindia.com> the defendants had verbatim copied the format, contents, layout, color scheme and source code of the plaintiff prior created regional section for India on the plaintiff's website. In this case the Court rejected the argument of the defendants that the provisions of the Indian Trade Mark Act 1999 would not apply to the domain names on the Internet. The Court relied on the *Doctrine of Passing Off* and combined with an analysis

136. (2004 (28) PTC 566)
137. 1999 PTC (19) 210 (Delhi).

of the working of the Internet the Court concluded that appropriation of the *"yahoo"* name by the defendants justified the action. The Court held that though a general term yahoo has acquired identity with the business of the plaintiff company and has strong association with the plaintiff's reputation and it thus needs maximum protection. The Court thus granted injunction restraining the defendants from using the word "yahoo" in its domain name.

In yet another landmark judgment *Rediff Communication Ltd. v.Cybertooth and Anr.*[138] deliberated upon the protection of domain names in India. The Single Bench judgment adds to the development of Indian Jurisprudence on domain names in India. The Court ruled "a domain name is more that an Internet Address and is entitled to the equal protection as trade mark. With the advancement and progress in the technology, the services rendered in the Internet site have also come to be recognized and accepted and are being given protection so as to protect such service provider of service from passing off the services rendered by others as his services." Rejecting all the arguments the Court was convinced that there was clear "intention to deceive" on the part of the defendants as they deliberately used the term "<rediff>" to trade on the goodwill and reputation of the plaintiffs as their field of operation was also common and hence there were strong possibilities of confusion.

§4. The Registration Procedure

I. General Considerations

184. The Internet encompasses every facet of life on earth, be it communication, trade, education, agriculture, science or technological development. It has reached the Government departments as a symbol of good governance and has become an impressive medium in politics. India following closely and impressively the advanced nations of the world has embraced the new medium of Internet. Domain names come as a facilitating factor for proliferation of the Internet in any country. To make the proliferation of the Internet easy and far reaching India adopted market friendly liberal policies. Especial consideration is to adopt the globally accepted policies and also procedure of registration so as to facilitate addition of domain names.

185. In India.IN is the allocated country code Top-level Domain (ccTLD).This helps not only the general masses but the government entities, businesses, organizations in establishing their Indian identity on the Internet thereby using a short and unique Domain Name. The overcautious registration policy and absence of contemporary processes and infrastructure for registration have so far not favored the much progress of the.IN Domain. Government therefore took no time in revamping the.IN Domain Name Registry in India to provide a greater thrust to its activities. Thus, the new policy has the following features:

138. AIR Bom. 27.

- Unlimited generic.IN registration will be offered at second level of domain name and also at the third level in the globally popular zones of domain name e.g.,.co. in,.net.in, and.org.in.
- Registration shall be by Registrars who will be appointed by the.IN Registry through an open process of selection which would be on the basis of transparent eligibility criteria.
- Registration shall be given by the Registrars following a competitive pricing policy and best market prices and the charges shall be different but affordable for both the third and second levels.
- The.IN Registry will adopt uniform Dispute Resolution Policy (UDRP) and will be assisted by a Dispute Resolution Committee to resolve disputes involving the Registry. It will also appoint Arbitrators to address disputes between Registrars and registrants.
- The entire process of registration shall be online and should be completed in less than twenty-four hours of the receipt of the request from the registrant.
- The.IN Registry will announce a "Sunrise Period" of ninety days to enable registered trademark owners, registered companies and owners of intellectual property having a legitimate interest in protecting their brand to secure registration of their Domain Names after due verification.
- The zones for Government, Military and Educational Institutions will be reserved for exclusive use by the respective organizations. Registrations for these departments will be offered by NIC, an organization nominated by the Ministry of Defense and ERNET.]
- The.IN Registry will have the authority to deny or suspend any registration if it conflicts with the sovereign national interest or public order.
- The names of Constitutional Authorities, States/Union Territories and specific names used by the.IN Registry will constitute the reserved category of names inaccessible by the public.

186. The NIXI: The National Internet Exchange of India presents a unique Domestic Internet Scenario in India with several large and small ISPs spread across a large geographical area. NIXI takes care of the concerns of large as well as the small ISPs at the same time keeping the larger national interest in mind by promoting domestic hosting of content as well as saving foreign exchange by keeping domestic traffic within India. The Traffic Routing and Tariff Policy is revised from time to time. NIXI is also given the responsibility of operating the.IN Registry to implement the new policy framework for.IN Domain Name by creating an.IN Network Information Center (INNIC). The INNIC under NIXI operates as an autonomous body which implements various policies of the Government; it maintains the.IN Domain and ensures its operational stability, reliability and security. The Registrars selected by the.IN Registry are from among or utilize the services of the ISPs connected to NIXI nodes.

II. Indian Domain Name's Typology

187. In 2005 the policies were liberalized which allowed unlimited second-level registrations under.in The India Registry has formulated new policies for the registration and administration of.IN domain names. The goal is to make.IN domain names easier to use and a way of making the Internet available to the common man. Following structure allows unlimited registration of domain names:

- in (available to anyone, used by companies, individuals and organizations in India);
- co.in (originally for banks, registered companies and trade marks);
- firm.in (originally for shops, partnerships liaison offices, sole proprietorships);
- net.in (originally for Internet service Providers);
- org.in (originally for non-profit organizations);
- gen.in (originally for general /miscellaneous use);
- ind.in (originally for individuals);

Six zones are fixed for use by prestigious institutions:

- ac.in (Academic institutions);
- edu.in(Educational Institutions);
- ernet.in (Previously for educational and research institutions);
- gov.in (Indian government);
- mil.in (Indian military).

The domain.nic.in is reserved for India's National Informatics Center (NIC) but other Indian agencies also use it.

III. Common Standards and Rules for the Registration of Second and Third-Level Domain Names

188. ERNET India is Domain Registrars for all the educational and research institutes. It will register Domains at second and third level in the following zones:

- ac.in (Academic);
- edu.in (Academic);
- res.in (Indian Research Institute).

The Internet Domain Name Registry receives Domain Name Service (DNS) Information from Domain Name Registrars, inserts that information into a centralized database and then propagates that information in Internet zone files on the Internet so that domain names can be found by users around the world via applications such as the world wide web and e-mail. .IN Registry is the official.IN Registry. It is appointed by the GOI and operates under NIXI.

IV. Registration of Third-Level Domain Names

189. Third-level domain names consists of three parts(like.in .co.uk names). For instance in the third-level domain name– example.com.cn– CN will be the top-level part COM would be the second-level part and EXAMPLE would be the third-level part which is registered by the user/applicant. In India there may be a registration at second level or at third level beneath generic category second-level domains. There is no restrictions on who can register second-level domains or most third-level domains; restriction under some specialized sub-domains.

§5. Cancellation of Domain Name Registrations

190. Once the Registrant gets his domain name he becomes its rightful user. However, there may be disputes between the Registrar and the Registrant. In such a case the matter will be referred to the Arbitrator. The dispute shall be conducted by the Arbitrator in accordance with the Arbitration and Conciliation Act 1996 and in accordance with the.IN Domain name Resolution Policy. The Cancellation of Domain name registration or its transfer shall take place in any of the following circumstances:

- First, at the end of the Arbitration proceedings the Arbitrator has power to cancel the registration of the Registrant.
- Second, the Registrar has the right to cancel the transfer of domain name registration to another holder if the transfer is made in violation of paragraph 12 of the Policy.

§6. Out-of-Court Dispute Settlement

191. Domain names have rightful claimants. Disputes are bound to arise when there is misuse of it by another or in other words cyber squatting is committed. A person who considers that a registered domain name conflicts with his legitimate rights or interest may file a complaint to the IN registry on the following grounds:

- That registrant's domain name is either identically similar or confusingly similar to his trade mark or service mark over which the complainant has rights.
- That the registrant has no rights in respect of it.
- That there is bad faith on the part of the registrant to have the registration of such domain name.

Thus, the registrant will have to submit to a mandatory arbitration proceeding in such a case and must follow the rules of the.IN Registrar. The following remedies are available to the complainant:

(a) Cancellation of the domain name of the registrant.
(b) Transfer of the registrant's domain name registration to the complainant.

192. These remedies are however insufficient. The IT Act 2000 is also silent on the point. However, section 66D of the newly amended (2008) IT Act which makes cheating by personation or by any communicational device a punishable offense can be applied to cyber squatting cases if the option of judicial courts is taken.

§7. Brief Reference to the Conflicts Between Domain Names and Trademarks

193. Trademarks are age old. Domain names are the product of the Internet. Trademarks have emerged as an established field of Intellectual Property;[139] domain names are acquiring the same status on the Internet though remarkable differences between the two still exist. Domain names are not only intangible but they are connected to a number of parties such as the registration authority, the website operator, the users of the worldwide web, etc.

194. The legal protection accorded to the trademarks is enshrined in the Indian Trade and Merchandise Marks Act 1958 as the trademarks are the main identifier to which the goodwill towards and reputation of a company are attached.

A registered trademark acquires twofold protection:

- Under the relevant law as in India under the Indian Trade and Merchandise Marks Act 1958 as also under the law of a country if it is registered there.
- Under the Common Law Doctrine of Passing off. Courts in India have abundantly applied this doctrine in a catena of cases.

195. Domain Names exist in a borderless world and hence are accessible globally. It is typical about domain names that once they are registered they enjoy global exclusivity and do not need separate registration in various countries. In such a situation a national legislation may not be adequate to protect a domain name. A domain name dispute gives rise to such issues which can be solved only by resorting to legal, technical and commercial principles. In recent times there have been situations where the infringement of a domain name has been treated similarly as a violation of trademark by the Courts. The dispute regarding domain names can be between the domain name and the trademark owners or between domain name owners/claimants *inter se*. A prior registrant can protect its domain name against the subsequent registrants. The defenses in respect of both the trade mark and the domain name disputes are the same.

In India no separate law deals with the dispute resolution in respect of domain names. Although the Trademarks Act 1999 is not having extraterritorial operation yet several judicial pronouncements (*Supra* paragraph 193) resorting to the Passing off Doctrine, etc. have extended strong and successful protection to domain names in India. The Courts in India are also free to apply Rule 2 of the UDNDR Policy which requires that for the registration of the domain name the applicant shows that the domain name does not infringe the "trademark rights" of another person and if it does

139. Ira Nathenson analogizes a domain name to property saying that law extends protection to domain names as well. Ira S. Nathenson- *"Jurisdiction over Squatters, Poachers and other Parasites"*, 58, U.Pitt.L.Rev.991 (1997).

so then it violates the Rule 2 and the Registrar can refuse registration of it. Thus, it is evident that a domain name though properly registered as per the requirements of ICANN is still subject to the Trade Marks Act 1999 if one proves that he has “rights” flowing out of the Act.

Part III. ICT Contracts

Chapter 1. Hardware Contracts

196. All the contracts including the hardware contracts under the ICT are controlled by the Indian Contract Act 1872. The hardware contracts on behalf of the government are implemented by the Department of Electronics and Information Technology. There are various schemes of the government, the most recent of which are the Electronic Hardware Technology Park (EHTP) and Export Oriented Unit (EOU).[140] Under the Foreign Trade Policy there are Deemed Exports in which the payment is made in Indian rupees. The supply of goods comes under the EHTP and EOU under the "Deemed Exports." Deemed exports shall be eligible for any/all of the following benefits in respect of manufacture of hardware goods qualifying as deemed exports. Such contracts shall be subject to the terms and conditions as given in Chapter 8 of Handbook of Procedures (volume I) 2009–2014 of the Department of Commerce, Ministry of Commerce and Industry.

140. Department of Electronic and Information Technology, Ministry of Communications and information

Chapter 2. Software Contracts

197. In India a good number of archaic legislations guide the commercial contracts. The Indian Contract Act 1872, the Sale of Goods Act 1930 are all pervasive and all types of contracts are guided by these legislations. The Information Technology act 2000 (amended 2008) is the latest law which deals with electronic commerce and as a consequence the software contracts are also guided by a combination of these laws. Contracts can be in the form of sale, assignment or license. First, the Sale of Goods Act 1930 deals with sale of all types of movable properties and it defines "goods" as "every kind of movable property other than actionable claims and money and includes stock and shares, growing crops, grass…" (section 2(7)) This definition includes both tangible and intangible property. The information in the software is of uncertain nature and hence uncertainty regarding its inclusion in the term "goods" was put at rest by the Supreme Court in the case *Tata Consultancy Services v. State of Andhra Pradesh.*[141]

In this case the Court ruled that computer software is included in the term "goods" notwithstanding the fact that computer software is protected as intellectual property and irrespective of the material form in which it is conveyed, e.g., in diskettes, floppy, magnetic tapes or CD-ROMS, whether canned (shrink-wrapped) or uncanned (customized), whether it comes as part of computer of independently branded or unbranded, tangible or intangible it is commodity capable of being transferred, transmitted, delivered, stored, processed, etc. Being a commodity which is sellable it is also taxable. Thus, the Court concluded that a software customized or non-customized fulfills these attributes then it is "goods" under the Sale of Goods Act 1930 and is hence guided by the relevant laws like the Indian Contract Act 1872, the Consumer Protection Act 1986 and shall also be subject to the different tax laws: central excise duty,[142] customs duty on imports[143] and royalty paid by the assessee for using the trade mark of another person.[144]

198. License Agreement: Licensing of software has come up as a substitute for contract of sale thus the software owners have become more prompted to opt for distribution transactions as licenses instead of sale.[145]A license gives more controlling power to the software owner. The license may have provisions relating to the person who may use the program, warranty, limitation of liability, distribution of the software, etc., as is evident in mass market licenses.[146] It may contain provisions relating to upgrading the program, access and Internet clauses, development and support contracts.

---

141. 271 ITR 401 (2004),418.
142. *Commissioner of Central Excise v. ACER India Ltd.* 137STC 596(2004)[SC]; [2001]4 SCC593.
143. *Associated Cement Company Ltd. v. Commissioner of Customs*, 124 STC, 59 (2001)[SC]; *State Bank of India v. Collector of Customs* [2000] 1 SCC 727, [2000]1Scale 72.
144. 35 *SPS Jayam and Co.* (2004) 137 STC 117[Mad].
145. Mtima Lateef, *Protecting and Licensing Software*; Copyright and Common law contract considerations, *The Computer and Internet Lawyer*, 22(3)(2005) 13.
146. Singsangob Anuya, *Computer Software and Information Licensing in Emerging Markets; The Need for a Viable Legal Framework* (Kluwer Law international, The Netherlands), 2003, p. 21, 68.

This gives universal rights to the owner other than the running of software in the purchaser's computer. This has also become an internationally acceptable phenomenon. Sale of off-the-shelf software may be termed as sale in which the title to the box containing disk, manual, etc., may pass to the buyer while the title to IP in the software remains with the owner. The purchaser obtains a license to use the software which is the main purpose of the contract. A software contract may be a license of both the physical carrier and the IP contained therein and in such a case the licensees is restricted from transferring it to the third person. Under the Copy right Act 1957 the right to rental, lease, lending, etc. is granted to the owner of the copyright in software. (section 14(b) (ii)). Consequently the licensee unless specifically authorized cannot rent or lease the software for profit, direct or indirect.[147] In India a contract is governed by the place where it is concluded and thus if it is applied on the software contracts then conflict of laws and multijurisdictional issues are bound to come up.

199. Enforcement of Software Contract-The legality and enforceability of software contracts are yet to be tested on a judicial level. The Copyright (Amendment) Act 2012 (27 of 2012) does away with the requirement of the contract being in written form or being signed. If the transaction is to be qualified as a sale, then the parties are free to determine the terms and conditions insofar these are not against public policy as followed in India. If the contract entails the delivery of a service, then the Consumer Protection Act 1986 will come into play for violation of efficient service as promised. The click-wrap agreements may involve more than one jurisdiction giving rise to issues like conflict of laws and extraterritorial application of the Indian Law. The legality of shrink-wrap agreements putting restrictions on the development, use, services may be called in question under the Competition Act 2002 (12 of 2003). The information Technology Act 2000 (21 of 2000) though deals with e-commerce would be applied to the software contracts in respect of IP issues is still to be seen. A license agreement to come under the law of contract must not be unconscionable or unreasonable bargain.

147. Mittal Raman, *Licensing Intellectual Property; Law & Management* (Satyam Law International, India), 2011, pp. 505–507.

Chapter 3. Turnkey Contracts

200. A turnkey contract is a business arrangement in which a project is delivered in a finished state. A developer is hired to finish the entire project without the inputs from the owner. The builder or developer is separate from the final owner or operator and the project is turned over only once it is fully operational. The term is also often used the technology industry most commonly to describe pre-built computer "packages" in which actions like audio editing is put together by the supplier and sold as a bundle.

A good number of companies in India give high quality turnkey electronics manufacturing Services, Defense Instruments and Medical Electronics, automotive electronics and Electronic manufacturing services, etc. operate in India. It often includes a computer with pre-installed software and various types of hardware and accessories.

Chapter 4. Distribution Agreements

201. The Distribution Agreement encompasses agreement between a company in need of having its products distributed and the distributor that specialized in providing that function. The distribution agreements are non-exclusive and exclusive. For ICT products exclusive distribution agreements are made as it involves highly sophisticated equipment and infrastructure. There is also distribution agreement for computer software and for other ICT products. All such distribution agreements are regulated by the Indian Companies Act 1956 and also by Companies Act 2013.

Chapter 5. Maintenance Contracts

202. In India maintenance contracts are considered to be service contracts. Like any other contract the maintenance contracts are also governed by the Indian Contract Act 1872.

Chapter 6. Facilities Management

203. In India outsourcing of individual services had started in early 1990s when Information Technology and Information Technology enabled Services (ITeS) had started gaining momentum in the country. However, integrated delivery of Facilities Management services through single point providers started only a decade ago. Presently Integrated Facilities Management (IFM) is a quite latest business offering in India.

Technology is playing a decisive role in the delivery methodology of FM services.

Outsourcing has gained popularity in the IT sector. The concept of facility management services gained momentum in India after the liberalization, privatization and globalization policies. The two main Facility Management Services and most of these Services are in the IT/ITeS/BPO/KPO and Banking and Finance sectors. In the IT Sector and in providing basic infrastructure the house keeping and security, manned guard are the main revenue gainers for the FM service providers.

At present there is no regulatory body to control the industry and the present labor laws like the Minimum Wages Act, Employees Provident Fund, etc. are applicable to FM industry also like any other industry.

There is also Total Facility Management (TFM) Services becoming popular where multiple sub contractors are avoided.

It is estimated that IT/ ITeS contribute more than 21% of revenue generated by the FM services market as more and more investments are seen in this sector. A Report forecasts that FM services market in India shall grow at a CAGR of 17.19% during the period 2016–2020.(Report inker, New York October 12,2016/PRNewswire/--)

Chapter 7. Network Services

204. The NIC is the premier information Technology Organization in India providing solutions for Information Management and Decision support in Government and corporate Center. It is the epicenter of various network services delivered to almost all the departments of the government both at the Central and state level. It provides network backbone to all the governmental organizations and offers a wide range of ICT services including Nationwide Communication Network for decentralized planning, improvement in government services and wide transparency of central and State governments. NIC assists in implementing IT projects and ensures latest technology to its users. It is actively involved in most of the IT enabled applications and has changed the mindset of the working community in the governments to make use of the latest state-of-the-art technology in their day to day activities to provide better services to its citizens.

205. Various Services by NIC – The NIC provides following services:

- Antivirus Services-Antivirus servers have been deployed across NICNET in every State and Ministry called Child Servers. They are all bound to a central console configured in NICNET HQ called the parent server.
- Business Intelligence (BI): The BI is providing services in the area of business intelligence solution to users across the government. It main aim is to provide facilitates to the users for better access to the information so as to extract knowledge from large base.
- CollabLand: NIC also provides software for digitization of survey of maps for computerization of Land Records. It can handle a variety of survey systems, extending from the conventional Chain and Theodolite method to the modern electronic Total Station (ETS) system.
- Domain Registration: As per the new Domain Name Policy released by the Department of Information Technology NIC is the exclusive registrar for GOV.IN country level Domain Registration.GOV.IN is reserved for registering domain names for all the Government Departments.
- Integrated Network Operations: Integrated Network Operations Center (INOC) is responsible for the constant monitoring and trouble shooting of network devices to ensure round the clock management of NICNETY. The INOC specializes in technical issues relating to network and guarantees a fast response.
- Messaging: Mails are accepted and sent in NICNET from a single entry point i.e., via the SMTP gateways. Over one million mails are transacted daily. Once a mail is accepted in the network based on its address, it is routed to the recipient server. Messaging services constitute one of the primary applications deployed across the network. They represent the front end of the network hence messaging services in NICNET need to integrate the application solution, the underlying network, proactive management and maintenance in a single source solution.
- National Data Centers (NDCs): The NDC meets the growing demand for state-of-the-art centers for hosting, protection of data with efficient backup and recovery solutions. Thus, there was a need to set up a strategic infrastructure those facilities

high availability, quick scalability, efficient management &optimized utilization of resources.

- NIC Certifying Authority: With the expansion of e-Governance NIC provides a PKI platform. As the nodal IT organization in the country it plays a pivotal role as it has established biometric sensor system and surveillance systems of international standard.
- National Knowledge Network (NKN)-The NKN is the state-of-the-art multi-gigabit Pan India network for providing a unified high speed network backbone for all knowledge-related institutions in the country. The purpose of such knowledge network can be linked to the quality institutions with requisite research facilities and a pool of highly trained officials.
- Video Conferencing: Established in 1995 it is the largest video conferencing network in the country. It is being upgraded by providing a High Definition video conferencing systems.VC services are decentralized by enabling such state unit to handle its own Multipoint videoconferencing sessions to meet local and state government requirements.
- Web Services – NIC is extending comprehensive World Wide Web services (http://webservices.nic.in) to Central and State Governments. Ministries and Departments in the areas of Consultancy, web design and development, web hosting, value-added web services for promotion of websites, enhancement of websites and training.
- SATCOM: NIC is the nodal information Technology organization for informatics development and networking in Government and Government-related organizations. It has established a satellite based nationwide VSAT Network called NICNET. Presently NIC, VSAT Network- NICNET has been offering network services over Ku-Band VSATS such as DVB Broadband and SCPC/DAMA/PAMA to its user organization for data, voice and video applications. SATCOM Division is providing VSAT connectivity for delivering the E –Governance services.

Chapter 8. Government Contracts

§1. General Information

206. As India emerges ahead in the area of ICT and as most of the Departments are predominantly held by the government in this area, it should not come as a surprise that commercial contracts between the government and private enterprises cover a major part of the commercial activities in the country. The Indian Contract Act 1872 is the major law which regulates commercial contracts and it hardly differentiates between contract which is purely between private individuals or contracts where one of the parties is the Government. However, the Constitution of India empowers the government to enter into contracts. Article 299 of the Constitution says that all the contracts entered into by the government shall be carried out and executed on behalf of and in the name of the President of India in respect of the contracts by the GOI and by the Governor in respect of the contracts entered into by the State Governments. The term "executed" does not – by itself – mean the execution of a formal contract, but a tender and its acceptance in writing made on behalf of the President or the Governor as the case may be and its execution in itself shall fulfill the requirement of Article 299 and a valid contract is formed. [148] The Supreme Court held in the case of *State of Bihar v. Majeed*[149] that "It may be noted that like other contracts, a Government contract is also governed by the Indian Contract Act yet it is a distinct thing. In addition to the requirements of the Indian Contract Act such as offer and acceptance and consideration, a Government contract has to comply with the provisions of Article 299. Hence, subject to the formalities prescribed by Article 299, the contractual liability of the Central or State Government is the same as that of any individual under the ordinary law of contract." There is hardly a distinction made by the Government and made by the private individual so far the formalities of the contract are concerned yet the government by virtue of Article 299 enjoys certain privileges. Again the Supreme Court held in *Bhikaraj Jaipuria v. Union of India*[150] that the provisions of Article 299 are mandatory and it saves the Government from unauthorized contracts and is based on public policy. Article 299 immunizes the President and the Governor totally from personal liability but the contractual liability of the government is on the same footing as the private individual.

207. Principles underlying Government Contracts: Reasonableness and fairness is the first underlying principle in a government contract. In a democratic set up it is unthinkable that the government can act arbitrarily using its power against the common man. The administrative authority must act in good faith The principle of reasonableness and fairness is also applicable in executive action and the Court undertaking the judicial

148. *State of Madhya Pradesh v. Firm Gopal Chand Sarju Prasad* –AIR 1972 MP 43.
149. AIR 1954 SC 786.
150. AIR 1962 SC 113; (1962) 2 SCC 880; *See also State of West Bengal v. BK Mondol & sons.* AIR!1962 SC 779; *Milan Chand v State of Madhya Pradesh.* AIR 1968 SC1218.

review can strike down such order which is in violation of it. [151] Public interest is the core of the governmental action. Whenever any contract is entered into the interest of the common man is paramount which should be taken care of by the government and equality which is the antithesis of arbitrariness must also be followed which is envisaged by Article 14 of the Constitution and which "pervades Article 14 like a brooding omnipresence"[152] and must be followed in all government procedures, contracts and actions.

§2. Hardware, Software and Maintenance Contracts

208. Over the last couple of decades India has taken long strides in the area of consumer demand which is also fueled by a phenomenal GDP growth. Demand for high technology products especially electronic products has also registered significant growth; the demand for electronics hardware in the country is projected to increase from USD 45 billion in 2009 to USD 400 billion in 2020 (source: Task Force Report).

209. The Centre of Development of Advanced Computing (C-DAC) for achieving High Computing a cluster of workstations are used. The Department has also developed hardware systems and commercial activity is going on in this respect. It is also aiming to take advantage of hardware technologies worldwide. The current generation of parallel systems uses a cluster of off-the-shelf workstations interconnected using high performance communication and switches developed by C-DAC which is supported by associated firmware and device drivers necessary for the integration of the hardware with the system software.

210. India is a signatory to the Information Technology Agreement (ITA-1) which is a plurilateral agreement of WTO. Developed member countries like the USA, European Union and Japan have proposed the scope and coverage of ITA. The Department of Commerce and the Department of Electronics and Information Technology of the GOI has started consultations with stakeholders. It mainly focuses on IT products comprising: (a) devices such as amplifiers, radios, media players, video cameras, IT office equipment, battery chargers, radio navigational devices; (b) parts and accessories like passive and active electronic components, connectors, switches, etc.; (c) consumables like magnetic tapes, optical discs, semiconductor storage devices, batteries used for powering IT goods, etc. India's stakeholders consultation is mainly focusing on 1) developing a definition of IT products; 2) identify products included in the list that have non-IT use; 3) basic economic characteristics of the products included in the list and manufactured in India; 4) identifying the products included in the list on which India can reduce tariffs to zero; 5) identifying products in which India has potential for export;6)implications on India's domestic industry of the proposed outcomes on non-tariff measures, such as SDOC standstill on third party certification, etc. [153]

---

151. *M/s/Pynites, Phosphates & Chemicals Ltd. v. Bihar Electricity Board.* AIR 1996 Pat 1.
152. *Maneka Gandhi v. Union of India.* AIR 1978 SC 597.
153. Annual Report 2012–2013: Commercial Relations, Trade Agreements and International Organizations; Ministry of Commerce and Industry-Department of Commerce- Government of India.

§3. Electronic Communication Contracts

211. The Department of Electronics and Information Technology of the GOI is the main body which carries out the contractual agreements in respect of electronic goods manufacturing on behalf of the President of India as per Article 299 of the Constitution. The Government has initiated several initiatives for the development of electronics sector in the country. The Government has recently approved National Policy on Electronics (NPE). The NPE aims at achieving a turnover of USD 55 billion of chip design, and embedded software industry, USD 80 billion of exports in the sector. The Policy also proposes to set up over 200 Electronic Manufacturing Clusters. To promote electronics sector the Government has plans to set up semiconductor wafer lab in the country and it has already become the hub for semiconductor design with nearly 2000 chips being designed per year. India is generating nearly USD 2 billion in revenue for chip design services.

212. The government also gives importance to the domestically manufactured Electronic Goods- (PMA) vide the Department of Electronics and Information Technology dated December 23, 2013. The policy is applicable to all government Ministries/departments except Defense. It will be applicable for procurement of electronic products made under all Centrally Sponsored Schemes and grants by Central government.

Part IV. Electronic Transactions

Chapter 1. Legal Status of Electronic Transactions

§1. Legal Framework

213. Founded on the Model Law on Electronic Commerce of the United Nations Commission on International Trade Law (UNCITRAL) the Information Technology Act 2000 (21 of 2000) was passed by the Indian Parliament. The IT Act has since been amended in 2008. The Act legalizes transactions carried out by means of electronic data interchange (EDI) and other means of electronic communication also known as electronic commerce. The IT Act 2000 also made consequential amendments in the Indian Penal Code 1860, the Indian Evidence Act 1872, Banker's Books Evidence Act 1891 and the Reserve Bank of India Act 1934.

214. Banking Laws: As a supplement to the IT Act a whole series of Acts and regulations and Notifications have been passed to augment the law regarding electronic fund transfer and online transactions in the country. The Payment and Settlement Systems Act 2007 (51 of 2007) The Act empowers the Reserve Bank of India (RBI) to regulate various payments and electronic settlement systems. As a sequence to the Act of 2007 the RBI issued the Payment and Settlement Systems Regulations 2008. These Regulations address various factors such as the need for the proposed system, the technical standards and design, credit policy, consumer interest, etc.

§2. Electronic Commerce and the IT Act

I. Legal Concept of Electronic Contract

215. With the proliferation of the Internet and in the fast moving and fast changing world of technology, commerce and industry could not opt to suffer. Globally laws were hastily formulated to catch up with the virtual world. Contracts hitherto were mostly concluded on paper but with the technological advancements paperless world is where now contracts of billions are concluded with the click of the keyboard. Traditionally speaking a contract is an agreement enforceable by law.[154]

154. Section 2(h) The Indian Contract Act 1872.

II. Scope of the Law

216. There are a number of legal intricacies involved regarding a finished contract: completion of offer and acceptance, formation of contract are still complex issues and its formation online remains a question of fact. The electronic contract is nowhere defined under the IT Act but it takes all the characteristics of a contract of the paper world namely offer and acceptance, competent parties, free consent, consideration and lawful object. The IT Act 2000 and the Indian Contract Act 1872 collectively guide the electronic contract.

III. Validity and Effectiveness of Contracts Concluded by Electronic Means

217. The main question is thus regarding the validity of the contract made online just like the contracts made in the paper world, the validity of an online contract depends on the same principles namely the time and completion of offer, the time and completion of acceptance and ultimately the formation of contract. This is because a contract is complete with the acceptance of the offer.[155]

Communication of offer and acceptance are complexities as different timings are destined for communication of acceptance as against the proposer and the acceptor. With the invention of telephones learned Denning LJ ruled[156] that the postal rule shall not apply to cases where the parties are face to face even though at some distance and in such a case “no contract will arise until the offeror receives the notification of acceptance.”[157] Today the online contract may well follow the postal rule as when the e-mail is “sent” it is out of the power of the acceptor and at this moment it binds the proposer as even timing is registered in online transactions and it will ultimately bind the acceptor the moment it reaches the offeror. A legal and valid contract is thus concluded.

IV. Electronic Contracts and Formal Requirements

218. The IT Act 2000 requires that three parties may exist in connection with a contract made online: (1) The Originator is the person who sends, generates, stores or transmits the electronic message or causes it to be sent, generated, stored or transmitted to any other person [section 2(1) (za)]. (2) The addressee is the person who is intended by the originator to receive the electronic message[section 2(1)(b)]. (3) The Intermediary with respect to a particular electronic message is any person who on behalf of another person receives, stores or transmits that message or provides any service with respect to that message [section 2(1) (w)]. Thus, so far electronic contracts are concerned there

155. Section 5 of the Sale of Goods Act 1930 also says that contract of sale is complete when an offer is accepted. *See* , AG Guest (Ed.*) Anson's Law of Contract*. 23rd ed., Oxford,1969) 44.
156. *Entores Ltd. v. Miles Far East Corpn.*, (1955) 2 all ER 493; (1955) 2 QB 327; (1955) 3 WLR 48.
157. Avtar Singh, Mercantile Law (8th ed., Eastern Book Company,2006) 31.

are three agencies involved though the contract is concluded only between the "'Originator' and the 'Addressee'".

219. Authentication Requirement: The authenticity and originality of the contract online and the identity of parties is secured by means of electronic signatures, encryption. This is a must to make the electronic contract valid and effective.

V. Evidence of Electronic Contracts

A. The Electronic Contracts and Its Evidence in the Litigation scope

220. While a paper document is the strong evidence of the contract in the online situation the evidence itself is intangible though capable of being produced in a law court. Thus, in electronic contracts technology permits the use of functional acknowledgements which would be equivalent to the traditional AD or Acknowledgement Due system. The provision of the IT Act dealing with acknowledgement of receipt is based on the assumption that acknowledgment procedures are to be used at the discretion of the originator. [section 12]. The Act is silent on the point whether such acknowledgement will amount to acceptance of the offer or not. Thus, in such cases the addressee shall either employ any other means to acknowledge receipt of the message or the conduct of the addressee shall be an indicator that he has received the intended message. In such a situation often the originator stipulates that the electronic record shall be binding only on receipt of an acknowledgement then unless an acknowledgement has been received the effect will be that the message was never send by the originator. If the originator does not stipulate that the message shall be binding only on receipt of the acknowledgement and the originator does not receive it then the originator can conclude that the message was never sent.

221. The Law of Evidence: The IT Act 2000 has made consequential amendment in the Indian Evidence Act 1872 making it suitable for electronic evidence in the Court. The amendment ensures that any transaction, activity, transmission, etc. made through electronic means shall be admissible in the law court. The relevant portions of the amended Evidence Act in respect of e-Commerce may be briefly understood as follows:

(1) Evidence means and includes all documents including electronic records produced for the inspection of the court. [section 3 (2)].
(2) Entries in the account books in electronic form maintained during course of business shall be relevant as per Court's opinion. [section 34].
(3) Opinion of the Certifying Authority who has issued the Electronic Signature Certificate is relevant. [section 47A].
(4) Admissibility of Electronic Records: Any information contained in an electric record which is printed on paper, stored or recorded or copied in optical or magnetic media produced by a computer shall be deemed to be a document and shall be admissible in any proceeding without the production of the original or further proof if the conditions given in the section are satisfied [section 65B].

B. Evidence of the Obligations Undertaken by the Parties and Intervention of " Reliable Third Parties"

1. Generally

222. Concluding commercial contracts traditionally necessarily involved only two parties; the offeror and the offeree. The proof of the contract remained with both the parties in paper form. The electronic transactions being totally an intangible affair, a mediator who could retain the e-document ensued as Reliable Third Parties.

Moreover the entire contract deed could be preserved in the form of an electronically signed document giving it not only authenticity but also a sort of permanence. Thus, the existence of Reliable Third Parties has come up as the hallmark of electronic transactions.

2. Intervention of "Reliable Third Parties"

223. The intermediary with respect to a particular electronic message is any person who on behalf of another person receives, stores or transmits that message or provides any service with respect to that message. The term according to the new amendment also includes telecom service providers, network service providers, Internet service providers, web-hosting service providers, search engines, online payment sites, online-auction sites, online-market places and cyber cafes [section 2(1) (H). The Information Technology (Amendment) Act 2008]. The definition of "intermediary" is intended to cover both professional and non-professional intermediaries. i.e., any person (other than the originator and the addressee) who performs any of the functions of an intermediary. In the Act "intermediary" definition is not as a generic category but with respect to each data message, thus recognizing that the same person could be the originator or addressee of one data message and an intermediary with respect to another data message.

VI. Formation of the Contract

224. The IT Act 2000 including the Amendment of 2008 is silent on the point of formation of the Contract. However, as the IT Act is based on the Model law (UNCITRAL) regard can be had to it regarding formation of the contract. The Model Law says that in the matter of contract formation an offer and the acceptance of an offer may be expressed by means of data messages. If the contract is formed by way of data message then it will not be denied validity and enforceability. [Chapter III, Article 11; Formation and Validity of Contracts- Model Law UNCITRAL].

A. Information to be Provided

225. There is no specific provision for the information to be provided by the parties in respect of the Contract in the IT Act 2000 (Amended 2008).

VII. Time and Place of Conclusion of the Contract

A. Moment of Conclusion of the Contract

226. Time and place of conclusion of the contract is important for more than one reason. The place of jurisdiction and the relevant rights and obligations of parties flow from it. In real world it was always an issue between parties but it could be resolved with little effort. The use of electronic communication techniques makes these difficult to ascertain. Moreover the location of certain communication systems like laptops where the message may be downloaded and viewed may change without notice. Thus, the IT Act reflects the fact that the location of information systems is irrelevant and sets forth a more objective criterion, namely the place of business of the parties. However, the provisions of the Act like contracts in the real world may override the terms of the contract between parties.

227. Relevant principles in the IT Act: The IT Act defines the time of dispatch or the commencement of the electronic transmission of the data message of an electronic record/message as the time when the data message enters an information system so as to be out of the power of the originator which may be the information system of an intermediary or an information system of the addressee. The IT Act lays down the following principles for time of receipt [section 13]:

- If the addressee does not designate any computer resource for receipt of the record or message receipt of the record/message occurs when the electronic record enters the computer resource of the addressee.
- If the addressee has unilaterally designated a computer resource in which case the designated system may or may not be an information system of the addressee for the purpose of receiving electronic records/messages receipt occurs at the time when the electronic record/message enters that designated computer resource.
- The Act also addresses the situation where the addressee designates a particular information system for the receipt of the record/message and the data message reaches an information system of the addressee that is not the designated system. In such a case there will be receipt of the message when the addressee retrieves the data message.

The term "entry" into the information system indicates the time of dispatch and receipt of the message. The data if not intelligible, like if it is "encrypted" form then too it is considered to be received.

B. Place of Conclusion of the Contract Entered into by the Electronic Means

228. As regarding the place of dispatch and receipt the electronic record/message is deemed to be dispatched at the place where the originator has his place of business and is deemed to be received at the place where the addressee has his place of business. Thus, for the implementation of the provisions of section 13 the following interpretation is made:

- If the originator or the addressee has more than one place of business the principal place of business shall the place of business.
- If the originator or the addressee does not have a place of business, his usual place of residence shall be deemed to be the place of business.
- "usual place of residence" in relation to a body corporate means the place where it is registered.

VIII. Brief Reference to the Applicable Law and Jurisdiction

229. The Information Technology Act 2000 (IT Act) will apply to all circumstances and types of transactions and documents other than those which are specifically excepted. The IT Act thus does not apply to negotiable instruments, power-of-attorney, trusts, wills or other testamentary dispositions, contracts for the sale of conveyance of immovable property or any interest in such property, any other class of documents or transactions which the Central Government (GOI)may notify in the Official Gazette [section 1(4)]. Along with IT Act the Indian Contract Act 1872 and the Sale of Goods Act 1930 would also guide the contract formation through electronic means.

230. The Act extends to the whole of India [section 1]. It also has extraterritorial jurisdiction. However, it is the law of the place which has the most proximate nexus with the contract. The parties have the freedom of choosing the law by which the contract and the issues arising there from are to be governed. Choice of law is available to the parties. As the IT Act is explicit in determining the time and place of the formation of the contract [sections 12 & 13] hence the parties to the contract by mutual consent can exercise the option of place of jurisdiction. The freedom of the parties is also subject to the substantive and procedural laws of the country. The Code of Civil Procedure 1908 limits the choice of the parties to some extent.

§3. Electronic Transactions, Retail Commerce and Protection of Consumers and Users

I. Generally

231. Electronic transactions are transactions, contracts and agreements concluded through electronic means. With the passing of the IT Act in 2000 electronic transmission and e-commerce has been legally recognized in India. A survey says that India is the tenth largest economy by nominal GDP and third largest by purchase power parity (PPP). Also on the electronic side the country has burgeoned into the world of ICTs with formidable impact. All the retail mechanisms like counter service, home delivery, door to door sale, self-service and digital delivery or online shopping are extensively used. Retail sales in India for scarce goods like gold, medicine and liquor are prevalent since 1900. A 2006 survey found that only 38% of retail stores in India believed they faced more than slight competition.[158] Retailing in India is one of the strongest pillars of the national economy and accounts for 15%16% of the GDP. India's retail market is estimated to be USD 450 billion and is one of the top five retail markets in the world by economic value.[159] The Indian Internet user base is expected to exceed 375 million unique Internet users by 2015 going by the 41%–43% annual growth rate. Electronic transactions are only augmenting the purchasing power of the retail consumer. Credit card holders and the debit card holders form the largest chunk of online buyers while online banking transfer and cash on delivery also show a considerable and constant rise.

232. Protection of consumers online is being addressed by the legislations of the real world. The Indian Contract Act 1872, the Consumer Protection Act 1986 and the RBI's continuous Regulations and Circulars also provide protection to the consumer.

II. Law on Regulation of the Retail Commerce

A. Introduction

233. The consumer is the pivot of the commercial world. The term consumer is not a new one though with the technological advancement it has gained vital dimensions. In India a number of laws have been protecting the consumer's interests, though in a sporadic manner, until 1986 when the law relating to retail commerce and consumer protection was consolidated into The Consumer Protection Act 1986. Before 1986 there were a number of Acts[160] which protected the consumer in a piecemeal manner and were quite specific in its application. Especially in the area of ICT the consumer availing services of not only mobile telephone but of cable TV and other online services has reached millions. Thus, the TRAI has also come up with regulations law to protect the interest of consumers in respect of communication services. Consumerism or government's concern to protect consumer interest has also gained momentum. In the newly enacted Competition Act 2002 there has been a neo-wave concern for the consumer.

B. Prior Information

234. Under the Consumer Protection Act 1986 the consumer has been accorded valuable rights among which is the right to be informed about the quality, quantity, potency, purity, standard and price of goods to save the consumer from unfair trade practices[section 6(b)]. Apart from this the TRAI has specifically been formulating

158. Md.Amin- *Competition and Labor Productivity in India's Retail Stores.* (2007) 1. World Bank, 57.
159. Rajan Kumar –*State of E-commerce Retail in India* (2013).
160. The Code of Civil Procedure 1908, The Indian Contract Act 1872, The Sale of Goods Act 1930, The Indian Penal Code 1860, The Standards of Weights and Measures Act 1976,The Motor Vehicles Act 1988, The Monopoly and Restrictive Trade Practices Act 1969 (now repealed).

Regulations and issued Directions[161] regarding providing prior information to the consumer as follows:

(1) All publication/Advertisement of tariffs shall be in a specified format and shall provide certain essential information.
(2) The pulse rate /tariff for premium rate service shall be published in all communication/ advertisements.
(3) The service providers shall inform customers in writing within a week of activation of service the details of his tariff plans.
(4) The service providers shall provide in printed material in English and Vernacular Language to customers at the time of enrolment the following:

- Full and complete tariff information sheet.
- The features of the service offered regarding rate and other value-added services.
- The terms and conditions in simple wordings.
- The rights of the consumers under TRAI.
- The common charter of service agreed upon by the service providers.

C. *Performance*

235. India has emerged as the world's third largest market for electronics. The smartphone market is reaping rich harvest, and a strong customer base. The overall Indian electronics industry is expected to grow at 9.9% CAGR to touch USD 94.2 billion by 2015.[162] These burgeoning demands are not satisfactorily met by the industry. Electronics imports now hold third place, behind oil and gold and are expected to reach USD 42 billion by the end of 2015

D. *Payment by Card*

236. Credit and Debit cards have been used domestically for many years. The RBI set up the Board for Payment and Settlement Systems in 2005.The vision was to consolidate and integrate the multiple systems with varying service levels into a nationwide uniform and standard business process for all retail payment systems. The National Payments Corporation of India incorporated in 2008 issued the Certificate of Commencement of Business in April 2009. It has the vision to be global in retail payment mechanisms. With the growth rate of 30% in the last five years in the card market, already 130 million cards are in circulation. Card Payments form an inseparable part of e-payments in the country as more and more customers make use of this for bill payment, transferring funds and shopping. The Debit Cards started in India in 1998 and since then it has taken an upgrade scale and there are nearly three-fourth of the total number of cards in circulation. Credit Cards though started much earlier have not shown much popularity though in the last five years there has been impressive growth in the number of credit cards by 74.3% between 2004 and 2008. Much use of

161. Circular No. 301-9/2006-Eco.,dated May 23, 2006 issued by TRAI.
162. According to the IESA-Frost & Sullivan Report

the credit cards is made in jewelry, dining and shopping segment. Recently there have been the introduction of co-branded credit cards which combine many services into one card where banks and other retail stores airlines, telecom companies enter into business partnerships.

III. General Law on Users and Consumers

237. The Consumer Protection Act of 1986 is a milestone in the socio-economic legislation in India. The main objective of the Act is to protect the interest of the Consumer by providing a speedy remedy to them and to lay down a different judicial mechanism for the redress after a complaint. An important change brought about by this consumer-friendly Act is that no court fee is required to be paid for filing an application for redress. It is the cheapest and the fastest remedy in the hands of the consumer. According to section 2(d) a Consumer is a person who is not only a purchaser of goods for consideration but who is also a user of services. The consumer need not be benefitted after full payment of the price but even if he has partly paid then too he enjoys the benefits of the Act. The term goods include all moveable goods but exclude "actionable claims". The "services" under it include banking, insurance, transport, processing, housing construction, supply of electrical energy, entertainment, boarding and lodging, Complaint can be filed not only by the consumer but by an organization as well.

238. The Procedure: The Act provides a three tier system starting from the District Forum (Claims up to INR 20 Lakh (2 million)) at the district level; then the State Commission (for claims above INR 20 lakhs (2 million) but less than INR 1 crore (10 million)) and then the National Commission (for claims above INR 1 crore (10 million). The complaint can be filed through a simple application concerning defective goods, deficiency in service, excess price, unhealthy and hazardous goods sale, etc. The remedies available to the consumer are; repair or replacement defective goods, refund of price paid for the defective goods of service, removal of deficiency in service, compensation or damages to be paid.

§4. Electronic Transaction Governed by Standard Clauses

239. The Standard Form Contracts or the pre-written contracts are well recognized by the Indian law. These are the contracts which are governed by the Indian Contract Act 1872, the major law of contract in the country and also by the Sale of Goods Act 1930. With the introduction of electronic commerce in the country the Information Technology Act 2000 recognizes all sorts of contracts which are concluded electronically. The national Banking systems and the electronic transactions are all concluded through standard clauses and the entire process is guided by the collective application of the above laws.

Chapter 2. Regulation of Electronic Signatures and Certification Services

§1. Introduction

240. Electronic signatures are new generation of signatures. In the new medium of information society originally nothing existed to match a human hand which lends originality, authenticity and legality to a document. On 30 June 2000, President Clinton became the first person to use electronic signatures when he signed the Electronic Signatures in Global and National Commerce Act (ESIGN)[163] using his electronic signature ID adducing validity and legal recognition to electronic signature for commercial and other online activities.

§2. Object of the Law

241. The Model Law on Electronic Signatures 2001 came as a sequel to the Model Law on Electronic Commerce (1996) keeping in view the increased acceptance of Public Key Infrastructure (PKI) system in the area of electronic signatures. India being a signatory to the UNCITRAL in 1996 came up with its first Internet specific legislation in 2000. Surprisingly enough the Information Technology Act 2000(21 of 2000) did not mention the term "electronic signature" instead it used the term "digital signature". It is only in 2008 that the term "digital signature" wherever appearing in the Act was repealed and at the same places the term "electronic signature" was inserted. Thus, the amended IT Act gives the definition of electronic signature as ".....authentication of any electronic record by a subscriber by means of the electronic technique specified in the Second Schedule and includes digital signature [section 2(ta)]. The amended Act however retains the definition of 'digital signature' in section 2(p)". The main object of the Amendment Act 2008 is that in the un amended IT Act 2000 there was no mention of the word "electronic signature" which was a great lacuna. However, as the Model Law on Electronic Signature 2001 urged its signatories to legislate on electronic signature hence to meet this objective the IT Act was amended in 2008.

§3. Legal Effects of Electronic Signature

I. General Statement

242. In 2000 the digital signature through the IT Act 2000 got legal recognition and commercial activities started moving online. The Act had earlier recognized digital

163. Isaac Bowman, "*The History of Electric Signatures Laws*", ESign Laws.

signatures based on asymmetric cryptosystems bringing them on par with manual signatures. However, the IT(Amendment) Act 2008 has now substituted the term "electronic signature" for the term "digital signatures".[164] With the popularity of electronic signatures globally there arose a need to provide electronic signatures with a legal framework so that they enjoy the same level of trust and confidence which has hitherto been the privilege of manuscript signature. In the history of electronic signature the Utah Digital Signature Act 1995 was the first ever legislation on the subject. There was growing legal skepticism about electronic signatures as it being a new technology and intangible too raised a number of suspicions. A 2006 progress report on the European Union Electronic Signatures Directive shows that there was slowing down of the spirit of users of electronic signatures. Factors like security fears, cost and complexity of the technology were some impediments in the acceptance of electronic signatures in the beginning. Countries like Germany and Thailand have also reported low acceptance of electronic signatures.[165]Thus, it was felt that legislation would not hamper instead it will facilitate it; it is said that "legislation can if properly written encourage rather than restrict, and promote rather than disable, the desirable policy goal of global e-commerce."[166] The formidable legal effect of electronic signatures globally can be categorized as follows:

- *The Evidentiary Issue*- It is the complex one. The mechanism to prove the electronic signatures in the law court is not as easy. Most digital signature statutes even in India create a presumption that the person, who owns a particular key pair used to sign a document in fact, did sign the document which is the ultimate purpose of PKI. But the difficulty arises from the fact that electronic signatures are impersonal by nature and its originality becomes a challenge and always shrouded with doubt. Misuse of private key cannot be ruled out. Even the original signor may often find it easier to escape from legal noose and disown it easily. [167]
- *Absence of Originals*- It is difficult to ascertain the originality of the electronic signature because after all it is the representation of some electromagnetic signals which is represented on the computer monitor.[168]
- *Absence of Physical Witnesses*- The electronic signatures cannot be proved with the help of natural witnesses i.e., the human beings. Hardly a person can testify

164. Amendments to the IT Act 2000; Section 2. In the IT Act 2000 (21 of 2000) (hereinafter in this part referred to as the principal Act'), for the words "digital signature" occurring in the chapter, section, sub-section and clause referred to in the Table below, the words "electronic signature" shall be substituted.
165. *See* , eGovernmentNews,"Take up of electronic signatures Remains Low in GermenyEPRACTICE,EU(120302008).http://www.epractice.eu/document/1276; Pascal Prud 'homme & Hassana Chira-phakul, "*E-Commerce in Thailand: A slow Awakening*" February 2009 Thailand Law Forum, http://thailawforum.com/articles/e-commerce.html.
166. Thomas J. Smedinghoff & Ruth Hil, Bro of Baker & McKenzie LLP,"*ElectronicSignatutre Legislation*", 14.
167. Chris Reed, "*Authenticating Electronic Mail Messages-Some Evidential Problems*" (1989) 52(5) Mod LR 649, 650.
168. LornaBrazell,-*Electronic Signatures Law and Regulation* (2004) 1999, Stephen Mason, *Electronic Signatures in Law* (2007) 461.

that the particular electronic signature is the creation of a particular person with as much ease as he does in the context of manuscript signatures.
- *Absence of Handwriting Experts*- Thus, handwriting experts which were of great help to the courts are conspicuously absent in the context of electronic signatures.

Thus, evidentiary uncertainty is the strange effect of electronic signatures, their intangible nature; requisition of a technician to prove it technically is also rare as the techno savvy is not easily available. Thus, in India too the IT Act 2000 made relevant amendments in the century old the Indian Evidence Act 1872 to make it admissible in the court, regarding presumption of electronic signatures, etc.[169]

II. Use of Electronic Signatures by Public Administration

243. The IT Act envisages the use of electronic records and electronic signatures by Public administration [section 6]. It provides for the Government and its agencies the use of electronic signatures. If any particular law requires 1) filing of any application or any other documents with any governmental office, authority, body or agency owned or controlled by the appropriate government or 2) the issue or grant of any license, permit, sanction or approval or 3) the receipt or payment of money in a particular manner then the filing, issuance, grant, receipt or payment if effected by electronic means will be deem to satisfy the requirements of law. The appropriate Government is empowered to prescribe rules for the manner and format in which such electronic records shall be filed, created or issued. It may also make rules for the manner or method of payment of any fee or charges for filing, creation or issue of any electronic record [section 6]. The IT Act also permits the retention of documents, records and information for any period of time in electronic form [section 7]. The requirement of publication of rule, regulation, etc.in Official Gazette will be deemed fulfilled if it is published in Electronic Gazette and the date of publication in the Electronic Gazette shall be taken as the date of its publication [section 8]. However, no one can insist that any Ministry or Department of Central Government or the State Government or any authority or body established under any law or funded by the Central or the State Government should be retained or preserved in electronic form or that any monetary transaction should be done in the electronic form [section 9].

§4. Certification Services and Products

I. Introduction

244. 1947 can be marked as the starting point of India's entry into the world of standardization of services and products. The Indian Standards Institution (ISI) was established as a society under the societies Registration Act 1860 to promote the adoption of national standards. In 1952 ISI was given the responsibility of operating

169. Section 65B, 67A, 73A, 85B of the Information Technology Act 2000.

a certification marking scheme under an Act of Parliament.[170] In 1986 the GOI felt the need to give a new thrust to standardization and quality control activities and to evolve a national strategy for giving appropriate recognition and importance to standards and for integrating them with the growth and development of production and exports in different sectors. As a result of these activities of the Government the Bureau of Indian Standards Act 1986 was passed and by virtue of which the Bureau of Indian Standards (BIS) was established on April 1, 1987.BIS is a founder member of the International Standard Organization (ISO). It represents India in ISO, the International Electro technical Commission (IEC) and the World Standards Service Network (WSSN).

245. Standardization Testing and Quality Certification (STQC)-was established in 1980 under the aegis of the Department of Technology, GOI. It started its services in the area of Testing and Calibration based on the need of small and medium sized electronic industry in the country. From a mere testing, Calibration and Quality Assurance support to electronics Hardware Sector, STQC has come up as a prime Assurance Service Provider to both Hardware and Software Sectors. STQC has established strong infrastructure and competent staff to provide quality assurance in addition to testing and calibration-related services. It is offering its value-added services in area of Information Security, software Testing /Certification and Development of National Level Assurance Framework and it is an internationally recognized Assurance Service providing organization.

246. Common Criteria Certification (CCC) – The India Common Criteria Certification Scheme (IC3S) is operated by the STQC, Department of Electronics and Information Technology (DEITY). It has the recognition by Common Criteria Recognition Arrangements (CCRA) as a Certificate Authorizing Nation. Consequently now IT Products tested and Certified in India up to EAL 4 are acceptable not only in India but also in other 26 other member countries of CCRA without re-testing under the mutual recognition arrangement. The purpose of the IC3S is to evaluate and certify IT Security Products and Protection Profiles (PP) against the requirements of Common Criteria Standards ver.3.1R2 at assurance levels EAL 1 through EAL 4. The Scheme ensures that security valuations of ICT products are performed to consistent globally – acceptable security standards like Common Criteria (CC) – an ISO 15408 Standard and certifications that are mutually acceptable globally under CCRA.

247. On August 30, 2013 India was accepted as a Certificate Authorizing participant by the Management Committee of the CCRA. With this 17 Certificate Authorizing Schemes operate under the CCRA.

248. Transition from ISO/IEC 27001:2013- It lays down new ISMS standards. Certified organizations willing to upgrade to new standard can make request to STQC for an assessment against new standard which preferably can be taken up during their surveillance recertification.

II. Scope of the Law

249. The Bureau of Indian Standards Act 1986 was given more autonomy as well as flexibility in its operations to achieve harmonious development of standardization

170. Resolution No. 1 Std. (4)/45 dated Sep. 3, 1946

activities. With the advent of technological innovations a new Department of Electronics and Information Technology was formed to carry out the Cyber Security Assurance Scheme of the GOI. The Certification Body was established under the official administration of GOI to meet the requirements of ISO Guide 65 and CCRA requirements and also to further the goal of the Government in supporting the trustworthiness of IT products. The Quality Manual Document [STQC/CC/DO1] is the one by which all Certification Body standard operating procedures are guided by it. It is applicable to the Certification Body Personnel and is also useful for CCTL personnel, product developers and sponsoring organizations.

III. Signature –Creation and Verification Devices

250. The STQC is also responsible for the testing and certification of biometric devices. This Scheme aims at instilling confidence in users regarding accuracy and authentic of such a device.

251. Signature verifications are of two types; static and dynamic. By static signature verification a signature is written offline such as bank checks and the system reads the image scanned and then verifies it. A dynamic signature verification system is when a signature is written onto a hand-held device such a tablet and is read at run-time and compared to the signatures in database of the person to check for authenticity. Most commonly used online signature acquisition devices are pressure sensitive tablets, digitizer and webcam. Smart pens are also widely used in signature verification systems which are capable of measuring forces at the pen-tip, exerted in three directions. Special hand gloves with sensors for finding finger bend and hand position and orientation and CCD camera-based approaches were also in signature acquisition The preprocessing depends on the device used.

IV. Electronic Certificates

A. Generally

252. STQC Certification Services was the first Third Party Certification Agency of Indian origin in India in 1991 to offer QMS (Quality Management System) Certification. With the introduction of innovative technologies the certification services have been expanded and presently Certification Service is provided in QMS Product Certification/ISMS/ITSM (Information Technology Management Service/Website quality/smart card/Biometric devices, etc. Certification is along the line of national and international norms and includes; Management system Certification Schemes, Product Certification Schemes, etc.

B. Certificate Suspension, Expiration and Revocation

253. Suspension-[171] Certification of a client may be suspended for a limited period at the discretion of Certification Body under the following circumstances:

- If the result of the surveillance shows minor non-conformance to the relevant system/Product requirements and the same is not cleared even after lapse of initial time period given for correction.
- If the surveillance result shows major non-conformance to the relevant system / Product requirements.
- If improper use of the Certificate of Registration or Logo/Mark is not rectified to the satisfaction of the Certification Body.
- If the certified supplier is not regularly involved in the activities for which he is certified.
- If there has been any contravention of the applicable requirements or rules of procedures of Certification Body.

Thus, the official suspension will be confirmed by the Certification Body in a registered letter to the supplier and it will also be posted on the website. Such order shall contain conditions to be fulfilled by the supplier failing which the certification shall be cancelled.

254. Withdrawal/Cancellation- The Certification Body shall cancel certification and withdraw the Certificate and authorization for the use of the Logo/Mark under the following circumstances:

- If the supplier fails to rectify the non-conformance within the given time.
- If the client does not or will not ensure conformance to changed rules of procedure of the Certification Body.
- If the supplier ceases to supply the product.
- If the supplier fails to meet the financial obligation to Certification Body.
- At the formal request of the supplier.
- In case of any other serious contravention of applicable requirements of rules or procedures defined by the Certification Body.

The official information of cancellation or withdrawal shall be made through registered letter and shall also be posted on the website.

C. Qualified Certificates

255. The Department of Electronics and Information Technology, GOI is empowered to issue certificate of qualification in the relevant field.

171. Safety Certification Scheme (S-Mark).STQC- - Standardisation Testing and Quality Certification Directorate-Department of Electronics & Information Technology-Government of India

D. The Electronic Identity Card

256. In 2008 a Unique Identity Authority was established by the Planning Commission and in 2009 India came up with its first in world system of ID Cards for more than a billion populations. Based on the smart card format the unique Identity included basic information like name, address, age, residence, education, annual income as well as photograph and biometric data in a digital format to make identification foolproof. The Government's aim was to eliminate the need for multiple identification mechanisms prevalent across various government departments. *Nasdaq-listed Infosys* technologies was given the charge of Unique Identification Scheme [UIS] for laying down plans, policies and its implementing so that all the citizens get Unique Identification Number by 2011.

ID Card and Smart Card testing Certification is carried by the Standardization Testing & Quality Certification Directorate (STQC) in association with the NIC. Smart Card is used in India for Driving License/Vehicle Registration Certificate (DL/RC), Multipurpose National Identity Card (MNIC), *Rashtriya Swasthya Bima Yojana* (RSBY) and Electronic Passport. The testing of Smart cards include contact and contact less cards like1) contact cards, Module(Chip with contact pads embedded in card)/Smart Cards, 2) Contact less Cards (with Chips & Antenna) on a plastic card.

V. The Provision of Certification Services

257. Directorate, Ministry of Communications & Information Technology promotes the Management System Certification scheme which is a third-party certification scheme of Information Security Management Systems (ISMS).The STQC also offers the testing and certification of information Security Products, Biometric Devices, Smart Cards and Websites. These schemes conform to the requirements of national and ISO. The Services offered are:

- ISO 27001 Information Security Management System (ISMS) Certification.
- ISO-20000-1IT Service Management (ITSM) Certification.
- Website Quality Certification.
- Common Criteria Certification.
- Smart card Testing and Certification.
- Biometric Devices Testing and Certification.
- Software and System Certification.

VI. Legal Status of Certification Service Providers

A. General Obligations of the Certification Service Providers

258. The various organizations and the Common Criteria Testing Laboratories (CCTL). Have the following obligations:

- Comply in every respect with the appropriate quality system standard requirements.
- No to claim or imply that the product or the process of service is certified.
- Use the logo/mark in accordance with the Certification body requirements.
- Not to use logo/mark in any manner which implies or leads to interpretation as certification of his product or process or service.
- No to make any change in the quality of the product which formed the basis of grant of certification.
- Notify the Certification body any changes of key personnel in relation to quality assurance, technology functions or senior management.
- Give access to assessment team meant for surveillance.
- Keep record of all customer complaint regarding quality, etc. of the certified product.
- Upon suspension, withdrawal or cancellation of the certification discontinue the use of certificate /logo/mark.
- Make all payments due in a timely fashion.
- Give access to Accreditation Agency of Certification Body at the time of surveillance.

§5. Voluntary Accreditation

259. The Accreditation Body is an independent organization responsible for assessing the performance of other organizations against a recognized standard and for formally confirming the status of those who meet the standards. The Common Criteria Test Laboratories (CCTL). The scope of Accreditation are the approved methods for which a CCTL has been accredited.

260. The Certification services are accredited for:

- ISO 9000 by Quality Management System(QMS) by National Accreditation Board for Certification Bodies(NABCB).
- ISO 270001-Information Security Management System (ISMS).
- ISO 20000-IT Service Management (ITSM)-Accreditation under Process.
- Product Safety Certification Scheme based on IEC standards-Accreditation under Process.
- STQC Certification is recognized by industry and MNCs PSUs, R&D and SMEs organizations.

NABCB is the signatory of Multilateral Recognition Arrangement (MLA) of International Accreditation Forum (IAF) Inc.; the NABCB accredited certificates issued by STQC Certification Services are valid worldwide. STQC, international recognition is augmented by its mutual recognition agreements with leading certification agencies across the world such as BSI; U.K.,TUV; Germany, JQA: Japan, KAITECH; South Korea, CEPREI; China, KEMA; Netherlands, etc. Organizations can also obtain EQNET certificate acceptable in all over the European Union. (EU).

§6. Certification of Secure-Signature –Creation Devices

261. Digital signatures are created with a Secure Signature Creation Device (SSCD). The authenticity of such a device thus becomes a customer concern. In India the IT Act 2000(Amended 2008) provides for the certification of digital signatures now newly termed under the amended Act as "electronic signature". The Act provides for the Controller of Certifying Authorities (CCA) who are entrusted with the responsibility of regulating the working of certification authorities who are in turn given the responsibility to issue the DSCs for electronic authentication of users. The CCA certifies the public keys of Certifying Authorities using its own private key which enables users in the cyberspace to verify that a given certificate is issued by a licensed Certifying Authority. For this it operates the Root Certifying Authority of India (RCAI). The CCA by virtue of section 20 of the IT Act 2000 maintained repositories which has now been deleted under the Amendment Act of 2008.[172] The CCA establishes the Root Certifying Authority of India (RCAI) to digitally sign the public keys of Certifying Authorities [section 18(b)]. The requirements fulfilled by the RCAI include; (1) the license issued to the Certifying Authority is digitally signed by the CCA. (2) all public keys corresponding to the signing of private keys of a Certifying Authority are digitally signed by the CCA. (3) That these keys are signed by the CCA can be verified by a relying party through the CCA's website or CA's own website. The RCAI is operated using SmartTrust software. Certification Practice Statement of RCAI guides the CCA personnel to perform Root Certifying Authority functions. The term "root" signifies the entire CA matrix including the software and its operations. The national Root Certifying authority uses a 2048 bit RSA key pair and the Certifying Authority entity uses a 1024 bit RSA key pair.[173]

262. Certifying Authorities in India – In India seven authorities are licensed as Certifying Authorities. These are: (1) Institute for Development and Research in banking Technology; (2) The Tata Consultancy Services, the first one to touch the INR 5 lakh (0.5 Million) mark; (3) National Informatics Centre Certifying Authority, a GOI organization; (4) *SafeScrypt*-result of sify technology; (5) MTNL TRUSTLINE; (6) Gujarat Narmada Fertilizer Company(GNFC); (7) *e-Mudhra* Certification Authority. t present in India the Premium SSL Genie is the only Global Certifying Authority[174] and it is the first company to have the global certification power.

172. Formerly under the IT Act the Controller had the job of maintaining a repository of all the certifying Authorities in the country. The National Repository of Digital Certificates (NRDC) maintained it under s. 20.

173. Dr. Sandeep Oberoi. "*India PKI Forum*", Presentation made at PKI Consortium Seminar, Nov. 8, 2007,4.

174. High Assurance four-step authentication and verification process that verifies the Domain Name and company legitimacy and provides up to USD 1,00,000 warranty and 256 bit encryption in just USD 49.99 per annum (2011). Premium SSL is the best option for e-commerce website with high value transactions and sharing of confidential data.

§7. Supervision and Control

263. Certification Body is a governmental organization responsible for carrying out Certification and for overseeing the day to day operation of IC3S. STQC Directorate is a part of Ministry of Communication & Information Technology, GOIIndia. It is the main governing body of the entire certification process and it provides the common criteria certification of IT products and protection profiles in a consistent, competent, credible and reliable manner. Its main policy is to achieve its organizational goal by establishing a system according to international requirements, certifying IT products, continuously reviewing and upgrading technical content of the activities in line with market need and adopting better methods /practices to provide better value to the clients. The management is responsible for carrying out general supervision for taking care of the implementation of governmental policies. The Certification Body establishes the procedures to control all documents and data related to the certification function.

Chapter 3. Legal Aspects of Electronic Banking

§1. The Provision of Electronic Banking Services

264. The proliferation of the Internet marked the demise of traditional money. Wealth in digital form is the most striking feature of electronic banking. Electronic banking has dealt with the great hassles of carrying money, transferring hard cash and of undergoing prolonged and cumbersome processes of money calculations. The payment system, money transfer is all not even for a farthing and above all the time taken is nanosecond. This banking revolution touched even the Indian society which responded to it in a fitting manner though a bit late. Computers replaced the lofty registers and even the Indian Banks were purged of piled up files. RBI, the fountain of all banking activities in the country, established in 1934 started issuing piecemeal regulations, Circulars and Directives to catch up with the digitization of banking system until in 2007 when the Payment and Settlement Systems Act 2007 empowered the RBI to regulate various payments and settlement systems. It authorizes the RBI to permit both gross and net settlement procedures. As a sequel to the said Act the RBI issued two important regulations namely Board for Regulation and Supervision of Payment Settlement Systems Regulations 2008 and Payment and Settlement Systems Regulations 2008. The RBI is empowered to prescribe various standards including the format for payment instructions, the timing and manner of funds transfer. The Act also defines "netting" and legally recognizes settlement finality. It thus states that a settlement, whether gross or net will be final and irrevocable as soon as the money, securities, foreign exchange or derivates or other transactions payable as a result of such settlement is determined. Legal recognition of netting is the pre condition for recognizing payment finality under the netting schemes.

265. Only forty-five Banks are providing electronic services out of which there are twenty-seven public sector banks and eighteen private sector banks:[175]

Banks	Number of Banks	Number of Electronic Banks
Private Sector Banks; NEW OLD	7 15	7 11
Public Sector Banks State Bank of India Nationalized Other Public Sector Banks	28 8 19 1	27 8 18 1
All	50	45

175. The Study is based on the Survey made in June 2008.

266. The Electronic Banking services in the country can be categorized as follows:

- *Internet Banking Services;* Balance enquiry and payment; transaction history; online transfer of funds; card to card transfer; Pre-paid mobile recharge; Buy and sell mutual funds; send money order anytime; open fixed deposit and recurring deposit; request of check book; stop payment request; request of debit cards; monthly bank account by e-mail; Reissue and debit of ATM Card; Link bank account to ATM Debit Card; renewal, premature closure of FD/RD; deactivate/activate ATM Debit card; change password; demat accounts; Loan details; interest rate updates; bills payment; online shopping; ticket booking; mobile top up; share trading; online tax payments; convert to EMI; online loans; customer correspondence; demonstration of I-Banking; corporate Internet Banking
- *Phone Banking Services-* Enquire your balance account; request for funds transfer; stop check payment instructions; mobile banking registration; latest interest and exchange rates.
- *Mobile Banking Services-*Account Balance; making payment; details of credit card balance; loan information; I-mobile; purchase and redemption of mutual fund units;
- Last three transactions.
- *ATM Services.* 24-hours access to Cash; transfer fund between accounts; view account balances and mini statements; pin change option.

267. The Act of 2007 provides for the following special type of electronic services:

- Electronic Funds Transfer (EFT) – It is defined as transfer of funds whereby a person instructs, authorizes or orders the bank to debit or credit an account maintained with that bank through electronic means and includes point of sale transfers, automated teller machine transactions, direct deposits or withdrawal of funds, transfers initiated by telephone, Internet and card payment [section 2(1)(c); Act of 2007].
- National Electronic Funds Transfer (NEFT) – It is a nationwide funds transfer system to facilitate transfer of funds from any bank branch to any other bank branch. The system has the concept of Centralized Accounting system and the bank's accounts, that are sending or receiving the funds transfer instructions gets operated at only Mumbai. The individual branches are spread all over the country.
- Real Time Gross Settlement (RTGS) – It is a funds transfer mechanism where transfer of money takes place from one bank to another on a "real time" and on "gross" basis. This is the fastest possible money transfer system through the banking channel. Settlement in "real time" denotes that transaction is not subject to any waiting period. "Gross settlement" means the transaction is settled on one-to-one basis without bunching with any other transaction.
- Payment systems- A Payment system is a mechanism that facilitates transfer of value between a payer and a beneficiary by which the payer discharges the payment obligations to the beneficiary. It enables two-way flow of payments in exchange

of goods and services in the economy. Payment System includes the systems enabling credit card operations, debit card operations, smart card operations, money transfer operations or similar operations but does not apply to stock exchanges or clearing [section 34 – Payment and Settlement Systems Act 2007.

§2. Brief Reference to Electronic Banking Contract

268. The Indian Contract Act 1972 envisages the principles of contract. Agreements entered into by parties including their mutual rights and obligations are governed by it. Banks providing Internet Banking services have been entering into agreements with their customers setting out the terms and conditions of the services. The terms and conditions include information on the access through User ID and secret password, minimum balance and charges, authority to the bank for carrying out transactions performed through the service, liability of the user and the bank, disclosure of personal information for statistical analysis and credit scoring, also non-transferability of the facility, notices and termination, etc.

Information Technology Act 2000 (21 of 2000) and The Negotiable Instruments Act 1881 (Amended by the IT Act 2000) are also applicable to such contracts. The IT Act in particular provides the legal basis for electronic transaction processing and it also stipulates the security features that are necessary to maintain the confidentiality, integrity and authenticity of such transactions. The IT (Amendment) Act 2008 provides legality for electronic signatures and encryption of data and enables the electronically stored data to be admissible evidence in the law courts.

§3. Electronic Money Institutions

I. General Statement

269. Since 1992 reformative activities in the banking sector have caught speed. The focal areas were deregulation, competition and adoption of international best practices. Banks and financial institutions were encouraged to play an effective role in strengthening economic growth. The main steps taken by the RBI comprised deregulation; improved prudential measures risk management as well as measures to develop financial markets. The monograph of the RBI on Payment systems in India (1998) sets outs objectives to conform to the international standards in the area of payment systems. With the constant effort of the RBI in the last two decades[176] the financial sector has been liberalized and is now more integrated with the global financial system. New institutions have been created and old institutions are strengthened.

270. Financial intermediaries in India can be categorized into four groups; commercial banks; cooperative banks; financial institutions and non-banking companies. Commercial and cooperatives banks are allowed to engage in a wide range of banking

176. Detailed in the *Vision Document for 2005–2008* and *Vision Document 2009–2012* reflect also the changes after the enactment of the Payment and Settlement Systems Act 2007.

and financial services. Financial institutions and non-bank finance companies are not allowed to accept deposits with a check issuance facility. Non-banking entities now under the PSS Act are permitted to provide certain payment services after due authorization from the RBI. At the end of March 2010 there were 169 commercial banks, 1,647 urban cooperative banks (UCBs), 31 state cooperative banks, 370 district central cooperative banks, four development financial institutions and 12,630 (June 2010) non-bank finance companies. The Rural Regional Banks (RRBs) formed under the Regional Rural Bank Act 1976 play a key role in rural institutional financing.

II. Electronic Money

271. Electronic money or E-money is a potential medium of exchange. It can be broadly defined as "an electronic store of monetary value on a technical device ... used for making payments to undertakings other than the issuer without necessarily involving bank accounts in the transaction, but acting as a pre-paid bearer instrument (European Central Bank 1998). These products could be classified into two broad categories namely: (a) pre-paid stored value card and (b) pre-paid software-based product that uses computer networks such as Internet. The stored value card scheme typically uses a microprocessor chip embedded in plastic card while a software-based scheme typically uses specialized software installed in a personal computer. The stored value cards is again of three types: single-purpose card, closed system (limited purpose card) and general purpose(multipurpose card). The single purpose card with a magnetic chip records the amount of funds and is designed to facilitate only one type of transaction, telephone calls, public transportation, etc. The closed system cards are generally used in a small number of well-identified points of sale within a well-defined location like corporate or university campus.

272. In an Indian economy where cash transactions are common, e-money helps saving costs from printing and minting of notes of small denominations while at the same time eliminates the handling, storing, transporting and insuring currency. E-money in the country also improves operational efficiency of the financial sector and extension of banking to the urban poor and rural communities other than facilitating e-governance initiatives of governments.[177]

III. Supervisory Regime

273. The Indian banking system consists of; commercial banks, cooperative banks, financial institutions (FI) and non-banking financial companies (NBFC). In the category of commercial banks there are even public sector banks, private sector banks and foreign banks. The State Bank of India and its associates, nationalized banks and regional Rural Banks (RRBs) are the creations of the Acts of Parliament. The Private Sector Banks are established under the Banking Regulation Act 1949. The cooperative credit institutions in the country are broadly classified into urban credit cooperatives and rural credit cooperatives while the rural credit cooperatives are further divided

177. Report of the Working Group on electronic Money- July 11, 2002- Reserve Bank of India.

into short-term and long-term cooperatives. The regulation and supervision of the financial system is carried out by different regulatory authorities. The RBI is the apex institution which supervises the major part of the financial system comprising commercial banks, Urban Cooperative Banks (UCBs), some FIs and NBFCs. Some of the Financial institutions in turn regulate and supervise other institutions in the financial sector like RRBs. Central and state cooperative banks are supervised by National Bank for Agriculture and Rural Development (NABARD). Housing finance companies are supervised by National housing Bank (NHB). The governmental Department of Company affairs(DCA) regulates deposit taking activities of companies other than NBFCs, registered under the Companies Act but not those which are registered under a separate law. The Registrar of Cooperatives (ROC) in the respective states is the supervisor. Central Government along with the RBI is the joint regulator in UCB multistate cooperatives and the Central government along with NABARD is the joint regulator in the multistate rural cooperatives. The respective Central and State Governments control the management while the RBI and the NABARD are concerned with the banking functions of the cooperatives. This dual control makes the supervision and regulation of the cooperatives effective. The Insurance Regulatory and Development Authority (IRDA) regulates the insurance sector while the capital market and credit rating agencies are regulated by Securities and Exchange Board of India (SEBI).

IV. Redeemability

274. The Reserve Bank of India Act 1934 does not contain any specific provision regarding redeem ability.

V. Waiver

275. The Reserve Bank of India Act 1934 does not contain any specific provision for waiver.

Chapter 4. Protection of Users of Electronic Services

§1. GENERALLY

I. Information Society Services

276. An information society can be described as the outcome of the smooth integration of ICTs with traditional media, a globally connected, knowledge-based society. The modern concept of ICTs has two dimensions; therefore ICT itself has become an instrument of social change and as an industry it has initiated economic revolution the world over. ICTs are octagonal in nature: connectivity, content, community, commerce, culture, capacity, cooperation and capital. Large swathes of the global population ranging from industry players, to users, from policy makers to economists are embracing the game-changing ICTs and are harnessing its fruits for improvement of life on earth and for the good of mankind. The developed countries – densely connected and with greater convergence – are the forerunners in transforming into information societies while the developing countries too have joined the race though in a modest manner. ICTs in developing countries are mainly being adopted in the areas of communications, education, agriculture, medicine, commerce, environment, urban development, etc. Not only that the information society services have affected the industrial or economic aspects of life but even the cultural, linguistic and political landscapes of even ancient countries like India are being changed. An agriculturally dominated country like India for instance had launched in 2000 the Indian Society of Agricultural Information Technology (INSAIT). The country in the agricultural area has not only passed through the green, yellow, white, blue revolutions but it is also undergoing cyber revolution. A village farmer in India has taken to the tremendous technological revolution and today he is no longer interested in the bullock-cart but has imbibed fully the ICT services in the art of agriculture.

II. Geographic Scope of the Law

277. There is no specific law to date for the information society services in India nevertheless the various regulations of the Department of Electronics, Ministry of Information Technology and the piecemeal regulations and Directives of various government departments regulate the activities of the information society in the country.

A. Service Providers Established in India

278. The Indian Information Technology and Information Technology Enabled Services (IT/ITES) has earned a global name for reliable and cost-effective delivery of services. Hence, India has become an outsourcing destination of choice in the world.

Indian IT companies have set up over 600 delivery centers across the world and are providing services in over 200 cities across 78 countries. As a proportion of national GDP the sector revenues have grown from 1.2% in 1997–98 to nearly 1.8% in 2013–2014. Consequently India is earning the reputation of "soft" power in the world and its leadership position in the global sourcing arena accounts for 55% of the global sourcing market size in 2013 as compared to 52% in 2012. The Department of Electronics and Information Technology is coordinating activities, promoting skill development programs enhancing infrastructure capabilities and supporting Research and Development for India's leadership position in IT and ITES services.

279. The growth of India in the area of ICT industry in 2014 has been recorded as 25%–30%, the highest in the world. The country has embraced the fruits of ICT in the best possible manner and has harnessed the excellence to the advantage of the Indian society. With an unstoppable population of more than 1.027 million and with the illiteracy rate of 35% the Indian society is transforming nevertheless. The ICT has impacted upon the country; it educates them formally or informally helping the country to become an information society. The application of ICT to the advantage of society covers all the facets of daily and national life.

280. There has been a phenomenal GDP growth leading to consumer demand as an inevitable partner of ICT, the electronics have made a long leap and going by current estimates the electronic products have registered a significant growth and demand for electronics hardware in the country is projected to increase from USD 45 billion in 2009 to USD 400 billion by 2020. (Source; Task Force Report). The Government has also come up with a number of initiatives to boost the electronic industry and has launched the NPE. The Policy aims at setting up 200 Electronic Manufacturing Clusters nationwide.

281. Information Society in India consists of IT Services[178] and BPO. The IT sector in the country is generating 2.5 million direct employments. The top five IT Services Providers are; *Tata Consultancy Services, Infosys, Cognizant, Wipro and HCL Technologies.* (Gartner).In 1991 the Department of Electronics created a corporation called software Technology Parks of India (STPI) a government –owned organization which easily provided VSAT communication alone.

Later in 1993 individual companies were allowed to have their direct link to abroad. VSNL introduced Gateway Electronic Mail Service in 1991, the 64 Kbit/s leased line service in 1992 and commercial Internet access on a big scale in 1992. By 1991 India was already on the path of globalization and international economic integration. The then GOI giving top priority to ICT formed the Indian National Task Force on Information Technology and Software Development. The Report of the Task Force and its recommendations were in conformity with the international bodies like the WTO, the ITU and the World Bank (Wolcott & Goodman; 2003). The New Telecommunications Policy 1999 liberalized the telecommunication sector and eventually passing of the Information Technology Act 2000(amended2008) gave legal recognition to all the IT activities in the country.

The economic effect of the technologically inclined services sector in India accounting for 40% of the country's GDP and 30% of export earnings in 2006 while

178. The IT Services sector was born in Mumbai in 1967 with the establishment of Tata Group in partnership with the Burroughs and the first Software Export Zone (SEEPZ) was set up in 1973.

employing only 25% of its workforce. Various cities in the country have become IT hubs. [179]

India signed a bilateral cooperation agreement with European Union (EU) on June 25, 2002 in the field of science and technology. The IT sector has led to massive direct and indirect job creation and has become a giant in outsourcing facing fierce competition from China and the Philippines. India with its IT potency was enabled to have commercial ties with the U.S. and the European Union (EU). However, the recent global financial crisis has affected India as well whereby hiring has dropped sharply and the employees are moving to sectors like the financial services, telecommunications and manufacturing industries.

B. Services Providers Established in the European Union or in the European Economic Area

282. The European Union Directive adopts the definition of Information Society Services (ISS) as any service for remuneration at distant points through electronic means at the recipient's request for service. The definition excludes radio broadcasting and television broadcasting services.[180] Under the Directive, Service Provider (SP) is any natural or legal person providing information service. The EC Directive[181] had the objective of creating a "legal framework to ensure the free movement of information society services between Member States." With the increase of companies offering telecommunication services, the increase of ISPs and with the use of commerce conducted between the Member States the Directive gained importance and relevance.

179. Bangalore is known as the *Silicon Valley of India* and contributes to 33% of Indian IT Exports and other cities like, Hyderabad Mumbai, Kolkata, Pune, Thiruvananthapuram (Trivandrum) are the major centers of IT Services in the country.
180. Article 1(2) of Directive 98/34/EC (Directive 98) as amended by Directive 98/48/EC.
181. Directive 2000/31/EC of the European Parliament and of the Council is the European Directive on Electronic Commerce issued on Jun. 8, 2000.

Part V. Non-Contractual Liability

Chapter 1. Negligence

283. Negligence is dereliction of public duty. It does not need any pre-existing legal or contractual obligation towards the aggrieved. It denotes an inadvertent act of a person which results in the harm caused to another. It is a term difficult to define though it is found both under the civil law and under the criminal jurisprudence. The authoritative definition is given by Ratanlal who says that negligence is the breach of duty caused by the omission to do something which a reasonable man guided by those considerations which ordinarily regulate the conduct of human affairs would do, or doing something which a prudent and reasonable man would not do. Actionable negligence consists in the neglect of the use of ordinary care or skill towards a person to whom the defendant owes the duty of observing ordinary care and skill by which neglect the plaintiff has suffered injury to his person or property.[182] Thus, by analysis the definition reveals three important ingredients of "negligence": (1) legal duty to take care; (2) breach of such duty; (3) consequential damage. In the landmark judgment of *Bolam*[183] it was explained that negligence in law means a failure to do some act which a reasonable man in the circumstances would do, or the doing of some act which a reasonable man in the circumstances would not do; and if that failure or the doing of that act results in injury then there is a cause of action. In the ordinary connotation the term "negligence" requires the prudence of a "reasonable" or "ordinary" man. Negligence in law comes in two principal forms: the civil negligence and the criminal negligence.

284. Civil negligence- Under civil law negligence is described as a breach of a legal duty of care; it denotes carelessness in a matter in which the law mandates carefulness.

Criminal negligence- In the *Santra* case the Supreme Court of India has pointed out that liability in civil law is based upon the amount of damages incurred; in criminal law the amount and degree of negligence is a factor in determining liability. Certain elements must be established to determine liability in any particular case, the motive of the offense, the magnitude of the offense and the character of the offender. In India under section 304A death caused by rash and negligent driving is mildly punished with imprisonment up to two years and with a fine and is not regarded as culpable homicide.

---

182. *Law of Torts*-Ratanlal&Dhirajlal- 24th ed., 2002 Justice GP Singh (ed.) 441–442.

183. *Bolam v. Friem Hospital Management Committee*, Queen's Bench Division 19576-2-1957. [1957] 1 WLR 582=[1957] 2 All ER 118.

285. Professional Negligence- Negligence by professionals especially by doctors has taken serious notes. In *State of Haryana v. Smt. Santra*[184]the Supreme Court held that every doctor has a duty to act with reasonable care and skill. The conduct of professionals was discussed by the Supreme Court in Jacob Mathew's[185] case. The Court said in the law of negligence professionals like lawyers, doctors, architects and others are included in the category of persons professing some special skill or skilled persons generally. When such professionals undertake a task they are expected to possess a particular degree of knowledge to call him as professional and the person with whom he deals is tacitly given the assurance that the task will be performed with reasonable degree of care and caution.

Although a professional does not assure cent percent success yet he will be held liable for negligence for one of two findings; that he was not possessed of reasonable skill which he professed to possess or he did not exercise it with reasonable competence. A case of *occupational negligence* is different from *professional negligence* and a simple lack of care or an error of judgment shall not hold the doctor liable.

286. Degree of negligence- The Delhi High Court held in 2005[186] that in civil law there are three degrees of negligence: (i) *lata culpa,* gross neglect (ii) *levis culpa* ordinary neglect and (iii) *levissima culpa*, slight neglect. Thus, every act of doctor shall not attract punishment. It is for the gross neglect for which the doctors shall be held liable. Doctors in India may not be held liable for their services individually or vicariously unless they come within the exceptions given in the case of *Indian Medical Association v. V.P. Santha.*[187]

The distinction between negligence, rashness and recklessness was very well made out by the Court in *Poonam Verma v. Ashwin Patel*[188] in which it said that a negligent person is one who inadvertently commits an act of omission and violates a positive duty. A person is rash who knows the consequences but foolishly thinks that they will not occur as a result of his act. A reckless person knows the consequences but does not care whether or not they may result from his act.

287. Legal Regime- A negligent act makes the doer liable under more than one law in India depending on the nature of the act and on the status of the defendant or accused. A simple case of negligence by a layman shall invite an action for damages under the law of tort. Then there are professionals especially from the medical field whose negligence may cost life or limb of the aggrieved. For this apart from damages under the law of tort criminal liability may entail imprisonment. There are certain provisions under the Indian Penal Code 1860 which exempt the medical profession if there is proved absence of *mens rea* or guilty mind. These are:

- Section 80- *Accident in doing a lawful Act-* Nothing is an offense if it is done by a person while doing a lawful act, in a lawful manner by lawful means by taking due care and attention. Thus, accident occurring in doing an act which lacks guilty mind will exempt the medical professional also.

---

184. AIR 2000 SC 3335.
185. *Jacob Mathew v. State of Punjab* – AIR 2005 SC 3180.
186. *Smt. Madhubala v. Government of NCT of Delhi* – 2005 (118) DLT 515.
187. AIR 1996 SC 550.
188. 1996 4 SCC 332.

- Section 88-Act not intended to cause death done by consent in good faith and for the benefit of the person and done with the person's consent concerned is not an offense.

288. However, when the negligence is so gross so as to endanger the life of the person concerned then the medical professional shall be held liable under the following provision:

Section 304A- Causing death by negligence – If anyone while doing a rash and negligent act causes adeath which does not amount to culpable homicide shall be punished with imprisonment up to two years or with fine or with both.

Quite recently under the new law the aggrieved consumer cum patient can claim damages under the Consumer Protection Act 1986. But under the same Act the free treatment by the doctors at a non-governmental, governmental hospital, health center, dispensary, etc. shall not be considered as "services" under the Consumer Protection Act 1986.

The National Consumer Disputes Redress Commission and the Supreme Court have held in several decisions that a doctor is not liable for the negligence or medical deficiency if some wrong is caused in his treatment or diagnosis if he acted in accordance with the practice accepted as proper by a reasonable body of persons. The Supreme Court held that a doctor's every mistake cannot be regarded as a negligent act and held in Dr. Laxman Balkrishna Joshi v. Dr. Trimbak Babnu Godbole[189] that if a doctor's act is "proper" then he cannot be held liable. In some cases the plaintiff can involve the principle of res ipsa loquitor or things speak for themselves. In such cases no proof of negligence is required beyond the accident itself. The National Consumer Disputes Redressal Commission applied this principle in Dr. Janak Kanthimathi Nathan v. Murlidhar Eknath Masane.[190] The principle comes into operation only when there is proof that the occurrence was unexpected that the accident could not have happened without the negligence or lapses on the part of the doctor and the circumstances conclusively show that the doctor and no other person was negligent.

189. AIR 1969 SC 128.
190. 2002 (2) CPR 138.

Chapter 2. Liability of Network Operators

289. A Mobile Network Operator or MNO is also known as a wireless service provider, cellular company or mobile network carrier. It is a provider of wireless communications services which owns or controls all the elements necessary to sell and deliver services to an end user including radio spectrum allocation, wireless networking infrastructure backhaul infrastructure, billing, customer care and provisioning computer systems and marketing customer care, provisioning and market organizations. MNO are obtaining revenue by offering retail service of its own brand, an MNO may sell access to network services at whole rates to MNVO. Mobile network operators thoroughly come under the Telecom regulatory Authority of India (TRAI). They are controlled mainly by the TRAI Act 1997 and the various rules and regulations which are updated and issued[191] almost every month or after regular intervals. The TRAI in its latest Directive has informed the multi network operators that the TRAI can intervene for the protection of interest of operators and to check the QoS of the operators.[192]The liability of such operators also falls under the Consumer Protection Act 1986.

191. For instance the latest one is –*The Standards of Quality of Service of Basic Telephone Service (Wireline) and Cellular Mobile Telephone Service(Third Amendment)Regulations 2014*(12 of 2014). F.No.305-01/2014-QoS. Date of Release- Aug. 21, 2014.

192. Regulation 24- *Standards of Quality of Service(Digital Addressable Cable TV Systems) Regulations* .2012 (12 of 2012)-Date of Issue- May 12, 2014.

Chapter 3. Liability of Service Providers

§1. GENERALLY

290. "Every Internet transaction requires the participation of multiple intermediaries, and may well involve more than two actors."[193] The Internet seems to flow between the user and the host yet no transaction is ended between the two parties exclusively. The postal carriers and telephone network are the predecessors of these online intermediaries though the automated transmission marks the dividing line between the two. The Internet is an amalgamation of human and non-human agencies that are equally important for its survival and when the question of liability regarding dissemination of illegal content arises the human face of the Internet is pinpointed for the arraignment. The virtual world of cyberspace is abounded with all the echelons of human society, be it artists, statesmen, organizations, businesses individuals or so to say criminals. Without the agency of human hand the virtual world will be reduced to nonexistent. The ISPs are the first ones who come to a lawman's mind when question of liability arises as they are "the 'glue' that binds the Internet together, via their supply of TCP/IP packet switching services, which allow third parties to communicate data packets across the 'network of networks'"[194] The liability of the ISPs is multifaceted and they are pinpointed not only for the content but they are also held strictly liable for the harm caused to the victim apart from the civil and criminal liability they entail. With the changing of the technological scenario it is being realized that the ISPs have taken multifold roles like that of access providers, network providers and hosts and with it the liability falls into different components depending on the particular role the ISP was involved in respect of the disputed act. Their liability basics are continuing to decline with the advent of automated technology; the greater the automation, the lesser is the role of these intermediaries and thus minimal is their liability area. The ISPs are the mediators, the carriers of information and are the online counterparts of telecommunications companies. Apart from serving the individuals, ISPs also serve large companies providing a direct connection from the company's networks to the Internet. ISPs themselves are connected to one another through Network Access Points (NAPs).[195]

291. Liability of ISPs in India-The liability of ISPs is determined by the IT Act 2000 and also by the guidelines issued in August 24, 2007[196] further amended in 2010.[197] Thus, according to Clause 33 the Guidelines are:

193. Chris Reed, ch. 2 "*From Each According to His Ability; Actors and Activities in the Internet World*" in *Internet Law: Text and Materials* (Cambridge University Press, 2004) 24.
194. Chris Reed, *Computer Law* (Oxford University Press,2003).
195. *See* , <http//www.pcwebopedia.com> TERM/1/ISP.html.>
196. Guidelines issued by DS Cell- DoT, Ministry of Communications and IT Government of India, New Delhi.
197. No. 820-1/2006/LR Vol (II) Dated Jan. 25, 2010 *Id.*

(1) ISPs must prevent unlawful content, messages from being carried on the network. In case of report of such obscene or objectionable content the enforcement agencies shall prevent its carriage.
(2) ISPs must ensure that content carried by them must not infringe "international and domestic cyber laws."
(3) Use of ISP network for anti-national activities would be construed as an offense under the Indian Penal code 1860.
(4) The ISPs are under obligation to follow the IT Act provisions failing which it will entail damages.
(5) ISPs must ensure and take care that their networks cannot be used to endanger or make vulnerable a networked infrastructure.
(6) ISPs must also ensure that their services are not used to break-in or attempt to break-in to Indian networks.
(7) ISPs must provide without any delay all the tracing facilities to trace nuisance, obnoxious call messages or communications transported through their network. Tracing facilities are to be provided to the enforcement department and to intelligence department, etc.
(8) ISPs are also under obligation to provide facilities to the government to counteract espionage, subversive acts, sabotage or any other unlawful activity.
(9) The ISPs must also maintain communication of privacy over their network. (Clause 34).

§2. Liability of Electronic Communications Service Providers

292. The Telecom and Regulatory authority of India is the main body which governs the liability of electronic communications providers. Telecommunication services under the TRAI Act 1997 has been defined as services of any description which includes electronic mail, voice mail, data services, audiotex services, videotex services, radio paging, and cellular mobile services and which is made available to the consumers by transmission of signs, signals, wires, etc. or by other electromagnetic means but does not include broadcasting services [section 2(k)].

§3. Liability of Information Society Service Providers

I. Generally

293. The IT Act 2000 is the sole law in India which explicitly mentions the law regarding the liability of ISPs. The law has undergone a massive change whereas the contours of the liability of the service providers have expanded; their obligations under the law are more defined and their exemptions circumscribed and conditional. The IT (Amendment) Act 2008 (10 of 2009), has inserted a catena of new sections connected with the liability of the intermediaries and their answerability before law. Chapter XII comprising section 79 has been replaced and the term "intermediaries" is redefined.

Apart from the IT Act 2000 rules made by the Central Government and the Guidelines issued by the Telecom Department also circumscribe such liability within the legal framework when at the time of issuing the license to provide service, the ISPs are not only bound to follow the guidelines but they are also to abide by the security conditions of the licensor i.e., the GOI. All these provisions define the limits of liability of the ISPs. An "intermediary" is defined under the Act as follows:

– 'intermediary 'regarding electronic records means any person who on behalf of another person receives, stores or transmits that record or provides any service with respect to that record and includes telecom service providers, network service providers, Internet service providers, web-hosting service providers, search engines, online payment sites, online auction sites, online -market places and cyber cafes [Section 2 (w)].

294. This definition of intermediary is an elaborate one and has explicitly mentioned even the different versions of service providers. It appears to be in consonance with the definition given by Graham J.H. Smith who for the first time identified the different roles the intermediaries play.[198] It is an improvement on the previous definition of the term given under the unamended IT Act in the sense that it has listed the names of various versions of the intermediaries and leaves no doubt regarding their existence. Moreover the term "cyber café" has also been separately defined in the Act to mean any facility from where access to the Internet is offered by any person in the ordinary course of business to the members of the public [section 2(na)]. This definition makes it easier for the law enforcers to fix the liability of an intermediary.

295. Exemption of Intermediaries- Section 79 of the IT Act gives conditional immunity to the intermediaries. The intermediary shall not be liable for any third-party information (information dealt with an intermediary in his capacity as an intermediary), data or communication link available or hosted by him if following conditions are satisfied:

(1) If the function of the intermediary is limited to providing access to a communication system over which information made available by third parties is transmitted or temporarily stored or hosted.
(2) The intermediary does not initiate the transmission.
(3) When he does not select the receiver of the transmission.
(4) The intermediary does not select or modify the information contained in the transmission.
(5) The intermediary observes due diligence and follows the guidelines issued by the Central Government or any of its agency.

However, the intermediary will not get the benefit of exemption if:

(1) He has conspired, abetted, aided or was induced whether by threats or promise or otherwise in the commission of the unlawful act.

---

198. Graham J. H .Smith & Bird & Bird, *Internet Law and Regulation* (4th ed. Sweet & Maxwell, London 2007).

(2) Even after receiving information and actual knowledge about the unlawful act, the intermediary fails to expeditiously remove or disable access to the material and has also in doing so, not tampered with any object which could serve as an evidence.

Thus, the exemption of the intermediary from being liable under law rests on several conditions. It is obvious that if the intermediary is proved to be a partner in the posting of the incriminating material, his exemption is nullified. It is to be noted that to make the intermediary liable, it is not necessary to prove his *malafides* in cyber security matters and the intermediary cannot claim exemption on the ground that he was not aware of the malicious and incriminating material. In fact to get the exemption certain physical acts should be proved like he did not initiate the transmission, did not select or modify the information.

296. New Legal Regime for the Intermediaries- The intention of the legislature behind the exemption of intermediaries is to encourage free flow of information and that unnecessary restrain on them would hamper the growth of technological and communicational innovations. But the misuse of the Internet and its criminalization has led to clothe this exemption with several safeguards. A perusal of the Amendment Act in the following sections shows that the scope of the exemption of the intermediaries has become limited and their freedom has to be enjoyed within defined legal limits:

- Section 6-A[199]- This section gives power to the Central Government or to the State Government to not only select the nature of service provided by the service provider but also to fix the service charges rates which are to be charges by such service providers. Thus, the service providers from the very beginning of their existence are not choosers and they have to abide by the orders of the government in this regard. The section in public interest also fixes the rates to be charged by them by law so that the innocent and the ignorant do not suffer at the hands of the service providers.
- Section 7-A-The section empowers the related authorities to inspect the related data and information which is in electronic form. Thus, by virtue of this section, whenever it is required by the enforcement department, the information stored or hosted by the intermediaries can also be the subject of audit and information.
- Section 43-A A body corporate which possesses, deals with or handles any personal data in a computer resource which it owns, controls or operates is negligent in implementing security practices which results in wrongful loss or wrongful gain to any person then such body corporate shall be liable to pay damages to the aggrieved.
- Section 67-A The section puts an obligation on the intermediaries to take care of preserved data. For this the Central Government is empowered to make rules in this regard. Any intermediary who violates such rules is held criminally liable the penalty for which may extend to imprisonment up to three years and with fine.
- Section 69-The Government has the power to order intercepting, monitoring or decrypting any information on the ground of national security, public order,

199. Inserted by virtue of s. 7 of the IT (Amendment) Act 2008 (10 of 2009).

friendly relations with foreign States, etc., and all the intermediaries are under duty to provide assistance and facilities to carry out the work of interception, monitoring, etc., failing which the intermediary may suffer imprisonment up to seven years and shall also be liable to pay fine.

- Section 69-A The Government may order blocking of the information for public access on the ground of security of India, defense of India, friendly relations with foreign States, public order or on the ground of prevention of any of these. For this the Government shall make rules and may order any intermediary or agency to block information failing which the intermediary may be punished with imprisonment up to seven years and shall also be liable to fine.
- Section 69-B- The Government can order any intermediary or agency to monitor traffic data for the sake of cyber security for identification, analysis, prevention of intrusion, spread of computer contaminant. The intermediary who does not obey or follow such orders may be punished with imprisonment up to three years and may be liable to pay fine.
- Section 70-B The Indian Computer Emergency Team(ICERT)for the sake of cyber security, order any intermediary to take precautions to maintain cyber security in the country failing which the intermediary may be punished for imprisonment up to one year or with fine up to INR 1 lakh (0.1 Million) or with both.
- Section 72-A – The dispelling of any information by the intermediary is rendered an offense. If any intermediary having entered into a contract with anyone to secure access to the personal information of such person discloses it to another person with the intention to cause wrongful loss or wrongful gain to someone then he will be punished with imprisonment up to three years or with fine which may extend up to INR 5 lakh (0.5 Million) or with both.

II. Liability of Intermediary Service Providers

A. Mere Conduit

297. This categorized liability of mere conduits as initiated by the Electronic Commerce Directive [200] is not separately defined under the IT Act. However, this role of the intermediary is covered under the new definition of "intermediary" by the IT (Amendment) Act 2008 –section 2(w) *supra.*

B. Caching

298. This role of the intermediary also comes under the definition of "intermediary" in section 2(w) of the IT (Amendment) Act 2008.

200. Liability of Intermediary Service Providers", European Union Directive (Feb. 8, 2000) also called E-Commerce Directive though not exhaustive on the point is yet a welcome step. It was to be implemented before Jan. 17, 2002. Ernst-Jan Louwers & Prpf.Corien E.J. Prins, *International Computer Law*, Vol. 2 (Lexis Nexis, 2004) 22-63.22.05[A].

C. *Hosting, Hyperlinks and Search Engines*

299. Section 2(w) of the IT Act specifically covers the liability of "...telecom service providers, network service providers, Internet service providers, web-hosting service providers, search engines, online payment sites, online auction-sites, online –market places, and cyber cafes."

§4. Liability of Certification Service Providers

300. It is an era of electronic communication the providers of certification services related to e-signatures are important in this regard. Electronic certificates are made trustworthy thereby. The EU directive 1999/93/EC introduces minimum liability regime to be adopted by various States.

§5. Liability of Domain Name Registrars

301. In India no specific legislation is available for the liability of domain name registrars. However, cyber squatters are not uncommon in India and disputes do arise between the registrant and the domain name holder. The Information Technology Act 2000 and the IT (Amendment) Act 2008 also lack any specific provision on the subject. However, in India disputes regarding domain name have arisen which were mainly between the registrant and the domain name holder. For this the Courts in India have resorted to the ICANN Policy and have also applied the Common Law (Doctrine of Passing off, etc.). As domain names are treated in a similar way as trademarks, the law relating to trademarks is applied by the courts. A Registrar provides direct services to the Domain Name Registrants. The Registrar database contains customer information in addition to the DNS information contained in the Registry database. Registrars process name registrations for Internet end users and send necessary DNS information to a Registry for entry into the Centralized Registry database and ultimate propagation over the Internet e.g., ERNET is the exclusive registrar for ac.in,edu.in, and res.in. .IN Registry is the official Registrar in India which facilitates the registration of domain names through its accredited registrars spread all over the word. The accredited Registrars in India fall under three categories: (1) IDN (Internationalized Domain Names) Accredited Registrars; (2) List of registrars; (3) Government registrars.

302. The ICANN has delegated IDN in seven Indian Languages to NIXI. These are: (1) *Devnagiri; (2) Bengali; (3) Telegu; (4) Gujarati; (5) Urdu; (6) Tamil;(7) Gurumukhi (Punjabi*). The Registry has the authority to deny or suspend a registration if it conflicts with the sovereign national interest or public order. As no specific law is available hence if the registrar violates this direction then he will be held liable either under the law of tort or under the Indian Penal Code 1860 for offenses like negligence, cheating, mischief, as the case may be.

Chapter 4. Product Liability

(1) In India "Product Liability" implies the liability of manufacturers, wholesalers, distributors and vendors for injury to a person or property as a result of defective or risky products. There is no product liability specific law but the various piecemeal legislations addressing the different areas of product manufacturing, contractual obligations, consumer protection, etc., collectively help the aggrieved. The product liability-related legal provisions never neglected the consumer although the specific law in this area is still pending. However, the liability is both civil and criminal. The various Acts are as follows:

(a) Consumer Protection Act 1986
(b) The Drugs and Cosmetics Act 1940
(c) The Drugs and Cosmetic Rules 1945
(d) The Drugs and Magic Remedies (Objectionable Advertisements) Act 1954.
(e) The Drugs and Magic Remedies (Objectionable Advertisements) Rules 1955.
(f) The Legal Metrology Act 2009.
(g) The Legal Metrology (Packed Commodities) Rules 2011.
(h) The Indian Contract Act 1872.
(i) The Sale of Goods Act 1930.
(j) Law of Torts.

303. Civil Liability – The following Acts are applicable in the area of product liability; Consumer Protection Act 1986, The Indian Contract Act 1872, The Sale of Goods Act 1930 and the Law of Torts. The protection of consumers was achieved in the country through socio-economic legislations as well by judicial pronouncements. The Consumer Protection Act 1986 is the most important and effective piece of legislation which is wholly consumer-centric. The Act gives the consumer the right to be compensated in the event of not only defective or harmful product but also for unsatisfactory or nil services. The Act envisages a parallel system of Redress which is not only quick and convenient but it is the cheapest remedy available. The redress forums are situated at three levels: District Forums at every District Head Quarter of India then the State Commissions in every state which have original jurisdiction regarding the value of the case and also have appellate jurisdiction to hear appeals from District Forums. Then there is one National Commission of India which is the highest body next to the Supreme Court only. It has original jurisdiction in respect of high valuation of the matter and then it is also empowered to hear appeals from the State Commissions. All these forums have the powers of the civil courts and dispense justice speedily. The remedies include not only return, repair or replacement of defective products but it also allows compensation to the aggrieved consumer. The procedure is simple and consumer–friendly as a complaint can be filed even on blank piece of paper which does away with the strict legal formalities to file a case.

304. Criminal Liability- There are a number of Acts like the Foods Adulteration Act 1954, The Food Safety and Standards Act 2006, The Drugs and Cosmetics Act

1940, The Indian Penal Code 1860, The Standards of Weights and Measures Act 1956, The Agricultural Produce (Grading and Marking) Act 1937; The India Standards (Certification Marks) Act 1952, The Bureau of Indian Standards Act 1986. As regarding criminal liability the laws provide not only a fine but also imprisonment in certain cases. Moreover, the biggest penal law of the country – the Indian Penal Code 1860 – is mostly attracted along with other specific legislations when the harm caused is a crime or when fraud and cheating are the means to violate such specific laws. Product liability falls under the Indian Penal Code 1860 under Chapter XIII and XIV *–Of Offenses Relating to Weights and Measures and Of Offenses Affecting Public Health, Safety, Convenience, Decency and Morals* respectively.[201] The Drugs and Cosmetics Act 1940 (DCA) was enacted to regulate the import, manufacture and sale and distribution of drugs and cosmetics. Both the Central and the State Governments maintain regulatory control over it and any contravention of DCA is punishable with imprisonment from six months to five years and fine ranges between INR 500 and 10,000. Harm caused due to harmful drugs will be punished with minimum imprisonment of ten years which may extend to life and the fine shall not be less than INR 10,000 or three times the value of the drug confiscated. If the death of the victim occurs then the fine amount shall be used for compensating the survivors of the deceased. The Drugs and Cosmetic Rules 1945 lays down restrictions on the importers of drugs regarding import of drugs which are prohibited in the country of origin and also to make declaration regarding the invoice, etc. of the drugs. The Drugs and Magic Remedies (Objectionable Advertisements) Act 1954 and The Drugs and Magic Remedies (Objectionable Advertisements) Rules 1955 also make it an offense to advertise products showing them to have magical qualities. Contravention of these laws would be met with -on first conviction imprisonment up to six months or with fine or with both and in case of second conviction with imprisonment up to one year or with fine or with both. The Legal Metrology Act 2009 (implemented 2011) The Legal Metrology (Packed Commodities) Rules 2011 provides that misquoting any price or publication of the weight, measures, etc. not in conformity with the actual weight of the product or the packing, selling, importing, distributing, delivering, etc. of the product the packing of which is not according to the prescribed procedure or standards then the wrongdoer shall be punished with fine ranging from INR 2,000 to 1,00,000 and or imprisonment from minimum three months to one year.

---

201. Chapter XIII- ss. 264–267; makes it a criminal offense, the fraudulent use of false instrument for weighing or measuring or selling false weight or measure. Chapter XIV- ss. 272–276 under which the adulteration of food or drink intended for sale, sale of noxious food or drink adulteration of drugs, sale of adulterated drugs or sale of drugs as a different drug or preparation, etc. The Indian Penal Code 1860.

Part VI. Privacy Protection

Chapter 1. Regulation of Personal Data Processing

§1. Legal Status of Data Protection

305. The birth of the virtual world as a result of the telecommunications and the Internet has raised alarms for the protection of personal data. The huge files containing the personal details of individuals regarding their health, service, property and a number of personal details has been totally replaced by the vast databases online. The secured paper files being static and confined to one place are replaced by online personal information which is accessible by at least certain authorized people and is also vulnerable to data intrusion, hacking and other data vandalism techniques. Data protection online thus becomes a crucial issue and all over the world laws have been formulated to secure data. Thus, data protection is a matter of concern not only at the personal level but also for defense, governments, businesses and other public works need data protection techniques and laws.

306. India presents a dismal picture so far as legal provisions regarding data protection are concerned. Thus, data protection law in the country can be found in scattered manner in the following provisions:

- Right to Privacy- Retrieved in Article 21 of the Constitution of India.
- The Public Financial institutions Act 1993.
- The Information Technology Act 2000.
- The Information Technology (Amendment) Act 2008.
- The Credit Information Companies (Regulation) Act 2005.
- The RBI Regulations under the CIC Act 2005.
- The Information Technology Rules 2009.
- The Information Technology Rules 2011.
- The Proposed Data Protection Bill (2006).
- The Indian Telegraph Act 1885.

The law has been piecemeal, starting from the year 2000 when the lone Information Technology Act 2000 (21 of 2000) was passed supplanted by the Information Technology (Amendment) Act 2008. Countering the stringent EU laws regarding data protection and realizing its conflict with the BPO industry in India, the GOI of late realized the need for having a suitable law to address the right to protection of personal data in the country. A need was felt to inculcate confidence among foreign investors and companies regarding data protection laws in the country. The amendment in the IT Act in 2008 was the first step towards having an effective data protection law making vandalizing of sensitive personal data a punishable offense (section 43A of the IT Act). Thus, empowered by section 43A the GOI promulgated ITR 2009 and 2011 consecutively to define "sensitive personal data or information" and "reasonable security practices and procedures" apart from formulating Rules on other related matters.

307. The GOI in order to uphold the law regarding data protection introduced a bill called Personal Data Protection Bill on December 8, 2006 in the *Rajya Sabha*, the upper House of the Parliament. The purpose of the Bill is to provide protection of personal data and information of an individual collected for a particular purpose by a Department or an Organization. The said Bill provides for compensation to the individual whose personal information has been vandalized, disclosed or used without his consent. There is also proposal for appointment of the Data Controllers to look upon the matters relating to violation of data protection laws.

The Bill is fashioned on the Data Protection Act of U.K. though it still needs to address India-specific issues. The Bill has not been passed into an Act to date.

§2. Definitions

308. Data-Data is defined as unprocessed information while information is defined as the data that have been organized and communicated in a comprehensible and meaningful manner. In the context of computers data, information and knowledge have become interchangeable words as all the information stored in the computer may be called data. "Data" under the Information Technology 2000 means a "representation of information, knowledge, facts, concepts or instructions which are being prepared or have been prepared in a formalized manner. Data is information which is processed in a computer system or computer network and can be in the form of computer printouts, magnetic or optical storage media, punched cards, punched tapes or information stored in the computer memory (section 2(o)).

§3. Scope of the Regulation

I. General Statement

309. Data Security Concerns- Finance, educational, legal, marketing, healthcare, telecommunication and banking services are all being outsourced into India. Thus, the Information Technology Enabled Services (ITES) where U.S. appears to be the biggest investor has expanded the area of data storage and data utilization at the same time raising alarms for security of such data. With globalization and a growing BPO industry in India the protection of data warrants legislation. Consumers of the BPO industry who hand over their personal information to the employees expect secrecy and security.

The cases of disclosing and handing over of the personal information of individuals to third parties for consideration and without the consent of the individual concerned have become a matter of concern. Most of the European Countries have data protection laws and they expect similar legal protection from countries with whom they are transacting. In such a case their Guidelines prohibit business with such countries which have no or weak data protection laws. Due to inadequate legal protection and weak privacy standards the Indian BPO industry has faced embarrassment.[202] Thus, lack of data protection laws have been a drawback for the India BPO industry which droops down to the lower level. Health care services, players in the retail financial sector, credit card transactions and banking services are largely the sensitive areas where data protection must be most stringent. In the Human Resource domain also personal information needs secrecy and security. So far Indian BPO outfits adhere to U.S. and European Regulations and Multinational Companies (MNCs) are made to comply with foreign Regulations. Thus, India is in need of a strong data protection law.

II. Personal Data

310. Internet has turned personal information of individuals into a treasure; a saleable commodity. The term personal data implies all the personal information of the individual which is collected by organizations and businesses under a contract or under some law. The GOI formulated the IT Rules 2011 in which there has been made a distinction between "sensitive personal data" and "personal data". The main object of the ITR 2011 is to put restrictions on the businesses in matter of handling personal data. Thus, as according to Rule 3 of ITR 2011 ***"Sensitive Personal Data"*** consists of the following:

(1) Password.
(2) Financial information comprising Bank account, Credit Card/Debit Card details.
(3) Physical, physiological and mental health condition.
(4) Sexual orientation; medical records and history.
(5) Biometric information.
(6) Any of the above details given to businesses for employment purposes.
(7) Any of the above information received by a body corporate for processing, stored or processed under lawful contract or otherwise.

Rule 2(i) defines *"Personal information"* as any information that relates to a natural person, which either directly or indirectly, or in combination with other information available or likely to be available with a body corporate is capable of identifying such person.

202. In June 2005 "The Sun" newspaper claimed that one of its journalists bought personal data details including passwords, addresses and passport data from a Delhi IT worker for GBP 4.25 each. Visit, http://news.bbc.co.uk/2/hi/south_asia/4619859.stm Earlier BPO Frauds in India include New York –based Citibank accounts being looted from a BPO in Pune and a call center employee in Bangalore peddling credit card information to fraudsters who stole USD 398,000 from bank accounts.http://www.atimes.com/atimes/South_Asia/HJ20Df01.html

However, the Rules do not explicitly differentiate between the "Sensitive Personal Data" and the "Personal Information" and thus unlike the U.K. data Protection act 1998 and its corresponding Rules the Indian law does not recognize different levels of stringency with regard to collection, transfer, disclosure and handling of "Personal Data" and "Sensitive Personal Data".

§4. Principles of Data Protection

I. Quality of the Data

311. The IT Act 2000 or the IT (Amendment) Act 2008 have no provision requiring processed and transferred data to be adequate, relevant and not excessive. However, as in respect of the Credit Information Companies (Regulation) Act 2005 the Government made Regulations and a duty is imposed on every credit institution to elaborate appropriate policy and safeguards procedure specifying the steps and security safeguards that must be adopted regarding collection, processing and colleting collecting of data and for security and protection of the data to ensure data accuracy and security.[203]

II. Right of Information in the Collection of Data

312. Any information that is freely available or accessible in public domain or furnished under the Right to Information Act 2005 or any other law shall not be regarded as sensitive personal data or information for the purposes of ITR 2011. (Rule 3 Proviso).

III. Consent of the Data Subject

313. Body corporate or any person representing it shall obtain written consent of the provider of the sensitive personal data or information through letter or fax or e-mail.(Rule 5; ITR 2011)

IV. Special Categories of Data

314. Personal information and Sensitive Personal Data or Information- "Personal information" is defined under Rule 2(i) while Rule 3 of ITR 2011 defines sensitive personal data or information. While "Personal information" means information in respect of a natural person which is sufficient to identify such person, sensitive personal data especially denotes that information which relates to: password; financial details of the person; physical or physiological conditions, sexual orientation; medical history; biometric information, etc. in respect of a person.

203. Regulation 20, Chapter III, Government Regulations under the CCI Regulation Act 2005.

§5. Data Security

I. General Statement

315. Data security becomes an important issue once it is collected whether under a contract or under some law. The IT (Amendment) Act 2008 is more concerned with cyber security and national security. For this elaborate arrangements are made for it. As regarding national security the intermediaries are made obligated to monitor, decrypt or intercept information flowing if so asked by the Government [section 69B IT (Amendment) Act 2008]. However, even the amended Act 2008 is silent on the specific point of data security. The Credit Information Companies (Regulation) Act 2005 contains privacy principle and envisages that every credit company or institution must ensure that the data relating to the credit information maintained by them is accurate, duly protected against any loss or unauthorized access or use or unauthorized disclosure.[204] Moreover the RBI Regulations[205] for the first time define "personal data" as "information about an identifiable individual but does not include the name, title or business address or telephone number of an employee of the credit company." (Chapter 1 RBI Regulations).

316. To enable the protection of information while in transit or in storage in order to safeguard the privacy of citizen's data and to decrease to decrease economic loss due to cyber crime or data theft is one of the objectives of the National Security Policy 2013 of the GOI.[206]

II. Security Document

The body corporate must have reasonable security practices and procedures and must have a comprehensive documented information security program and information security policies that contain managerial, technical, operational and physical security control measures that are suitable for the nature of information which is to be protected. If they implement such practices and policies then they will be considered to have complied with such procedures. In the event of an information security breach such body corporate shall be required to demonstrate that they have implemented security control measures as per the documented information security program and information security policies.

317. One of the Security Standards is the International Standard IS/ISO/IEC 27001 on "Information Technology –Security Techniques – Information Security Management System- Requirements." The body corporate or a person on its behalf who have implemented IS/ISO/IEC 27001 standard or the codes of best practices for

204. Section 19 Credit Information Companies (Regulation) Act 2005.
205. Regulations made by the reserve Bank of India in exercise of power conferred by s. 37(2) of the Credit Information Companies (Regulation) Act 2005.
206. File No. 2 (35) 2011 –CERT- Ministry of Communication and Information Technology – Department of Electronics and Information Technology –Notification on National Cyber Security Policy 2013 (NCSP-2013).

data protection as approved by ITR 2011 8 (3) shall be taken as complying with reasonable security practices and procedures provided it has been regularly certified or audited by an independent auditor who is approved by the GOI. (Rule 8). Such audit shall be carried once in a year or when such body corporate undertakes significant up gradation.

318. If an industry association whose members are self-regulating by following other than IS/ISO/IEC codes of best practices for data protection shall get its codes of best practices approved by the GOI.(Rule 8(3))

III. Functions and Obligations of Employees

319. Obligations- The body corporate or any person on behalf of the body corporate must provide a policy for privacy and disclosure of information. The body corporate or its representative who collects, receives, possesses, stores, deals or handles information of provider of information shall provide a privacy policy regarding handling and dealing of such personal information including sensitive personal data or information. Such policy must provide for view by such provider of information who has supplied such information under a lawful contract. Such policy as published on the website of body corporate shall have following features:

- Clear and easily accessible statements of its practices and policies.
- Type of personal or sensitive personal data or information so collected.
- Purpose of collection and usage of such information.
- Disclosure of information including sensitive personal data or information as provided in Rule 6.
- Reasonable security practices and procedures as provided under Rule 8. (Infra paragraph 397).

IV. Security Officer

320. The National Cyber Security Policy 2013[207] urges all private and public organizations to designate a member or senior of the Department as Chief Information Security Officer (CISO) responsible for cyber security efforts and initiatives.

V. Record of Incidents

321. Large scale cyber incidents may not only disturb the government, users and stakeholders but it will also greatly harm the Critical Information Infrastructure (CII). The political will has shown inclination to contain the cyber threats and a lots of activities, programs and planning is on the way to mitigate the occurrence of cyber

207. File No. 2 (35) 2011 –CERT- Ministry of Communication and Information Technology – Department of Electronics and Information Technology –Notification on National Cyber Security Policy 2013 (NCSP-2013).

incidents. The National Cyber Security Policy 2013 is a big step forward. The Policy aims to create a cyber-security framework.

It urges all the organizations, service providers to earmark a budget for implementing cyber security initiatives and to prevent occurrence and recurrence of cyber incidents.

The Policy introduces Cyber Security Management Plan dealing with cyber-related incidents. It also mandates cyber security drills and exercises to enable assessment of the security posture to test the preparedness to deal with the cyber security incidents.

VI. Identification, Authentication and Access Control

322. Identification-The Controller of Certifying Authority (CCA) has the power to checking the identification of end users, and providing them with service. The process of confirming the identity of a person is facilitated in public key cryptography by means of certificates.

323. Authentication -Authentication of the data is achieved by the use of electronic signatures as envisaged in the IT (Amendment) Act 2008 [section15]. The authentication of the electronic record shall be effected by the use of an asymmetric crypto system and hash functions[208] which envelop and transform the initial electronic record into another electronic record [section 3 IT Act 2000]. The authentication of the data is achieved by electronic signature or by electronic authentication technique which is considered reliable and is found in the Second Schedule of the IT Act 2000. For this the electronic signature or the electronic authentication technique shall be regarded reliable if (i) the signature creation data or the authentication data are within the context in which they are used linked to the signatory and to no other person; (ii)the signature creation data and the authentication data were under the control of the signatory and no other person. The Central government in this respect is empowered to prescribe the procedure or the purpose of ascertaining the person whose electronic signature is intended and the Government can also add or omit any electronic signature or electronic authentication technique form the Second Schedule [section 3A –IT (Amendment) Act 2008].

324. Access- The Controller of Certifying Authorities (CCA)or any person authorized by him having sufficient ground to suspect that any contravention of the IT Act, rules or regulations has been committed shall have access to any computer system, any apparatus, data or any other material connected with such system. This is done with the purpose of searching or causing a search to be made for obtaining any information or data contained in or available to such computer system. The person in charge of such computer, apparatus shall provide all reasonable technical and other assistance which is necessary [section 29 IT Act 2000].

208. The hash function means an algorithm mapping or translation of one sequence bit into another, generally smaller set known as "hash result" so that the electronic record yields the same hash result every time the algorithm is executed with the same electronic record as its input making it computationally infeasible i)to derive or reconstruct the original electronic record from the hash result produced by the algorithm ii)that two electronic records can produce the same has result using the algorithm.(Section-3 Explanation IT Act 2000)

VII. Audit

325. The audit of reasonable security practices and procedures shall be carried once a year by an auditor who is approved by the GOI. Audit can also be carried when the body corporate or a person on its behalf undertakes significant up gradation of its process and computer resource. (Rule 8(4)). Moreover it is provided in the amended Act that the audit of documents and records provided by any law shall be applicable for audit of documents or records in electronic form [section 7A-IT (Amendment) Act 2008].

326. The Government also dedicates itself to periodic audit and evaluation of the adequacy and effectiveness of the information infrastructure to see that it is appropriate according to the regulatory framework. (National Cyber Security Policy 2013).

VIII. Tests with Real Data

327. The National Cyber Security Policy 2013 also urges organizations to create an infrastructure for conformity assessment and certification of compliance to cyber security best practices standards and guidelines (for example, ISO 27001 ISMS Certification, IS system audits, penetration testing /vulnerability assessment application security testing, web security testing.). The Policy also encourages all entities to periodically test and evaluate effectiveness of technical and operational security control measures.

§6. Duty of Secrecy

328. Body corporate or any person on its behalf which collects the information must keep the information secure as per Rule 8. It must have a documented information security program and information security policies; must follow the International Standard IS/ISO/IEC 27001 on Information Technology- Security Techniques-Information Security Management System-Requirements".

329. The Public Financial Institutions Act 1993 obliges a banker to keep secret about the accounts of its customers. In the case of *Kattabomman Transport Corporation Ltd. v. State Bank of Travancore & Ors*[209] the court ruled that among the duties of the bankers towards their customer is the duty of secrecy which arises out of banker – customer relationship.

§7. Disclosure of Data

330. – Disclosure of sensitive personal data or information by body corporate cannot be made to the third party without the prior permission from the provider of

209. AIR 1992 Ker. 35.

such data who delivers such information under a contract. Such disclosure can be made without such permission if:

- It was agreed to such disclosure in the contract.
- Such disclosure becomes necessary for compliance of some legal obligation.
- Disclosure is made to Government Agencies who are authorized to obtain such sensitive personal data or information for the purpose of verification of identity or for prevention, detection, investigation including cyber incidents, prosecution and punishment of offenses.
- Disclosure can also be made if it is ordered by any law.

§8. International Movement of Data

I. General Statement

331. The Indian companies acting as "data importers" may enter into contracts with "data exporters" to adhere to a high standard of data protection. These contracts are binding and may fulfill the requirements of overseas customer (s) national laws. Thus, if the data exporter in the EU and the data importer in India use the standard contractual clauses of the Commission of 2001 the data importer is expected to honor its undertakings under the contract and treat the data with the level of data protection and limitations reflected in the contract. The Indian Contract Act 1972 guiding the commercial contracts may entitle the aggrieved to damages for violation of contract or disclosure of data. Recently outsourcing /BPO contracts are also incorporating clauses on international arbitration for dispute resolution. Such contracts often provide choice of law provision which may include arbitration rules of UNCITRAL, ICC London Court of International Arbitration (LCIA). Indian outsourcing and BPO companies are also accepting process of mediation to resolve the dispute. Thus, companies are agreeing to dispute resolution by non-binding mediation under the International Mediation Rules of the International Center for Dispute Resolution of the American Arbitration Association. (ICDR).Some Indian companies like WIPRO, INFOSYS, and TCS active in the IT/BPO sector presently have a very stringent policy dealing with the protection of their client's information and all the employees are contractually bound to protect the confidential information of the client.

II. Specific Provisions Ruling the Transfer to Countries which Provide an Adequate Level of Protection

332. A body corporate or any of its representative may transfer sensitive personal data or information including any information to any other body corporate or to any person in India or in any foreign country provided assurance is given by such transferee body corporate or person regarding the level of data protection as required by the ITR 2011.(Rule 7) Such transfer can be made under the following two situations:

- That such transfer is necessary for the performance of contract between the body corporate and the provider of information. or
- Where the provider of such information has given consent to such transfer.

III. Specific Provisions Ruling the Transfers to Other Countries

333. The IT Act 2000 and the Rules are silent on this point.

§9. Access to Data on Behalf of the Controller

334. The IT Act 2000 is silent on the specific point. In the Credit Information Companies (Regulation) Act 2005 it is provided that the credit information companies and credit institutions and the specified users must establish security procedures in accordance with the rules under the said Act. The credit company must arrange for all its employees to sign a declaration of fidelity and secrecy and to handle credit information on a "need to know" basis and to transfer the information through a secure medium.

§10. Rights of Data Subjects

I. General Statement

335. Individual privacy is the victim of the Internet. As the individual logs in his personal information goes viral. E-Commerce, social media, banking services, traveling, and medical services *inter alia* have made the individual transparent in the Internet age. Nevertheless human beings by nature preserve their personal details and would never allow publicity of it. This is known as the individual privacy. The various legislations in India do respect the rights of the data subjects though no exhaustive law is still available. Apart from right to privacy which flows as a fundamental right from the Constitution of India (Article 21; Case Law) the various legislations aim to protect the rights of data subject like the right to protection and secrecy of data, the right to know the purpose of collection of data and the right to be compensated in case of unauthorized disclosure of data, etc.

II. Challenging Assessments

336. Individual privacy faces many challenges in the cyberspace. Apart from the traditional services the upcoming cloud services also pose challenges to the privacy of the individual. Cloud computing on the one hand gives added facilities to the owner of the data namely that data is available to him from anywhere in the globe and the users, the cloud service providers and even the regulators are attracted by it. But on the other hand it is raising grim privacy and other challenges. Today more and more services like document creation, storage, workflows, e-mail; office applications like accounting, HR purchase, CRM among others are being delivered from the Cloud. India with its booming economy, growing domestic IT market and USD 60 billion IT and BPO industry is uniquely positioned to benefit from cloud computing both as a hub for delivering Cloud services and as a consumer of cloud services. The worldwide cloud services revenue is expected to reach USD 148.8 billion in 2014 (Gartner). The National Telecom Policy 2012 also plans to address speeding up of cloud computing and adopting policies to ensure rapid expansion of these services at par with international standards. The benefits of cloud computing however are not without certain challenges involved in it. These can be enumerated as follows:[210]

- Data Security and Privacy.
- Compliance Issues.
- Legal and Contractual issues.
- Challenges in Migration.
- Lack of clarity in pay per use model.
- Integration of cloud-based applications with legacy systems.

III. Rights of Access, Rectification and Cancellation

A. General Statement

337. In the Internet Age collection of personal data has become a way of life. For innumerable services personal information is gathered by body corporate and government agencies to provide various services to the individual. The information so provided however remains the right of the individual. Thus, data protection becomes an important legal issue. Collection of such information is however clothed with legal protection and with a number of rules and regulations. The consent of the data provider is a must and it has the condition attached that such sensitive personal data or information shall not be collected unless there is some lawful purpose to do so. When the information is so collected by body corporate or any other person on its behalf then such person must ensure that the person providing the information is fully aware of the fact of obtaining the information; the purpose to collect it; the identity of the recipients and agencies handling the information must also be disclosed to such person. The body corporate gathering such information must not retain it for longer than is required for the purpose for which it is collected. (Rule 5 ITR 2011).

B. Right of Access

338. Every data subject who provides information shall be given an option not to provide the sensitive personal data or information. Once the information is provided the body corporate shall not be responsible for the authenticity of the information. Body corporate or any person on its behalf shall permit the providers of information as and when requested to have an access to and review the information they had

210. *Data Protection Challenges in Cloud Computing*-Data Security Council of India (DSCI).2010.

provided. (Rule 5(6).There is also in respect of the Credit Information Company's obligation to allow the person concerned or the (data subject) to make available the data to him and to make correction or amendment according to his wishes.

IV. Right of Rectification and Cancellation

339. Once the information is provided by the provider of information at any time while availing the services of such body corporate they shall have an option to withdraw its consent given earlier. Such withdrawal shall be in writing. As a result of such withdrawal the body corporate shall no longer be under obligation to provide goods or services to such provider of information. (Rule 5).

V. Right to Compensation

340. Compensation for failure to Protect Data- Where a body corporate which is possessing, dealing or handling any sensitive personal data or information in its computer resource is negligent in implementing the reasonable security practices and procedures and thus causes wrongful gain or wrongful loss to any person such body corporate shall be liable to pay damages by way of compensation to the person so affected (section 43A- IT (Amendment) Act 2008).

§11. Sectorial Provisions

I. Files in Public Ownership

341. The Copyright Act 1957 secures the rights of an author over his work, creation, etc. However, there is still certain government work or data which is although copyrighted yet the following work is exempted from it and is regarded as under public ownership:

- Act of legislature.
- Reports of Committees, Councils, Boards or body appointed by the Government.
- Judgment or order of a Court/tribunal.

342. Also there will be fair dealing with a literary dramatic, musical or artistic work which is for the purpose of; a) research and study;2) for criticism or review;3) for reporting current events;4) the judicial proceedings; 5) performance by amateur club or society; 6) the making of sound recordings of literary, dramatic or musical works.

II. Files in Private Ownership

A. Data Included in Sources Accessible to the Public

343. The National Data Sharing and Accessibility Policy -2012 of the GOI[211] gives importance to data sharing for the good of the community and fosters a technology-based data management culture. In response to the Principle 10 of United Nations Declaration on Environment and Development (Rio De Janeiro– June 1992) which supported that every member of the community should have access to the information concerning the environment and that the Government must make arrangement to make provision for wide availability of information; and in response to the Indian Right to Information Act 2005 [section 4(2)] which says that State must provide *suo moto* information to the public at regular intervals by all means including the Internet, the National Data Sharing and Accessibility Policy 2012 is formulated. Different types of data sets available both in geospatial and non-geospatial form by different ministries and departments are to be marked as shareable data and non-shareable data. The accessibility by the public may fall into different categories according to Policy 2012 such as: (1) open access which should be easy, and user-friendly; (2) Registered Access which is accessible only on special request and when authorized by the department concerned; (3) Restricted Data- Certain data can be declared as restricted by the government and will be accessible only if allowed by the Government. A state-of-the-art data warehouse and data archive with online analytical processing (OLAP) capabilities providing a multi-dimensional and subject-oriented view of the data will be arranged. The data so uploaded remains the property of the ministry or department concerned. The Department of Science and Technology will serve as the nodal agency and shall work in close collaboration with the Department of Information Technology by creating data gov.in through NIC.

344. The National Portal of India is the official website of the GOI designed, developed and hosted by the NIC under the aegis of the DEITY, the Ministry of Communications and information Technology. It is developed as the National E-Governance Plan (NGEP) of the GOI. The main purpose is to provide a single window access to the information and services being provided by the Indian Government for public access.

B. Provision of Information Services on Credit Worthiness and Credit Scoring

345. Credit information bureaus are a repository of information about the credit history of the borrowers. They assign credit scores to the customers and on the basis of which they decide their creditworthiness. The Credit information Bureau (India) Ltd. (CIBIL) was formed in 2004. Although the credit is being used globally for multipurpose but in India it is largely used in space lending since 2007. The establishment of CIBIL is a sincere effort of the Government and the RBI to improve the functionality and stability of the Indian financial system by containing non-performing-assets (NPAs)

211. Registered No. DL(N)-04/0007/2003-05. The Gazette of India –No.11-New Delhi Saturday Mar. 23, 2012.

while improving grantor's portfolio quality. It was promoted by the State Bank of India (SBI), Housing Development Finance Corporation (HDFC), Dun& Bradstreet Information Services India Pvt. Ltd .and TransUnion International Inc. to provide comprehensive credit information by collecting, collating and disseminating credit information regarding both the commercial and customer borrowers to a closed user group of Members. The credit environment is changing in India while the *Equifax* and *Experian* credit bureaus are part of it. The RBI also granted operating license to High Mark Credit Information Services the only start up in this oligopoly. High Mark launched India's first micro finance bureau in 2011 and is flourishing as world's largest micro finance bureau.

C. Processing for the Purpose of Publicity and Market Research

346. Market research and Information Network Scheme was launched by Ministry of Agriculture in March 2000. The Scheme is being implemented through Directorate of Marketing and Inspection in collaboration with National Informatics Centre. The Ministry of Agriculture, GOI has framed procedures and guidelines for marketing Personnel in different states under Marketing Research and Information Network.

347. Indian Market Research Bureau (IMRB) established in 1970 is a multi-country market research, survey and business consultancy firm that offer a range of syndicated data and customized research services.

§12. Liability of Controllers and Processors of Personal Data

348. A body corporate or any person on its behalf must lay down a policy for privacy and handling or dealing with the personal data or sensitive personal data of the individual or provider of information. (Rule 4).[212] Such a policy shall be made public. Such body corporate must also have a documented security program and implement security control measures like the International standard IS/ISO/IEC 27001 on information Technology – Security techniques –Information Security Management System-Requirements " is one such standard referred to in sub-rule(1) (Rule 8).

349. The mishandling of personal data or the disclosure of its content is a punishable offense. In this respect in India not only the intermediary but any other person obtaining information under a legal contract is liable for breach of the contract for not maintaining the privacy of the information provider and shall also be criminally liable. If such intermediary or the person concerned with the intent to cause wrongful loss or unlawful gain to someone, without the consent of the information provider discloses the information to any other person shall be punished with imprisonment up to three years or with fine which may extend to INR 5 lakh or with both [section 72A Information Technology (Amendment) Act 2008].

212. The Information Technology (Reasonable Security Practices and Procedures and sensitive personal data or information) Rules 2011.

Chapter 2. Protection of Telecommunications Privacy

§1. Confidentiality of the Communications

350. Legal Provisions- Communications between individuals requires not only confidentiality but legal protection too. However, privacy of individuals in communicational situation is not a new concept in India and the ancient law on Telegraph secures to its commuters that level of privacy which was required at that time. Privacy has become a universally recognized right and especially in the modern world of telecommunication and Internet it is relevant as never before. Today though India lacks a specific privacy legislation nevertheless it has secured right to privacy in sporadic and different legal provisions as follows:

- Article 21 of the Constitution of India protects the right to privacy.
- Section 24 of the Indian Telegraph Act 1885 (13 of 1885) prescribes a criminal penalty of one year's imprisonment for any person who intrudes or trespasses on telecom premises in order to "unlawfully learn" the contents of any message. Section 25 of the said Act makes it an offense to damage, remove, tamper with or touch any telegraph equipment with the intent to intercept a message or acquit one with contents thereof. The punishment is imprisonment up to three years or fine or both.
- Section 427 of Indian Telegraph Rules 1951 provides that phones should not be used to disturb, irritate or annoy persons or to transmit any message for communication which may annoy a person.
- Rule 513 of the Indian Telegraph Rules 1951 prohibits use of telex for the transmission of indecent, annoying, obscene or illegal messages.
- In 1997 the Supreme Court of India directed the RBI to employ measures to reduce unsolicited calls on the ground that the right to privacy is a fundamental right.[213]
- As result of the Supreme Court Guidelines in the PUCL Case the GOI invoked section 7(2) (b) of the Telegraph Act to codify the applicable guidelines for communications surveillance. Consequently in 1998 rule 419-A was inserted in the Telegraph rules 1951 which provides that all directions for interception under section 5(2) of the Telegraph Act must be issued by a competent Officer.
- The TRAI issued a Consultation Paper on November 20, 2006 which defines Unsolicited Commercial Communications (UCC) to include telephone calls on fixed or mobile phones, SMS, MMS, video or voice mail and any other form of electronic communication vial telecommunication services. It has also introduced specific regulations for setting up a national Do-Not-Call-Register (DNCR).

213. *People's Union for Civil Liberties (PUCL) v. Union of India and Anr.* AIR 1997 1 SCC 301.

I. Interception of the Communications by the National Intelligence Agency

351. Right to privacy though now a constitutionally recognized right in India is not absolute. It is subject to national security, defense requirements, security of communicational installations, and terrorism. Law enforcement Agencies frequently monitor and intercept telephone conversations. However, the surveillance by intelligence agencies has often become a subject of political debate and supporters of individual privacy also often question the limit and ground of interception of communications, tapping of phonic conversations, and tracking of electronic communications by the intelligence agencies. However, the power to monitor and intercept by the intelligence agencies is backed by legal provisions and at such a situation the privacy rights of users and the due-process rights of private network owners takes a secondary position. The Supreme Court of India through many landmark judgments has tried to strike a balance between the requirements of the law enforcers and the privacy rights of the citizens. Apart from the PUCL case the Supreme Court restricted cellular companies from making unsolicited calls. As a result of this landmark judgment the RBI through its Circular [214] to various banks ordered that the telemarketers who are registered with the Department of Telecommunication (DoT) are to be employed by them.

II. Statutory Basis for Surveillance

352. Surveillance and interception by government agencies to establish rule of law and to secure national interest has the force of law. in the following sections interception by intelligence agencies is backed by law.

A. Section 5(2) of the Indian Telegraph Act 1885 (13 of 1885)

353. Section 5(2) of the Indian Telegraph Act 1885- Under this section the GOI, any state government or an authorized Government Officer can order the non-transmission, interception, detention, disclosure of messages about a particular subject on the following grounds:

(1) In the event of public emergency.
(2) In the interest of public safety.

354. Although the above ground/grounds may exist but the action taken must also be justified on the following other grounds:

- Sovereignty and integrity of India.
- State Security.
- In the interest of friendly relations with foreign States.
- Public Order.
- Incitement to an offense.

214. RBI/2008-09/177 DBOD No. FSD.BC.45/24.01.011/2008-09

The Proviso to section 5(2) reads that press messages intended to be published in India from government-accredited correspondents shall not be intercepted or detained unless their transmission is prohibited.

B. PUCL v. Union of India

355. People's Union for Civil Liberties v. Union of India is the landmark judicial pronouncement on the surveillance and interception of communications by the government agencies. The petitioners, a civil liberties group countered the said section 5(2) by pleading that there was telephone tapping by the agencies and that the said section was unconstitutional as it lacks adequate safeguards for monitoring and interception. The Government took the pleas that State security will be in jeopardy if the said section is declared unconstitutional as telephone tapping is undertaken only in exceptional circumstances. The Court associating the surveillance and telephone tapping with the right to privacy said that it is the fundamental right of the citizens under Article 21 of the Indian constitution and that telephonic conversation is a matter of privacy and should not be interfered with without a legally justified ground. Referring to the fact that India being a signatory to the *International Covenant on Civil and Political Rights* also required that the privacy of the individual should not be interfered with arbitrarily. The Court however ruled that public emergency and public safety are essential requirements for the government to legitimately monitor telephonic conversation. The Court observed that section 7(2) (b) of the Indian Telegraph Act 1885 authorizes the GOI to make rules for prevention of improper interception and issued detailed guidelines to the government to protect communication privacy. [215]

C. Rule 419-A of the Telegraph Rules

356. As a corollary to the judgment of the Supreme Court of India in the PUCL case Rule 419 A was inserted in the Telegraph Rules. Rule 419A basically contains the guidelines issued by the Court regarding interception of the communication by government agencies. Rule 419-A is stringent and takes every precaution to maintain communicational privacy. It has been amended recently in 2014.

357. Telegraph (Amendment of 2014)Rules 2014-[216] Rule 419-A is replaced by the following new Rule in which it is confirmed that no interception shall be made except by:

- In case of GOI – By an order of the Secretary to the GOI in Ministry of Home Affairs-
- In case of States- By an order of the Secretary to the government of the State –In charge of the Home Department.

215. Paragraph 34 & 35; *People's Union for Civil Liberties (PUCL) v. Union of India and Anr.* AIR 1997 1 SCC 301.

216. Ministry of Communications and IT; DoT – New Delhi- the January 28, 2014. In exercise of powers conferred by s. 7 of the Indian Telegraph Act 1885 (13 of 1885), the Telegraph Rules 1951 are amended.

- In unavoidable Circumstances – by an order of the officer not below the rank of a Joint Secretary.
- In emergent cases the interception:

  (a) In remote areas where prior direction for obtaining the order for interception is not feasible, or
  (b) For operational reasons obtaining of prior direction is not feasible.

358. Then in such cases prior approval of the Head or second senior most officers of the authorized Security and Enforcement Agency at the Central level and in the case of State approval of the officer not below the rank of the Inspector General of Police should be taken. The competent authority shall be informed of the interception by the approving authority within three working days and the interception to be carried out within seven days failing which the message shall not be intercepted. The officer concerned must also look for other means to get the information and issue the order of interception only if it is not possible to obtain information through other means. An order by the competent authority shall contain reasons for such order and shall be forwarded to the Review Committee within seven working days. The directions shall specify the name of the officer to whom the content of the message is to be disclosed. The direction of interception shall remain in force up to sixty days and shall in no case extend beyond a period of 180 days from the date of issue of such direction. The directions for interception shall be issued to the designated authorized officers who are granted license under section 4 of the Telegraph Act in writing or in secure electronic form. The authorized officer to intercept must maintain a detailed record of the entire operation, the name of the person whose message has been intercepted, the copies of the message, the duration of the interception, etc. The Telegraph authority shall designate nodal officers of the Authority or of the Service Providers. Every fortnight a list of the authorized interceptions shall be forwarded to the Secrecy and Enforcement Agency and the officers carrying out the interception activities shall maintain full secrecy and confidentiality regarding the intercepted message so as to maintain the privacy rights of the citizens. The Service providers shall be responsible for the actions of their employees in respect of violations of license conditions and will have to suffer fine or cancellation of license if found guilty. Review Committees shall be formed by the GOI and the concerned State Government comprising high level officials. The Committee in their respective areas shall meet every two months and review the intercepting orders and test the legality of such orders in the light of the Telegraph Act. The intercepted messages shall be destroyed within two months of the discontinuance of such interception and shall not maintain the record and intercepted message beyond six months unless required for functional requirements.

D. Private Licensees

359. Surveillance by private licensees also became prevalent with the expansion of telecommunication services in the country. Today private licensees have greater coverage in the mobile services area than the two giant government departments; the *BSNL* and the *MTNL.* Private licensees are under obligation to assist the government agencies in the matter of monitoring and interception activities. The private telecom network providers are also duty bound to maintain communicational privacy of individuals. In the landmark judgment of *Amar Singh v. Union of India*[217] in which the petitioner was aggrieved by its telephone tapping by the private network provider M/S Reliance Infocom Ltd sought to protect his right to privacy under Article 21 of the Constitution. The Supreme Court ruled that interception is an invasion of privacy and it must be carried out only after ascertaining the genuineness of the interception direction and if service provider without being sure of the genuineness of the direction carries out the interception fails in its public duty and infringes upon the individual's right to privacy.

360. GOI's Guidelines to Private Licensees- Inspired by the observations of the Supreme Court of India in the Amar Singh's case the Government issued following Guidelines to the private telecom networks in the country:

(1) All private licensees must maintain 24-hour arrangement to ensure proper processing of interception requests from security and law enforcement agencies and must designate a nodal officer to carry out related duties.
(2) The nodal officers shall be held responsible for receiving and acknowledging requests where prior approval of competent officers under section 419-A has not been obtained.
(3) Every fortnight the nodal officers must receive confirmation of such interception requests from the nodal officers of enforcement agencies.
(4) Licensees must provide interception facilities to the state police in respect of roaming subscribers' communications. For interception facilities of non-roaming subscribers out of their state must be provided with the approval of the Home secretary concerned.
(5) Access service providers must use prescribed encryption algorithms in their GSM networks.
(6) Where interception requests are issued in emergency cases in rural areas for operational reasons, retroactive confirmation of these requisitions must be obtained from the competent officials within three days.
(7) Licensees must maintain secrecy and for this must assign the work to senior most officials of their department so that utmost care is taken to prevent communicational leakage from law enforcement and security agencies.
(8) Service providers must carry out internal checks to ensure that there is not unauthorized interception and that full confidentiality and secrecy of interception authorizations are made.
(9) Service providers must ensure verification of their mobile subscribers and pre-paid cards to prevent misuse of mobile services for terrorism and anti-national activities.

217. [2011] INSC 491 (11May 2011). Civil Original Jurisdiction WP (Civil) No. 39 of 2006.

361. Guidelines to OSPs- From time to time the DoT issues guidelines to the Other Service Providers [218]regarding their operational activities in the country.

E. Unlawful Interceptions

362. The Indian Telegraph Act 1885(13 of 1885) regards "unlawful learning" the contents of any message as a punishable offense (section 24) and the tampering or damaging of any equipment with intent to prevent or obstruct transmission is also regarded an offense (section 25). But in the case *RM Malkani v. State of Maharashtra*[219] the court ruled that section 25 is not applied to cases where one person on phone allows another to hear and record the statement. [220]

§2. Personal Data Protection

363. There is no such concept as "personal data" though the term "data" has been defined in the IT Act 2000. India still lacks the much-needed data protection law though there have been in 2011 the recent Rules[221] which define "sensitive personal data". However, there is a long pending proposal in the form of "Right to Privacy Bill"[222] as proposed by the GOI. Data under the IT Act is defined as "a representation of information, knowledge, facts, concepts or instructions which are being prepared or have been prepared in a formalized manner and is intended to be processed, is being processed or has been processed in a computer system or computer network, and may be in any form (including computer printouts magnetic or optical storage media, punched cards, punched tapes) or stored in the memory of the computer"[section 2(1)(o), The Information Technology Act 2000]. In the amended Act ample provisions are added to protect the data and personal information of the subject.

364. Right to Privacy is an important facet of the data protection under which the personal details of individuals raise questions regarding its security and secrecy. It is a right which is recognized globally and from ancient times. In India it has been

218. The Services like call centers, network operation centers, tele-marketing, tele-education, tele-medicine, e-commerce using infrastructure provided by various access providers are being registered under Other Service Providers (OSP) category as provided in National Telecom Policy 1999. Office

Memorandum No. 18-7/2007-OSP- Government of India, Ministry of Communications and IT, DoT, New Delhi. Dated the June 2, 2008.

219. AIR 1973 SC 157, (1973) 1 SCC 471.

220. In this Case the Police recorded the statement of the accused during a telephonic conversation on the basis of which the Court convicted him under anti-corruption statute. The Court held that the Police did not damage or tampered with the telephonic equipment by attaching a telephone recorder to it.

221. Rule 3- The Information Technology (Reasonable Security Practices and Procedures and sensitive personal data or information)Rules 2011. Published in the Gazette of india,Extraordinary. PartII, s. 3 subs. (i) of dated the April 11, 2011. Ministry of Communications and Information Technology – Government of India –New Delhi.

222. Ministry of Personnel, Public Grievances & Pensions, Right to Privacy Bill, Release ID- 74743 dated Aug. 18, 2011.

a right though cherished and treasured yet it is still to occupy a place of pride in the law books of the country. Time and again the Supreme Court of India has culled this right to privacy out of Article 21 of the Constitution of India which includes the fundamental right to life and personal liberty yet the right has not been separately recognized in any other law.

365. Personal data has been commodified in the Internet Age. It is susceptible to vandalism, hacking and has become a subject of sale and purchase. Apart from causing wrongful loss to the provider of information it is also considered as a serious breach of his Right to privacy. Thus, under the Indian law it is a punishable offense to cause breach of confidentiality and privacy. Not only the common offender but the Certifying Authorities and Government Agencies are punished for the breach of privacy as follows.

366. The breach of confidentiality has two dimensions:

- *Breach of confidentiality of private information* which is received from subscribers by the authorities entails criminal liability; the punishment is imprisonment up to two years or with fine upto INR 1 Lakh or with both (section 72 IT Act 2000).
- *Disclosure of Information in breach of lawful contract or data vandalism* – Any person including an intermediary who providing services to a person under a lawful contract secures access to personal information and thereby discloses such information to any other person in order to cause wrongful loss or wrongful gain to any one is guilty of data vandalism and shall be punished with imprisonment up to three years or with fine up to INR 5 lakh or with both (section 72A -IT (Amendment) Act 2008).

§3. Rights of Users and Consumers

I. Traffic Data

367. Traffic data has been defined under the newly amended IT Act as any data identifying any person or computer system or computer network or location or from which the communication can be transferred. It includes communications origin, destination, route time, data, size, duration or type of underlying service and any other information [section 69B-(4) (ii) The IT (Amendment) Act 2008].

368. Mobile Traffic Data – Mobile traffic data in the country soared by 92% to around 25 petabytes in 2012 on the back of higher 3G uptake on account of cheaper traffic. Data consumption by 3G users had tripled in one year which shows the high speed with which data consumption has increased in the country. Currently a 3G user consumes 434 MB of data per month on an average while a 2G user consumers 115 MB per month. The 3G price reductions in May mid 2012 has boosted its upgrading and the price differential between 3G and 2G has reduced from 7X (start of 2012) to 2X (end of 2012). 3G now constitutes one –third of all mobile data as compared to one-fourth of all data in mid 2012. Mobile data growth in the country is in line with the similar growth globally and it is expected that by 2020 the operators need to service

1GB data per user per day. The Smartphone penetration in the country is just 6%, 50% of all mobile data (2G and 3G) is generated through these phones, while feature phones contribute 30% of all mobile data. Study shows that the growth of the Smartphone subscribers was one of the highest in the world in 2012.[223]

II. Itemized Billing

369. Charges for calls in message rate or measured rate system shall become payable only when the consumer receives the bill. The Telegraph Authority lays down the rates and the periods for which the bill is to be paid (Rule 439 The Indian Telegraph Rules 1951).

Computer-based itemized mobile bills are admissible in evidence. Itemized bills or the hard copy of bills to the post-paid subscriber are nothing but human/readable averment of electronic document or data. Allegations regarding its authenticity were not accepted by the court. Itemized bills are acceptance of liability and /or acknowledgment for amount due and payable.[224]

III. Presentation and Restriction of Calling and Connected Line Identification

370. This facility is provided to the subscribers by the service providers. TRAI has issued Direction[225] in connection with the Charges for Calling Line Identification Presentation (CLIP). CLIP is a value-added service and cannot be made compulsory for the subscribers. All monthly fixed recurring charges which are compulsory for a subscriber under one head should include charges for CLIP as well. Consent of the subscriber in availing the value-added services is compulsory.

371. Change in 2014- The service provider can now charge for CLIP facility but it cannot be made compulsory in the tariff plan. When CLIP facility is subject to charge then the subscriber should be given option by the service provider to give his consent for it which should be done in a transparent manner.

IV. Automatic Call Forwarding

372. Call Forwarding Facility is an advantageous for the busy people which is available both on fixed line and mobile phones. Earlier the call forwarding facility was provided on nominal charges. Cell One which is the BSNL, Mobile phone service, gives to its subscribers opportunity to utilize this facility. Using the menu function the subscriber can activate call forwarding facility for the following four options; all calls, if busy, if no reply, if not reachable/switched off. All calls forwarded are billed the

223. Press Trust of India Report – Dated Wednesday May 22, 2013.
224. *Vodafone Essar Ltd. V. Raju Sud,* II (2012) BC 141 (Bom).
225. Direction No. 301-49/2005-Eco dated August 23, 2007. The TRAI.

same way a regular call is billed. However, calls forwarded to the Cell One Voice Mail are not charged for airtime.

Policy Change- The State -owned Telecom giant BSNL provides for call forwarding facility to its subscribers free. Pan India the 3G mobile service operator with the object of having a seamless mobile connectivity launched the "Unlimited Free Call forwarding" service for all its subscribers. It offers the facility to the pre-paid subscribers without any "call charge" for forwarded calls. For post-paid subscribers the facility of Call forwarding is on nominal monthly charge. Earlier the Call forwarding Facility via SMS, STV, Boosters was for limited cities which have now been extended to all telecom circles in India. [226]

§4. Unsolicited Communications

373. Unsolicited Commercial Communications (UCC) is the dark side of the huge expansion of the telecommunications services the world over. It is not only an irritant for the mobile consumers but it is also taken as an invasion of their privacy. Indian Telecom Industry with 900 million subscribers has become the second largest wireless market in the world. Low tariffs and easier ways to reach the grassroots level consumers has made direct calling a preferred means for telemarketers. To curb the menace of UCC and to solve this problem of consumers the TRAI formulated The Telecom Commercial Communication Customer Preference Regulations 2010 (effective September 27, 2011). There have been a number of amendments to the Regulation 2010.[227] In these Regulations Unsolicited Commercial Communications have been defined as: any message through telecommunications service which is transmitted for the purpose of informing about, or soliciting or promoting any commercial transaction in relation to goods, investments or services which a subscriber opts not to receive. But such messages do not include; message regarding financial transaction as a result between the parties, messages relating to charities, national campaigns, messages on the direction of the Government, etc.

374. Implementation Status- To carry out the Regulations a framework was worked out by the TRAI in which the National Do Not Call (NDNC) Registry is

226. Telecom Talk- November 15,2011.
227. Amendment to Principal Regulations dated 14-12-2010
Amendment to Principal Regulations dated 28-12-2010
Amendment to Principal Regulations dated 31-01-2011
Amendment to Principal Regulations dated 28-02-2011
Amendment to Principal Regulations dated 18-032011
Amendment to Principal Regulations dated 5-9-2011
Amendment to Principal Regulations dated 25-10-2011
Amendment to Principal Regulations dated 31-10-2011
Amendment to Principal Regulations dated14-05-2012
Amendment to Principal Regulations dated 5-11-2012
Amendment to Principal Regulations dated 23-05-2013
Amendment to Principal Regulations dated 24-05-2013
Amendment to Principal Regulations dated 22-08-2013
Amendment to Principal Regulations dated 03-12-2013

required to be maintained by the Department to list subscribers who do not wish to entertain UCC. All Telemarketers are required to be registered in the NDNC Registry as per the Regulations. A unique 1909 number has been fixed for Telemarketers to receive the requests of subscribers for UCC. Any subscriber requesting for not receiving UCC shall stop getting such calls after expiry of forty days. If a subscriber gets such UCC even after forty-five days then it can lodge a complaint to his service provider. Service Providers are also duty bound under the Regulations to facilitate and dispose of such complaints promptly.

375. The Telecom Portal- The Telecom Commercial Communications Customers Preference Portal is a data base furnishes a variety of useful knowledge for the customers. The customers who do not want UCC can dial or SMS to1 909 (Toll free) and get registered in any one of the Categories:

- Fully Blocked Category
- Partially Blocked Category.

For Fully Blocked Category the customer can opt for no messages at all and for the Partially Blocked Category the customer can choose from the following seven categories giving nod for any of his preference from the category of; Banking/Insurance/Financial Products/Credit Cards-1/Real Estate-2/Education-3. The consumer can accordingly send his preference to receive or block the particular UCC.

§5. User's Terminal Devices for Storing and Retrieving Information

376. Data communication moves on online protocol which is the gift of the Internet. Such protocol involves transmission of digitized data between two or more online processing locations and is an integral part of the modern information and retrieval systems in terms of their online access. Users can access the network through terminal devices attached to a node and the data travels on the network through the switching nodes. Conventional telecommunication links for data transmission are used by converting digital signals into analog signals by a process called "Modulation" with the help of the modem. Currently there has been development of an Integrated Service Digital Network (ISDN) which handles all telecommunications requirements like voice, data, telemetry, facsimile and video without discrimination.[228]

377. Network Scenario in India – NICNET, INDONET, VIKRAM are the three networks which comprise the general network in India and specialized networks are ERNET, and the networks supported by NISSAT such as CALIBNET, BONET, DELNET, MALIBNET, BALNET AND HYDLIBNET. NICNET the pioneer satellite-based network set up under the aegis of the Planning Commission of India, the GOI was to provide services to the Government and its various departments for decision-

228. V.Rajaraman –Professor-, *Supercomputer Education & Research Centre Indian Institute of Science, Bangalore 560 012* [This is a revised (24.11.08) and updated version of an article which appeared in Technorama (Institution of Engineers, India) Vol. 49 [T], No.3, December 1999, pp.4–10]

making, etc. The INDONET engineered by the Computer Maintenance Corporation of India Ltd (CMC) has an integrated information management and distributed data processing facility which aims to provide facility for distributed data processing on all India basis for large organizations in the network using CMC computers for their data processing operations. VIKRAM is the packet switched public data network under the DoT.

378. User's Terminal Devices- The following are the various methods of storing and retrieving information as used in India:

- Textual data- Books and journals and other information such as patents, international standards, etc. stored in a digital form in a computer's disk store. It can be stored either by way of photograph a page or by scanning the image. The scanner digitizes the image storing a 0 for white and 1 for a dark sport. This form of storage is known as a bit mapped form and is a common method to store old books, manuscripts, etc. The other way of string a text is to represent each character by its ASCII Code.
- Numeric Data- It consists of tables of various types like physical property data of various materials, data from experiments, astronomical tables. Such numeric data stored digitally may be used by curve fitting programs, spread sheet programs, etc.
- Graphics Data- This kind of information is in the form of maps, photographs, drawings, land records, etc. The simple way to store it is by scanning the image and then storing it. The other methods are coding and storing maps, drawings, etc., which abstract information contained in them. Thus, maps may be stored using longitude/latitude as coordinates of cities, a linked list depicting road network, etc. Such storage is easier to retrieve.
- Photographs- These are stored in bit mapped from using compression algorithms to reduce storage space. Formats known as bmp, tif, gif and jpeg are commonly used.
- Audio Data- It can be digitized, compressed using a commonly accepted standard compression algorithm called MP 3 format and stored. Musical scores may also be coded and stored along with the audio data.
- Video Data- It needs extra storage space due to need for repeating frames at least thirty times per second. Thus, the data is compressed in such a way that when decompressed the original data is recovered. Common standards like the MPEG-4 (Motion Picturcs Expert Group- Version 4) compress a ninety minute video movie to occupy 7 Gigabytes.

  A user can access from anywhere using a terminal or a computer connected to the network. Newest technology helps popular music downloads through iPod; You Tube; and e-book reader called Kindle are some of the other terminal devices.

§6. Retention of Data

379. In the digitized world mammoth amount of information can be easily preserved. The question arises then as to of what use will be of such preserved information. Basically for law enforcement agencies the world over, data retention is a favored practice. As it helps investigation and in collection of evidence. This being serious objective data retention is favored but an established standard is required for it. In 2006 the European Union passed the Data Retention Directive which requires European ISP to retain telecom and Internet traffic data from customer's communications for at least six months and up to two years.

380. The GOI has established a data retention regime[229] in which retention requirements for service providers are found in the ISP and UASL licenses which are grounded in the Indian Telegraph Act 1885.

381. ISP License- According to the ISP license[230] eight categories of records are required to be retained for security purposes in which duration of retention is also often indicated. Thus, according to the ISP License each ISP must maintain the following:

- Users and services- A log of all users and their services will be made available to the Telecom Authority in real time (section 34.12).
- Outward Login and Telnet-A log of every outward login or telnet through an ISP's computer shall be made available in real time to the Telecom Authority (section 34.12).
- Packets- Copies of all packets originating from the Customer Premises Equipment of the ISP must be available in real time to the Telecom Authority (section 34.12).
- Subscribers- A complete list of subscribers must be made available on the ISP website with password controlled access available to the authorized Intelligence Agencies at any time (section 34.12).
- Internet Leased Line Customers- A complete list of Internet leased line customers and their sub-customers consisting of name of customer, IP address allotted, bandwidth provided, address of installation, date of installing/commissioning and name of contact person with his e-mail, etc. must be given. This should be available on a password protected website (section 34.14). The password and login must be furnished to the various authorities in the Department of Telecommunication. (DoT). The information must be accessible to authorized government agencies (section 34.14).
- Diagram records and reasons- A record of complete network of set up at each of the Internet leased line customer premises along with details of connectivity must be posted at the website of the service provider. Details of other communication links like the PSTN, NLD, ILD, WLL, GSM and reasons for taking the links by the customer must be recorded by the service provider before activation of the link. These records are also subject to inspection (section 34.18).
- Commercial Records- All such commercial records must be maintained for a year (section 34.23).
- Location- The service provider should be able to provide the geographical location of any subscriber whenever asked for (section 34.28(x)).

---

229. Elonnai Hickock, *Data Retention in India*, Posted January 30, 2013.

230. Government of India – Ministry of Communications and IT; Department of Telecommunication. License Agreement for Provision of Internet Services.

- Remote Activities- A complete audit record of the remote access activities must be retained for a period of six months and must be furnished to the Licensor when asked for (section 34.28 (xv).)

382. UASL License-[231] For security purposes customer transactions are required to be preserved and there are about twelve categories of such information. In some cases the duration of retention has been indicated while in others merely presentation of records on the orders of the authorities has been directed. Thus, the ISPs are directed to retain the following information:

- Numbers- Calling /Called Party mobile /PSTN numbers are to be furnished when required (section 41.10).
- Interception Records- Time, date and duration of interception is to be provided (section 41.10).
- Location- Location of target subscribers, Cell ID should be provided for location of the target subscriber when required (section 41.10).
- All Call records- It includes;1) Failed call records- 2) Roaming subscriber records (section 41.10).
- Commercial Records- All commercial records regarding communications exchanged on the network must be retained for one year (section 41.17).
- Outgoing Call records- A record of checks made on outgoing calls made by customer who are making large outgoing calls day and night to various customers must be maintained (section 41.19(ii)).
- Calling Line Identification- A list of subscribers including address details using calling line identification should be preserved in a password protected website accessible only to government agencies (section 41.19(iv)).
- Location – the Service Providers must also provide the geographical location of the subscriber when asked for (section 41.20 (x)).
- Remote access activities- Full audit trail for six months of the remote access activities pertaining to the network in India must also be retained (section 41.20(xv)).

383. Data Retention Practice in India – On September 10, 2012 the Centre for Internet and Society sent an RTI to MTNL and BSNL regarding certain queries. As response to this BSNL replied that it stores at least three types of information including; IP session information- connection start/end time, bytes in and out (three years offline) and Bill copies for post-paid and recharge/top up billing details for pre-paid for six months. MTNL responded that it retains five types of information including; text message details for one year, Call detail records for one year, Bill copies for post-paid for one year, recharge details for pre-paid for three months and location of the mobile number if it has used the MTNL/GSM/3GCDMA network for one year.

231. Government of India –Ministry of Communication & IT- DoT- License Agreement for Unified Access Service after Migration from CMTS- Amended Dec. 3, 2009.

§7. Directories

384. Every consumer is entitled by way of right to a telephone directory containing the list of telephone subscribers and their telephone numbers free of charge. However, the authorized agency for publication of integrated telephone directory for fixed line telephones shall supply the integrated telephone directory for fixed line telephones on charge basis. The charges shall not exceed as specified in the license or as fixed by the TRAI from time to time. (Rule 452-The Indian Telegraph Rules 1951). The Telephone directory cannot be published by anyone except with the permission of TRAI. (Rule 458- The Indian Telegraph Rules 1951). For every subscriber one line entry containing the details like the telephone number, the initials, the surname and the address of the subscriber or user are allowed free of charge. (Rule 453- Indian Telegraph Rules 1951). Extra line or extra entry may be allowed on charges as fixed by the TRAI from time to time. (Rule 455 – The Indian Telegraph Rules 1951).

§8. Electronic Signatures and Data Protection

385. Silicon chips have changed the concept of document and of signatures. The word “writing” gets new forms and dimensions and a totally new concept has emerged in its place. “Data”, “information”, “Message” become synonyms for “documents”. Traditionally speaking the originality and authenticity of a document was verified through a signature. In the computer situation nothing is copy, everything is original hence a question arose regarding the authenticity or originality of data preserved in the computer. The easiness of putting a signature through pen on the paper was lacking in the computer situation. With the digitization of the world of information, the big hurdle was the protection of data in the computer. Thus, the functional equivalent of the manual signature was badly needed. The Model Law on Electronic Signatures[232] came as an answer although the form requirements were given importance and an electronic record is made to have the same levels of reliability, traceability and inalterability as they exist in the paper document. The susceptibility of electronic data being vandalized and being an object of various types of cybercrimes necessitated the need to secure it electronically. Electronic signatures are but a technique to give reliability and protection to data. Electronic signatures are officially defined by the Model Law on Electronic signatures (2001) as: “…data in electronic form in affixed to or logically associated with a data message and to indicate the signatory’s approval of the information contained in the data message.”[233]

386. Indian Law- Information Technology (Amendment) Act 2008-India being a part of the global technological boom came up with its first computer specific legislation in the year 2000 when it enacted the Information Technology Act 2000 (21 of 2000). The term “electronic signature” was missing from this Act and it is only in

232. Model Law on Electronic Signatures adopted by the UNCITRAL 56/80. Resolution adopted by the General Assembly [on the report of the 6th Committee 9A/56/588)] in its 85th Plenary meeting on 12-12-2001.

233. Article 2, Definitions; Part I UNCITRAL Model Law on Electronic Signatures with Guide to Enactment 2001,1.

2008 that the term "digital signature" is replaced by the term "electronic signature." The Amendment Act 2008 opens with the words:

> 2.In the Information Technology Act 2000 (hereinafter in this Part referred to as the principal Act), for the words 'digital signature' occurring in the Chapter, section, sub-section and clause referred to in the Table below[234], the words 'electronic signature' shall be substituted. The amended ection 2 of the IT Act gives the definition of electronic signature in the following words: "electronic signature means authentication of any electronic record by a subscriber by means of the electronic technique specified in the Second Schedule and includes digital signature.'

387. Data Protection – Data protection did not receive proper legal treatment until the passing of the IT (Amendment) Act 2008.The amendments made in respect of electronic signatures have now given legal protection to data stored in the computer. In the IT Act 2000 the lone section entailing civil consequences for data vandalism was section 43. Under this section fine of a maximum of INR 1 crore was prescribed for unauthorized access, downloading the copies, extracting data, introducing viruses into the computer system were treated as computer vandalism. The IT Amendment Act 2008 comes up with more stringent penalties and regards data vandalism as a criminal offense under section 43A and 72 A.

388. The PKI Scenario in India – The IT Act 2000 had earlier recognized digital signatures based on asymmetric crypto systems bringing them at par with manual signatures. The IT (Amendment) Act 2008 has now substituted the term "electronic signature" for the term "digital signature". The Act provides for the Controller of Certifying authorities who are entrusted with the responsibility of regulating the working of the certification authorities who are in turn given the responsibility to issue the DSCs for electronic authentication of users. The CCA certifies the public keys of Certifying Authorities using its own private key which enables users in cyberspace to verify that a given certificate is issued by licensed Certifying Authority. For this it operates the Root Certifying Authority of India (RCAI). The CCA by virtue of section 20 of the IT Act 2000 maintained repositories which have now been deleted under the Amendment Act 2008.[235]

The requirements fulfilled by the RCAI include:

(1) The license issued to the Certifying authority is digitally signed by the CCA.
(2) All public keys corresponding to the signing of private keys of a Certifying Authority are digitally signed by the CCA.

---

234. Table: (1) Class (d),(g),(h) and (zg) of s. 2; (2) s. 5 and its marginal heading; (3) Marginal heading of s. 6. (4) Cls. (a), (b), (c), and (e) of s. 10 and its marginal heading; (5) Heading of Chap. V; (6) Cls. (f) and (g) of s. 18; (7) Sub-s (2) of s. 19; (8) Sub-Ss (1) and (2) of s. 21 and its marginal heading; (9) Sub-S. 3 of s. 25; (10) Cl. (c) of s.30.; (11) Cls (a) and (d) of sub-ss (1) and (2) of s. 34.

235. Formerly under the IT Act, the Controller had the job of maintaining a repository of all the Certifying Authorities in the country. The National Repository of Digital Certificates (NRDC) maintained it under s. 20.

(3) That these keys are signed by CCA can be verified by a relying party through the CCA's website or Certifying Authority's own website.

The RCAI is operated using SmartTrust software. Certification Practice Statement of RCAI guides the CCA personnel to perform Root Certifying Authority functions. The term "Root" signifies the entire certifying Authority matrix including the software operations. The National Root Certifying Authority uses a 2048 bit RSA key pair and the Certifying Authority entity uses a 1024 bit RSA key pair.[236]

236. Dr. Sandeep Oberoi, "*India PKI Forum*", Presentation made at PKI Consortium Seminar, Nov. 8, 2007, 4.

Part VII. Computer-Related Crime

Chapter 1. General Legal Development

389. The Rise of Computer-Related crime-The Internet has a global face. The computers hand in hand with the Internet swept the globe in less than two and a half decades. It invaded every nook and corner of life on earth and today life is unimaginable without computers and the Internet. The technological innovations had already started perforating the legal fabric by the middle of the twentieth century. The evolution of computer had taken the path of sophistication and technical excellence. The first ever Electronic Numerical Integrator and Computer (ENIAC) was switched on in February 1946. The invention of computers is a boon yet the".... cases of computer abuse began to be documented from the outset".[237] By the late 1970s "crime by computer" was serious enough problem to merit new criminal statutes[238] but the Internet proliferation and unstoppable growth of technology did not have such an impact as it is having today. Slowly and gradually computers were emerging as an indispensable household gadget but at the same time it also became a new weapon in the hand of criminals. The year 1960 can be called as the genesis of the field of computer law; it was the time when large mainframe computers were dominated by IBM and other seven companies[239] which together were termed by Douglas W. Jones as *Snow White and the Seven Dwarfs.* Also this was the year when the first legal article on computer law by Roy N. Freed was published.[240] The article depicts the awakening of the legal mind to the importance and relevance of computers in the legal world.

390. If cyber crimes are taken to be crimes committed through the agency of automated machines, a school of thought without hesitation regards early nineteenth century as the date of first known cybercrime.[241] The term *cyber* relates to machines.[242]

237. Donn. B. Parker, *Crime by Computer* (Charles Scribner's sons, New York 1976); Martin Wasik, *Crime and the Computer* (Oxford University Press, US 1991).
238. Richard C. Hollinger, "*Computer Crime*" in Clifton D. Bryant (ed.), *Encyclopedia of Criminology and Deviant Behaviour* (Vol II, Brunner-Routledge, Taylor & Francis Group,2000)76–81.
239. Often referred to as BUNCH; Burroughs, Univac, NCR,ControlData,Honeywell, plus GE and Xerox make it seven.
240. Roy N.Freed, "*A Lawyer's Guide Through the Computer Maze*" (November 1960 The Practical Lawyer.
241. http://cybercrime.planetindia.net/intro.html.
242. *Concise Oxford English Dictionary* defines *cybernetics* as "the science of communication and automatic control system in both machines and living things." The term *"cyberspace"* was first coined by the science fiction author, William Gibson in his novel *Neuromancer*in 1982 and by this time, the term cyber had entered common parlance.

The term cyber crime or computer-related crimes can be traced back to early eighties when the Internet was expanding and the *Worm of the 88* can well be given the status of the first registered computer-related crime ever committed.[243] The development of computer-related crime can be divided into four distinct focal periods[244] as follows:

- 1946–1976- The first period called the discovery period which describes the computer-abuse phenomenon.
- 1977–1988 The criminalization periods which aimed at correcting various deficiencies in criminal law.
- 1988–1993- The almost five-year long third period revolved around demonization of the hacker, the perpetrator who made unauthorized entry into computer data.
- 1993- To date is the present period when the Internet expansion has clouded the entire globe and users have started discovering the baneful effect of computer and Internet, criminals have taken Internet as a means of minting money by exploiting the power of Internet to access indecent and obscene material there.

Such exploitation has given birth to a number of *neo crimes* unknown to the world of law. The first computer crime law was enacted in the State of Florida in 1978 in response to an indigenous computer fraud perpetration the year before at the Flagler Dog Track in Hialeah.[245]

391. General Legal Development- The year 2004 can be recalled as the year of dramatic growth of the computer-related crimes where the "waning influence of the boy hackers keen to make a name by writing fast-speeding virus on windows" is observed.[246] Countries that started booking the cybercriminal under traditional laws soon started realizing the inadequacy of such laws to the new generation of crimes.

From 1983 to 1985 an ad hoc committee of the Organisation of Economic Co-operation and Development (OECD) discussed the need for international harmonization of criminal laws with respect to computer-related economic crime. After joint deliberation with the working party on Information, Computers and Communications Policy (ICCP), a final report was published in 1986.[247] The European Committee on Crime Problems, established in December 1985, published a report in September 1989 which produced guidelines for national legislatures on a "Minimum List of Offenses Necessary for Uniform Criminal Policy" where eight offenses of computer misuse were listed. The *McConnell International Report* says that until 2000, fifty-two countries that were surveyed, thirty-three had not updated their laws and only nine had enacted legislation

243. http://cybercrime.planetindia.net/intro.html
244. Richard C.Hollinger, "Evidence that Computer Crime follows as Guttman-like Progression" Sociology and Research72: 199-200.
245. Richard C.Hollinger, "Evidence that Computer Crime follows as Guttman-like Progression" Sociology and Research72: 199-200.
246. Cybercrime General, http://www.diplomacy.edu/.>.
247. Computer-Related Criminality: Analysis of Legal Policy in the OECD Area", (Report DSTI-ICCP 84-22 of 18-4-1986.)

to address five or fewer types of cybercrime while ten had updated their laws to prosecute against six or more of the ten types of cybercrime.[248]

Thereafter in 2001 the Cybercrime Convention organized by the Council of Europe urged countries to curb the menace by legislating specifically. The United Nations Commission on International Trade Law (UNCITRAL) adopted the Model Law on electronic Commerce in 1996. The Model Law basically a civil law in its paragraph 3[249] also created criminal liability for infringement of the provisions of proposed legislation thus requiring signatory nations to legislate also on the subject of criminal offenses. Thus, the legal activity to control the computer-related menace was already unleashed. The countries which were pioneer in this direction were the U.S. and the U.K. and a brief reference to these will complete the general legal development in this respect.

392. United States- The country with the highest connectivity and the home of the Internet was the pioneer one to start legal battle against computer-related crimes. Act after Act, rigorous surveys, extensive crime reporting mark the formidable response of the U.S. to these crimes. The number of cyber incidents reported to the Computer Emergency Response Team (CERT) speedily followed the up graph. Though earlier there were tailor-made legislations yet their application in the law courts was yet to be tested. The crime specific piecemeal legislation to meet the emergent situation is the hall mark of the US response to these crimes. For instance there have been separate laws for computer fraud, privacy breaches, national security, online obscenity, spamming, online forgery, etc.

393. United Kingdom- The ever-soaring computer-related crime graph and the loss of billions of wealth did not spare even the most advanced nations. U.K. too suffered the strokes of the technological crimes and its response came promptly which can be summarized in two phases. In the first phase the traditional laws were *per se* applied to criminal activities online in a number of cases like *R.v. Preddy,*[250] *(Preddy) and R. v. Gold.*[251] but it was difficult for the courts to apply the real life provisions to automated situations.[252] The second phase was when the need to legislate specifically on computer-related crime was felt. The Law Commission Report on "Computer misuse" published in October 1989 and certain other recommendations led to the passing of the Computer Misuse Act 1990. The U.K. Audit Commission Report showed

248. "Cybercrime,and Punishment? Archaic laws Threated Global information" (McConnell International Report, December 2000) http://www.mcconnellinternational/com.

249. Paragraph 3 itself mentions the criminal liability and the logic behind the creation of such liability saying that

To prevent possible misuse arising out of transactions and other dealings concluded over the electronic medium, it is also proposed to create civil and criminal liabilities for contravention of the provisions of the proposed legislation.

The Model Law on Electronic Commerce 1996; The General Assembly of the United Nations Resolution No. 51/162, Jan. 30, 1997, recommended that all States should give favorable considerations to the said Model Law when they enact or revise their laws.

250. (1996) 3 All ER 481.

251. (1987) 3 WLR 803(1988) 2 All ER 186.

252. Preddy illustrates the types of problem raised when trying to apply traditional criminal concepts to acts involving intangible information. Ian J. Lloyd & Moira J. Simpson, "*Computer Crime*" in Chris Reed (ed.), *Computer Law* (3rd ed., Universal Law Publishing) 279.

a whopping increase from a total of seventy-seven incidents of computer crime in 1984 to a total of 510 such incidents in 1998.[253] As the story of crime increase continued the U.K. too continued with the legal responses by making new such laws. The National Hi-Tech Crime Unit is set up to check the rise[254] cooperation of Russia and China is continuing and the National Information Commissioner has been given new powers to fine companies up to GBP 5,000 for breach of Data Protection Act apart from a number of other steps which are being taken in this direction.

394. India – India showed commendable activity in accepting the new technological changes and thus soon it joined the league of countries in responding to the new computer situation. To start with the country first established separate information Technology Ministry in the year 1999. It came up with its first cyber legislation namely the Information Technology Act 2000 (21 of 2000). The Act basically meant to legalize commercial activities online was the country's first step to address the computer-related infractions and vandalism. Soon it was realized that the brief provisions relating to the computer infractions are inadequate and thus in 2008 the IT Act was amended this time addressing separately and specifically the menace of computer-related crimes. The Highlights of the newly amended law in respect of computer-related crimes can be summarized as follows:

(1) Major amendments are made in the criminal area. A host of new cybercrimes like child pornography, obscenity, depiction of sex explicit act, violation of privacy, cheating by personation, identity theft, cyber terrorism, sending offensive messages have been introduced. (Chapter XI IT (Amendment) Act 2008).
(2) Offenses under the Act are categorized into bailable and cognizable which has been done for the first time under the Act. This will give the law enforcement agencies more freedom to act.
(3) Attempts and abetments of offenses are also recognized as offenses under the Act.
(4) The amendments are more investigation friendly and even officers of the rank of an Inspector can investigate instead of only the Deputy Superintendent of Police as it was in the unamended Act.
(5) Terms like "cybercafé", "e-mail", "communication device" have been defined thus enlarging the area of law to apply to Internet situations.
(6) Cyber security has been addressed well. Elaborate provisions are introduced to safeguard cyber infrastructure in the country. For this provision for the establishment of a National Nodal Agency; the Indian Computer Emergency Response Team (ICERT) has been constituted.
(7) The term "intermediaries" has been defined to include within its area a number of other service providers so as to enlarge the liability-susceptible class in cyberspace.
(8) National security has been given an upper hand. For this monitoring, intercepting and decryption of flowing information has been made mandatory by the intermediaries and any person in charge of a computer source on the directions of the proposed governmental agency. Failure to follow the directions has been made an offense.

253. Steven Furnell, *Cybercrime: Vandalizing the Information Society* (Addison-Wesley, 2004) 27.
254. Established on Apr. 28, 2010.

(9) The Amendment makes provision for including a technocrat in the judicial bench.
(10) To make the evidence more acceptable and reliable, the report of the electronic Evidence Expert has been made relevant under the evidence law by making relevant amendment.

395. Thus, to make a technology-centric law the amendments in 2008 make a positive headway to meet the legal exigencies and about more than two dozen new provisions have been added to cover the situations were left out by the original IT Act 2000.The IT Action Plan of the GOI is striving towards the goal of making India the forerunner in the new technological age.

Chapter 2. Application of Substantive Criminal Law to the Area of ICT

§1. Offenses Against the Confidentiality, Integrity and Availability of Computer Data and Systems

I. Illegal Access and Illegal Interception

A. Illegal Access

396. Information and data stored in the Computer is the subject matter of crimes which are computer-related. It is a new age crime and can be committed in two ways; by internal means and by external means. Hacking is the most common and the oldest way to make illegal access to the data stored in the system. The Indian law though does not define the term "hacking" yet the various actions comprising it have been made punishable. Section 43 of the IT Act 2000 says that if an act (i) destroys, deletes or alters any information residing in a computer resource or diminishes its value or utility or affects it injuriously by any means or (ii) steals, conceals destroys, or alters or causes any person to steal, conceal destroy or alter any computer source code used for a computer resource shall be liable to pay damages by way of compensation not exceeding INR 1 crore (10 million). This section is to be read with section 66 of the IT Amendment Act 2008 which says that if a person does any act as defined under section 43 *dishonestly*[255] *and fraudulently*[256] then he shall be punished with imprisonment up to three years or with fine which may extend to INR five lakh (0.5 Million) or with both. Previously under the IT Act 2000 the illegal access entailed only civil action by way of damages but in the amended Act 2008 if the access has been done dishonestly and fraudulently then it is declared as a punishable criminal offense.

B. Illegal Interception

397. - Intercepting information or data which is stored in a computer or is in the course of transmission means the aural or other acquisition of the contents of any information through the use of any means, including an interception device so as to make some or all of the contents of an information available to an unauthorized person and it includes its monitoring, viewing, examination or inspection of the contents or

255. "Dishonestly" means – Whoever does anything with the intention of causing wrongful gain to one person or wrongful loss to another person is said to do that thing "dishonestly" s. 24 the Indian Penal Code 1860.

256. "Fraudulently"- A person is said to do a thing fraudulently if he does that thing with intend to defraud but not otherwise s. 25 The Indian Penal Code 1860.

its diversion to any other unauthorized destination.[257] Interception of information during the course of transmission is permissible in the interest of national security or in the interest of general public, etc. This is authorized under law if it is done by authorized agencies and in the prescribed manner. Any other person or way of making an interception has been made an invasion of individual's privacy and is punishable under law. Thus, if interception is not done by authorized person then it becomes illegal interception. Thus, any person without authorization (under Rule 3 & 4 of the Rules 2009) intentionally or knowingly intercepts, or attempts to intercept or authorizes or assists any other person to intercept or attempts to intercept any information in the course of its occurrence or transmission will be guilty of illegal interception.

C. Related Crimes

398. The computer-related crimes are committed mainly by causing injury or harm to the data stored in the computer. However, the IT (Amendment) Act 2008 introduces a number of other related crimes which are often committed along with or as a result of computer data interference. These are:

- Identity theft- Anyone who fraudulently or dishonestly uses any electronic signature, password or unique identification figure of another is said to commit the offense of identity theft. The offense is punished with imprisonment up to three years or with fine upto INR 1 lakh (0.1Million) (section 66-C).
- Cheating by personation- It is a traditional offense as defined under the India Penal Code 1860 when a person disguises himself as another and by doing so causes wrongful loss to another. The offense when committed by using a computer resources or communication device then the offense is punishable under the IT Act with imprisonment up to three years and with fine up to INR 1 lakh (0.1Million) (section 66-D)

II. Data Interference and System Interference

399. Data interference – The data stored in the computer is the most vulnerable and any interference, damaging, deleting, etc. is a punishable offense under the IT (Amendment) Act 2008. The offenses relating to Data interference can be summarized as follows:

- Section 43 (IT Act 2000)- Civil nature provision deals with tampering with computer source document-; accesses, downloads, copies or extracts data computer data base on information from such computer, computer system, or computer network; introduces any computer contaminant or virus; damages any computer, computer system or computer network, data database; disrupts computer system or computer network; provides unauthorized access to any person to facilitate

---

257. Rule 2(l) the Information Technology (Procedure and Safeguards for Interception, Monitoring and Decryption of Information) Rules 2009. Notification G.S.R. 780 (E), Government of India, DoT, New Delhi the Oct. 27, 2009.

access to a computer, shall be liable to pay damages by way of compensation not exceeding INR 1 crore (10 Million).

- Section 65- (IT Act 2000)- Tampering with computer source documents – Where anyone knowingly and intentionally causes another to conceal, destroy or alter any computer source code used for a computer, computer program, computer system or computer network shall be punished with imprisonment up to three years or with fine up to INR 2 lakh (0.2 million) or with both.
- Section 66 (IT Amendment) 2008- Acts defined under section 43 when committed dishonestly and fraudulently then the offense is punishable with imprisonment up to three years or with fine up to INR 5 lakh (0.5Million) or with both.

III. Misuse of Devices

400. IT (Amendment) Act 2008- The offense of sending offensive menacing false messages through communication device, etc. or causing annoyance, hatred enmity, insult, injury, etc., or e-mail causing annoyance, inconvenience then the newly inserted offense is committed which is punished with imprisonment up to three years and with fine (section 66-A).

401. Dishonestly and knowingly retaining stolen computer resource, communication device is punishable with imprisonment up to three years or with fine up to INR 1 lakh (0.1 Million) or with both (section 66-B IT (Amendment).

402. Cyberterrorism- Anyone who by means of computer resource threatens the sovereignty, integrity unity or security of India and causes injury or damage to or disruption of services to the general public or adversely affects the CII[258] or gains access to any data or data base connected with security of India commits cyber terrorism and shall be punished with imprisonment which may extend to life imprisonment (section 66-F).

§2. Other Computer-Related Offenses

I. Computer-Related Forgery

403. Online forgery is an offense which needs little effort as compared to offline forgery. It is usually not resorted for money but it is also employed for "glory or a spirit of devilment, cocking a snook at experts and purchasers."[259] Like other countries in India too forgery has been an offense under substantive criminal law. As defined under section 463 of the Indian Penal Code 1860 as making of a false document with any one or more of the intents mentioned in the said section. The traditional offense

258. Critical Information Infrastructure (CII) means the computer resource which the incapacitation or destruction of which shall have debilitating impact on national security, economy, public health or safety.
259. "Caslon Analytics Profile Forgery, Fraud and Forensics", http://www.caslon.comau/siteuse.htm.

has a reference to "document" or "part of a document" in the said section. The technological boom and the instances of forgery through computer rendered the said section inadequate for the purposes of digital forgery as the term "document" could be applied to computer data and information stored therein which was transient in nature. Thus, to make the said section workable in the online situation as well amendments were made in the said section by the IT Act 2000. These amendments made electronic record as also an instrument of the offense of forgery. The relevant section 470 says Forged[260] [document or electronic record]. – A false [document or electronic record] made wholly or in part by forgery is designated "as forged document or electronic record." Thus, not only paper document but an electronic record which is intangible in nature can be the object of forgery.

404. Section 463- Forgery –[261] Whoever makes any false document or false electronic record or part of a document or electronic record, with intent to cause damage or injury, to the public or to any person, or to support any claim or title or to cause any person to part with property, or to enter into any express or implied contract, or with intent to commit fraud or that fraud may be committed, commits forgery. "This definition after the amendment includes "the making of any false electronic record or part thereof with intent to cause damage or injury to the public or to any person". Traditionally speaking, the offense of forgery is said to be committed when the maker of its knows that the document is not genuine but represents it as genuine with the object of defrauding someone. When such false making is done through using the digital means such as "desktop publishing systems, color laser and inkjet printers, color copiers and image scanners" which "enable crooks to make fake, with relative ease checks, currencies, passports, visas, birth certificates, ID Cards, etc."[262]

405. Section 464 of the Indian Penal Code 1860 is also amended by the IT Act 2000 and also by the IT (Amendment) Act 2008. The amended section describing the "making of false document" says that a person is said to make a false document or false electronic record who dishonestly and fraudulently makes, sings or seals a document or its part or makes or transmits any electronic record or affixes any electronic signature on any electronic record or who makes any mark to give authenticity to any document or electronic record. The section also regards the cancellation, alteration of any document or electronic record or affixing of electronic signature on it to be taken as made by any person living or dead as making of false document or electronic record. In the third place the section also regards the making of a document when anyone causes a person of unsound mind, or a person under intoxication or a person under deception to put his signature or electronic signature on any document.

Thus, the section comprehensively covers the case of digital forgery where it also clarifies in Explanation 3 that the expression "affixing electronic signature" shall have the same meaning as it appears in section 2 (I) (d) of the IT Act 2000. The effect of technology on the offense of forgery has been tremendous as computer technology by its very nature reduces the burden of handwritten documents and simplifies the job of the writer. Mass copying which hardly can be termed as copy requires nanoseconds

260. Substituted by the IT Act, s. 91 & Schedule I for document.
261. Substituted by the IT Act, s. 91 & Schedule I for document.
262. Steven Furnell,*Cybercrime: Vandalizing the Information Society* (Addison-Wesley, 2002) 235.

and the identical replica of the original makes the job of a law enforcer a challenging one.

II. Computer-Related Fraud

406. Jack Blum says, "International fraud, commercial fraud, money laundering and tax evasion will be the most important enterprise crimes of the future".[263]Unlike U.S. and U.K. where fraud or "wire fraud" has been separately defined and dealt with [264]there is no separate provision for "wire fraud" in the IT Act 2000. This can be analogized with the fact that under the Indian Penal Code 1860 which is the major substantive penal in India, fraud is neither defined nor it is considered as a separate offense under the Code. Under Indian penal provisions fraud is not an offense but it is taken as a mental condition which is present in many other crimes. Under IPC a person is said to do a thing fraudulently if he does that thing with intent to defraud but not otherwise. (section 25, The Indian Penal Code 1860). In the words of Sir James Stephen fraudster's own "advantage" is the principal object whether or not the victim has suffered some loss or injury. The IT Act 2000 has no mention of the word "fraud" or "fraudulently" but in The IT (Amendment) Act 2008 section 66 read with section 43(i) reveals that to commit an offense under it, one has to prove that the act of intrusion into any computer data was done dishonestly and fraudulently. section 415[265] of IPC defines cheating and can be compared with U.S. law regarding wire fraud in the Computer Fraud and Abuse Act 1986 which enumerate "false pretenses" and "intent to defraud" as ingredients of the offense of fraud with the use of interstate wire communications as yet one more ingredient. As IPC is a traditional law, only an amendment in section 415 can bring it along the lines of the U.S. law where "the use of interstate wire communications" is included as one of the ingredients of fraud committed via the Internet. After the amendment section 415 should read as this; "Whoever, by deceiving any person, fraudulently or dishonestly, by electronic communication or otherwise, induces…" section 415 can then be independently applied to the Internet Fraud where there has been no concomitant computer intrusion. However, in cases[266] where fraud is committed by vandalizing the communication system and by infusing malicious programs and codes, section 415 read with sections 43, 65 or 66 whatever the case may be can be applied.

263. Sherry I. Louise, "*Crimes and Corruption in the Digital Age*" March 1998 Journal of International Affairs.

264. Recommendations of the U.K. Audit Commission and the Computer Fraud and Abuse Act (US 1986).

265. Section 415- Whoever by deceiving any person, fraudulently or dishonesty, induces the person so deceived to deliver any property to any person, or to consent that any person shall retain any property, or intentionally induces the person so deceived to do or omit to do anything which he would not do or omit if he were not so deceived, and which act or omission causes or is likely to cause damage or harm to that person in body, mind reputation or property, is said to cheat.

266. The most popular of such cases is credit card fraud. Then there are bogus online investment schemes, market manipulation schemes where fraud is committed by hacking into the computer system of other users.

§3. CONTENT-RELATED OFFENSES:

407. The pornographic content on the Internet calls for a separate category of content-related crimes.[267]Aberrant activities online have provided an easy opportunity to the criminals to make money in total disregard of the cultural and moral ethos of the human society. Obscenity comes up as the most popular crime committed online and which has given a bad name to the blissful Internet. Obscenity is not a new offense and traditionally speaking no civilized society regards indecent expressions, visuals, representations or acts as acceptable. This is because such obscene acts drive one to commit similar crimes. Cockburn CJ in R. Hicklin in 1868 said the test of obscenity is "…..whether the tendency of the matter charged as obscene is to deprave and corrupt those whose minds are open to such immoral influences, and into whose hands a publication of this sort may fall."[268] The Supreme Court of India in *Ranjit D. Udeshi v. State of Maharashtra* [269] has observed that the test of obscenity laid down by Cockburn CJ should not be discarded and held that obscenity in India is treating sex in a manner appealing to the carnal side of human nature or having that tendency. Under traditional Indian Penal Code 1860 sale of obscene material is regarded as an offense (section 292).

408. Online Obscenity- The IT Act 2000 was deficient in addressing obscenity which is committed online but the IT (Amendment) Act 2008 has done away with this lacuna and obscenity and other sex-related offenses as new sections have been added to address these crimes. The earlier section 67[270] was the only section which dealt with obscenity in a limited manner and it also did not distinguish between child pornography and mainstream pornography. The section was deficient in many ways; it said nothing about the knowledge of the offender, i.e., it says nothing whether in cases where such an offending material is hidden in the cache memory of a system of which the offender is unaware, what will be his liability in such case. Second, the section uses the word persons and omits to mention the age of such a person. It only means that A who is a matured person of 50 if the material published, depraves and corrupts his mind, hearing or reading such an offending material, the offense is not committed. Does the section aims at particular application. Here the prosecution may take the help of section 293 of the Indian Penal Code 1860. Third, the section also omits to clarify as to what is "obscenity".

409. The IT (Amendment) Act 2008 (10 of 2009) has reformed the law of online obscenity in India to a greater extent. The combined effect of sections 66-E, 67, 67-A

267. Cybercrime Convention 2001.

268. (1868) LR 3 QB 360,371.

269. AIR 1965 SC 881: (1965) 2 Cri LJ 8.

270. Section 67 – (IT Act 2000)- *"Publishing of information which is obscene in electronic form.-* Whoever publishes or transmits or causes to be published in the electronic form, any material which is lascivious or appeals to the prurient interest or if its effect is such as t tend to deprave and corrupt persons who are likely, having regard to all relevant circumstances, to read, see or hear the matter contained or embodied in it, shall be punished on **first** conviction with imprisonment of either description for a term which may extend to five years and with fine which may extend to INR 1 lakh and in the event of a **second** or subsequent conviction with imprisonment of either description for a term which may extend to ten years and also with fine which may extend to INR 2 lakh."

and 67-B is that online obscenity has been brought within the legal regime and it also differentiates between "child pornography" and "mainstream pornography". Section 67 provides punishment for publishing obscene material in electronic form. The new section 67 in descriptive manner is the same as the old section but it differs from it in two ways: First, in the marginal heading the word "transmitting" is inserted. Second, the quantum of punishment has been changed as the term of imprisonment has been decreased while the amount of fine has been increased in both the first and second convictions. The section is deficient in the fact that like the traditional section 292 of the Indian Penal Code 1860 the present section 67 too does not define the content of the term "obscenity". As regarding the punishment it is not only twofold but it is also stringent i.e., for the first time commission of the offense the punishment includes both fine and imprisonment and for a subsequent commission the quantum of this punishment is doubled which is more severe as compared to the Indian standards. Like fraud and other crimes, in the matter of Internet obscenity too, the provisions of traditional obscenity laws as contained in section 293 of the Indian Penal Code 1860 will be helpful as to when it comes to prosecute persons dealing in cyber pornography that is applicable to persons under the age of 20 years. Other Acts like the Indecent Representation of Women (Prohibition) Act 1986 and Young Persons (Harmful Publications) Act 1956 can also be invoked in the matter of Internet Obscenity.

410. Section 67-A The new section inserted by the IT (Amendment) Act 2008 comes out with the explanation that an act which depicts sex appealing activities in electronic form is also punishable. The new section thus enlarges the area of obscenity and includes within it, depiction of sex activities. It is for the first time that any Indian law defines such type of offense thereby indicating indirectly that depiction of sex-related act in public is intolerable, prepares the weak minded to commit an offense and is morally degrading and hence an offense. The punishment given here is tow-tier which only shows that the fear of graver punishment may deter the criminal to commit the offense for the second time.

411. Section 67-B- The section inserted by the IT (Amendment) Act 2008 differentiates between "child pornography" and "mainstream pornography". The section is an exhaustive one and dwells well on the subject of child pornography. It elaborately describes as to what constitutes child pornography and is a pioneer law provision in the country in the sense that the time –tested IPC the term "child pornography" does not occur. The reason is well understood in the context of India as India is a religiously dominated society where morality and spirituality are deep-rooted. Going to the extent of indulging in physical exploitation with the underage is though not ruled out but publicizing the same and making it a profession was hitherto unknown to it. While the underage are physically and economically exploited their use before the public eye and their depiction for public show has been scant in India. A law on such a subject was not so eagerly required until the Internet made it not only common among the masses but the foreign websites aided in its popularization. The section 67-B makes it an offense not only the publication or transmission of it but also the creation of, the browsing and downloading of these objectionable materials though posted by others as an offense. The section provides grave corporal punishment (five years imprisonment on first conviction and seven years imprisonment in the case of second conviction). The pecuniary punishment is also heavy (maximum of INR 10 lakh (1 Million) in both types of convictions. As under section 292 of the Indian Penal Code 1860 section 67 of the IT Act and also under Proviso to section 67-B the exceptions are the same which say that the provisions of section 67 and 67-A shall not extend to any book, pamphlet, paper, writing, drawing, painting, representation of figure in electronic form if the publication is justified for public good or is in the interest of science, literature, art, or learning or other objects of general concern or which is preserved for bonafide heritage or religious purpose. These exceptions are inserted in view of the rich cultural heritage of India which is the spirit of India and in this respect no distinction is made between obscenities in the virtual or real world.

412. Section 66-E and Privacy- Section 66-E as inserted by IT (Amendment) Act 2008 relates to obscenity as it is the result of violation of privacy as well. The section talks of physical privacy and the projection of any physical part of a person without his or her consent. The section makes it an offense. Section 66-E (e) also describes as to what is violation of privacy in the phrase "under circumstances violating privacy" means circumstances in which a person can have a reasonable expectation that he or his physique is not under public eye or general surveillance.

413. Child pornography being connected with social issues has been frowned upon not only by India but even by advanced countries like the U.S. and the U.K. where the growth of Internet has provided the child pornographers with a distribution vehicle which is perceived to be relatively anonymous.[271] In India some positive steps have been taken in this direction. The Bombay High Court Committee gave its recommendations in its report on 30 January 2002 which was in pursuant to a letter sent to the Hon'ble Chief Justice of the Bombay High Court. A Committee was formed which had the two aspects; Educational and Regulatory. In the Educational category the committee deals with awareness among Internet users through e-mail, newsletters online content, hotlines and help desks. In the Regulatory category, there are the ISPs, cybercafés and online portals which provided communication services who were asked by the Committee to block objectionable sites, prevent minors from accessing unsuitable material on the Internet and preventing the publication of pornography from cyber cafes.

§4. Offenses Related to Infringements of Copyright and Related Rights

414. Infringement of Copyright – Copyright in a work is deemed to be infringed when any person without a license granted by the owner does anything which is the exclusive right of the owner. Where a person reproduces the work of another in any material form he infringes the copyright.[272] It is not necessary that the infringed part would be a verbatim copy of the original work of another but it is enough if it resembles with the original in a substantive manner. [273] Thus, under the Copyright Act 1957 copyright in a work shall deemed to be infringed in the following cases:

---

271. Yaman Akdeniz, " The Regulation of Pornography and Child Pornography on the Internet" (1997) 1 Journal of information, Law and Technology.
272. *Fatehsingh Mehta v. OP Singhal,* AIR 1990 Raj 8.
273. *RG Anand v. Deluxe Films,* AIR 1978 SC 1613.

(a) When any person without a license or in violation of it or in violation of any condition of the license does the act which is the exclusive right of the owner or permits for profit any place to be used for the public communication of the work then such communication constitutes infringement of the copyright unless he does it not being aware that such communication shall constitute infringement. Infringement shall also be committed when anyone takes the infringing copies for sale/hire, displays, distributes for trade to the extent that it prejudicially affects the owner's rights, or exhibits it in public or imports in into India (section 51 Copyright Act 1957). All the reproduction of a literary, dramatic, musical or artistic work in the form of a cinematograph film shall be deemed to be an "infringing copy."

415. Acts not to be infringement- Section 52 of the Copyright Act 1957 has been elaborately amended in 2012 to include computer program and electronic transmission in the area of copyright infringement. Certain Acts are not considered to be infringement of copyright. These are:

(a) A fair dealing with any work which is not a computer program for private use, research, criticism, review, reporting of current affairs.
(b) Making copies, backup copies or adaptation of a computer program by the lawful possessor for preservation or for the purpose for which such program was made.
(c) The doing of any act necessary to obtain information for operating interoperability of an independently created computer program by a lawful possessor.
(d) The observation, study or test of computer program to determine the ideas and principles which underline any program.
(e) The making of copies or adaptation of the computer program for non-commercial personal use.
(f) The transient or incidental storage of a work or performance purely in the technical process of electronic transmission or communication to the public.
(g) The transient or incidental storage of a work for the purpose of providing electronic links, access, etc. if not prohibited by the right holder.
(h) Reproduction of any work for judicial proceeding.
(i) The reproduction or publication of any work prepared by the Legislature for the use of the members of that Legislature.
(j) The reproduction of any work in a certified copy made or supplied according to law.
(k) The reading or recitation in public of reasonable extracts from a published literary or dramatic work.
(l) The publication in a collection mainly of non-copyright matter meant for instructional use to the limit of two such paragraphs within a period of five years.
(m) Reproduction of any work by a teacher or pupil in course of instruction or examination, etc.
(n) The performance of a literary or dramatic work in the educational program of such institution.
(o) The causing of a recording to be heard in public by the residents of a closed place or room.

(p) The performance of a literary dramatic or musical work by a club or society.
(q) The reproduction of an article on current topic in a newspaper or magazine.
(r) The storing of work in any electronic medium for non-commercial public library.
(s) The making of not more than three copies of a book of a library for non-commercial use if the book is not on sale in India.
(t) The reproduction of an unpublished work for research or study if kept in a library or museum provided it is made more than sixty years from the date of the death of the author.
(u) Reproduction of any matter published in the Official Gazette or report of any Committee appointed by the government unless it is prohibited by the government or any judgment of the court.
(v) The reproduction or translation in any Indian language of an Act or rules, etc.
(w) The making or publishing of a painting or drawing of a work of architecture.
(x) The inclusion in the cinematograph film any artistic work which is in public domain
(y) The making of a three-dimensional object from a two-dimensional artistic work for industrial application, etc.
(z) The construction of a building or structure in accordance with architectural drawing.
(aa) The exhibition of any literary or artistic work reproduced in a cinematograph film after the expiration of the term of copyright therein.
(ab) The making of an ephemeral recording by a broadcasting organization of a work for which it has right to broadcast.
(ac) The performance of a literary dramatic or musical work during a religious ceremony or official ceremony of the government or during a marriage ceremony.
(ad) The adaptation, reproduction, issue of copies or communication to the public of any work in accessible format for the benefit of the disabled.
(ae) The importation of copies of any literary or artistic work such as labels, company logos which is purely incidental to other goods being imported lawfully.

416. The copyright infringements under the Copyright Act 1957 entail both civil remedies and offenses:

(a) Civil Remedies- Whenever copyright in any work is infringed the owner of the copyright shall be entitled to all such remedies by way of injunction, damages, accounts and otherwise as provide by law. The cost of all parties in the suit shall be within the discretion of the court. (section 55).
(b) Offenses – Any person who knowingly infringes or abets the infringement of:

    (1) the copyright in a work or any other right conferred by this Act (except the right conferred by section 53A) shall be punished with imprisonment for a term which shall not be less than six months but which may extend to three years and with fine which shall not be less than INR 50,000 but which may extend to INR 2 lakh (0.2 Million).

Modified Provision- Where the infringement has not been made for commercial gain then the court for special reasons impose a fine of less than fifty thousand or an imprisonment less than six months. (section 63).

(2) Enhanced Penalty- Anyone who is once punished under section 63 is convicted of the same offense for the second or subsequent time then the minimum period of imprisonment shall be one year and maximum of three years while the minimum fine will be INR 1 lakh (0.1 Million) which may extend to three years (section 63-A).

(3) Use of infringing Copy of Computer Program- Anyone who knowingly makes use on a computer of any infringing copy of a computer program shall be punished with imprisonment for not less than seven days but which may extend to three years and with fine which shall not be less than INR 50,000 and which may extend to INR 2 lakh (0.2 Million). If the use of the copies is not for commercial gain then the Court may for special reasons to be recorded may not pass on sentence of imprisonment and may impose a fine which may extend to fifty thousand rupees. (section 63-B).

417. Related Rights- The Copyright Act 1957 gives certain other rights to the author. Where there are several owners in one copyright then each of them shall be having his separate right in it and he can individually enforce it by means of any suit or action to the extent of his right. In this regard he may not make other owners of the right a party to it (section 56). There are also author's special rights. Independently of the author's copyright the author of a work shall have special rights in respect of the following:

(a) To claim authorship of the work.

(b) To restrain and claim damages in respect of any distortion, mutilation, modification or other act in relation to his work if such distortion and modification is prejudicial to his honor and reputation. But the author shall not have the right to restrain or claim damages in respect of any adaptation of a computer program to which section 52(1) (aa)[274] applies. Such right may also be exercised by the legal representatives of the author (section 57). Section 57 is a special provision for the protection of the special rights of the author. The object of the section is to put the intellectual property on a higher footing than the normal objects of copyright. Section 57 is coached in broad terms and hence cannot been restricted to "literary" expression only. Visuals and audio manifestations are directly covered.[275] The section speaks of "author's special rights" and does not speak of

274. Section 52(1)(aa) – (The following acts shall not constitute infringement of copyright)...... The making of copies or adaptation of a computer program by the lawful possessor of a copy of such computer program from such copy: (i) in order to utilize the computer program for the purpose for which it was supplied; or (ii) to make backup copies purely as a temporary protection against loss, destruction or damage in order only to utilize the computer program for the purpose for which it was applied.

275. *Mannu Bhandari v. Kala Vikas Pictures Pvt. Ltd.*, AIR Del 13.

publisher's or owner's special rights. "action prejudicial to his honor or reputation" within the ambit of section 57(1) (b) is also referable to the author only.[276]

276. *Wiley Eastern Limited v. Indian institute of Management* 1995 PTR 53 (Del).

Chapter 3. Application of Criminal Procedure Law in the Area of ICT

§1. Search and Seizure of Stored Computer Data

418. The IT Act 2000 envisages special procedure for investigation of computer-related crimes. It empowers the officer of the rank of Inspector to handle the investigation in the amended section 78 which states:

> 78- Power to investigate offences (amended 2008) – Notwithstanding anything contained in the Criminal Procedure Code 1973 (2 of 1974), a police officer not below the rank of Inspector shall investigate any offence under this Act.

The words "Deputy Superintendent of Police" has been replaced by the term "Inspector" which shows that the investigation of computer related crimes will be as easy and expedited as any other ordinary crime so that the lack of will power to prosecute commonly found in the people is reduced to some extent. The Section is merely a declaratory one which reposes the responsibility of investigation of such computer-related crimes in senior officials. There is a felt need to have a technology expert and a computer savvy person to handle the job of investigation and an otherwise competent officer but with amateur skills in the field of computer technology could inadvertently but irretrievably damage the data.[277] Search and seizure, being an inseparable part of investigation are treated separately in the IT Act 2000. In traditional crimes too when the suspects do not easily cooperate in investigation then coercive methods are adopted. The Code of Criminal Procedure 1973 initially sends summon to the person concerned to produce the required evidence. If summons do not work then the Court can issue orders to the police for search and seizure of documents and things.[278] Computer-related crimes though committed in intangible world, have some physical appliances like the hard disks, the CPU, the monitor, magnetic tapes and a good number of software which could be quite valuable in reaching an investigative conclusion. The IT Act 2000 thus in Chapter XIII, Section 80 envisages certain rules regarding search and seizure of such incriminating objects in which power of Police officer and other officers to enter, search etc. (amended)[279] are given. The Section authorizes a police officer not below the rank of an

277. SC Agarwal, "Cybercrime: Prevention & Investigation" April-June 2002 Indian Police journal 85.
278. Prof. KN Chandrasekhran Pillai & RV Kelkar, RV Kelkar's *Criminal Procedure* (3rd ed Eastern Book Co.(1993)140.
279. The words "Deputy Superintendent of Police" are replaced by the word "Inspector" by the IT (Amended) Act 2008.

Inspector whether authorized by the Government of India or by any of the State Government to enter, search and arrest any person without warrant who is reasonably suspected of having committed an offence under the Act. The term public place includes any public conveyance, hotel, shop or any other place where general public has free access. The person so arrested shall then be presented before a Magistrate having jurisdiction or before the Officer-in-Charge of a police station. The Section also allows the application of the relevant provisions of the Code of Criminal Procedure 1973 to entry, search or arrest made under this section (Section 80 IT (Amended) Act 2008). The mentioning of the word "public place" in the section presumably excludes a private home from it. The section is conspicuously silent on the point of domestic homes understandably for the reason that in the year 2000 computer systems were not so easily used or available in the homely surroundings. India is on the path of Information Superpower and today even a humble domesticity can boast of having a computer setting in the house. In such cases the search and seizure operation may suffer a setback if one goes by the true wordings of the section. In such situations the traditional provisions contained in Section 47 and Section 100 of the Criminal Procedure Code 1973 will need to be applied. The said Section 100 has three important aspects; firstly, it makes obligatory upon the occupant of a closed place to afford facilities to the investigative authorities, secondly, the authorities should be armed with proper authority to conduct the search and thirdly, procedures have been designated "to obtain as reliable evidence as possible of the search and to exclude the possibility of any concoction, or malpractice of any kind".[280] Thus the traditional law too insists upon the originality of the material collected.

The most crucial question in computer-related crime investigation is the reliability of digital evidence. This is the work less of a law expert and more of a technology expert. The 2008 Amendments in the IT Act have given due importance to this fact and thus Section 45-A has been inserted in the Indian Evidence Act 1872 (1 of 1872) whereby the opinion of the Electronic Evidence Expert (EEE) has been made admissible by the court. Handling of information and data and keeping it in its original form until it reaches the court needs extra care and precautions. There is the danger of the evidence being manipulated at the hands of the dishonest but technologically expert person. The trustworthiness of the evidence depends much on the way it is collected. For this computer forensics is being recognized as a new branch of forensic science and which "is the scientific collection, examination, analysis and presentation of information held on or retrieved from storage media in such a way that it can be used as potential legal evidence."[281]

280. *Emperor v. Balai Ghosh*, AIR 1930 Cal 141.
281. *Morgans v. Director of Public Prosecutions* (2001) 1 AC315.

§2. Interception

419. The IT (Amendment) Act 2008 empowers the Central or State government to authorize its officers to order interception or monitoring of any information generated, transmitted, received or stored in any computer resource. The grounds of interception are: (1) interest of sovereignty; (2) integrity of India; (3) defense of India; (4) security of the State; (5) friendly relations with foreign States; (6) public order; (7) prevention of incitement to the commission of any offense; (8) for investigation of any offense. The procedure of interception shall be prescribed by the government. The subscriber or intermediary or any other person is under obligation not only to facilitate access to the computer resource but also to intercept or monitor or decrypt the intended information. The intermediary who fails in it shall be punished with an imprisonment up to seven years and shall also be liable to fine [section 69]. The government can on the above grounds order the blocking for public access any information which is being transmitted. The intermediary who fails in it shall be punished with an imprisonment up to seven years and shall also be liable to fine [section 69A].

420. Both the Indian Telegraph Act 1885 (ITA) and the Telegraph Act (TA) also provide for interception. The TA creates two levels of circumstances that must be met before the interception of communications can take place. It is mainly for the sake of public emergency or safety or for sovereignty or integrity of India for preventing incitement of an offense. The ITA allows interception for investigation of an offense also. The ITA allows for the interception, monitoring and decryption of information while TA allows only for interception of communications. The ITA makes it obligatory upon the intermediaries for disclosing decryption keys if so asked by the nodal officer. The intermediary must also destroy records pertaining to the interception within two months of discontinuance unless it is required further for some investigation, criminal complaint or legal proceedings. If interception is required beyond the jurisdiction of a State Government then the Secretary in charge of the Home department will request permission from the Secretary of Ministry of Home Affairs.

§3. Jurisdiction

421. Jurisdiction is the worst casualty of the technological spree. The jurisdictional issues involved in organized crimes have become "…much more common in computer and Internet crimes."[282] India like most of the Western countries has a deep-rooted legal infrastructure with non ending convergence and connectivity. The basic traditional principles of jurisdiction as recognized by the world over are well received in India in the Civil Procedure Code 1908 (CPC) and the Criminal Procedure Code 1973 (CrPC). The major procedural criminal law the CrPC is a time-tested law and envisages the basic rule of criminal jurisdiction. (sections 177–189). The basic rule says that every offense shall ordinarily be tried by the court within whose jurisdiction it is committed (section 177). The rule constructed about a century ago is one of expediency.[283]

282. F. Lawrence Street, Mark P. Grant, *Law of the Internet* (Lexis Nexis,2004) 7.04,7–18.

283. Prof. K.N. Pillari & RV Kelkar, RV Kelkar's *Criminal Procedure* (3rd ed. Eastern Book Co., 1993) 140.

At the time it was formulated t time when the world of crime was not only real but it was also limited and confined and such basic rule was applied without any hurdle. These wordings when being repeated today show how drastically the world has undergone a change and so have the practical considerations. If the wordings are seen in the context of the Internet, the legislators will now have to consider the size of the cyberspace; the distance of courts from the place of crimes now running into thousands of miles; and the vicinity of crime expanding globally. The section though appears to be an antique piece of law is still successful in the real world. But as connectivity has increased and as online activities are increasing the basic rule is devoid of practicability. Application of CrPC is confined to the territory of India which in itself limits its scope. It also has certain exceptions like it is applied to the whole of India except the State of Jammu & Kashmir, Nagaland and other Tribal Areas.

422. Cumulative Effect of CrPC, IPC and IT Act- The applicability of legal rules to crimes committed in cyberspace is the interplay of several Acts. In U.S. too, the pre-Internet rules of jurisdiction which emanate directly from its constitution are being applied in matter of Internet jurisdiction. As cybercrimes transcend the physical frontiers, the question of jurisdiction becomes a complex one. Chapter XIII of CrPC concerning jurisdiction in the criminal area covers also the situations where a crime even in the real world is not committed in one single area. Sections 178–189 enlarge the ambit of "local jurisdiction." This is to minimize the inconvenience and hardship which may result from strict adherence to the rule given in section 177.

423. Apart from dealing with the offenses committed within India the CrPC also supplements section 4 of the IPC which contains the extension of the IPC to exterritorial offenses. The extraterritorial extension of IPC is twofold; *first,* it concerns the person or citizen of India and *second,* it concerns the place namely, the aircraft and ship. The IT Act 2000 amends section 4 of IPC and includes the word "computer resource" in it explaining its meaning. The amendment says that "computer resource" term shall mean "computer, computer system, computer network, data, computer database or software" as given in section 2(1) (k) of the IT Act 2000. This amendment makes the jurisdictional rule in IPC as applicable to Internet situations. Computer-related crimes being borderless crimes have defied the fundamentals of jurisdiction yet suitable amendments make the traditional provisions useful and practical. Thus, the newly added sub-section (3) in section 4 IPC gives importance to the place where the "computer resource" is situated. While sub-section (1) gives importance to the "person" or "citizen" and sub-section (2) gives importance to the vessel registered in India. On the same principle, the place where a computer resource, namely the hardware is situated is given importance. This once again conforms to the "extraterritorial" principle embodied in the section. An analysis reveals that a person, no matter wherever he is or to whatever country he belongs, if his movement at the keyboard makes a change or affects any computer resource in India in the form of an offense then the CrPC will extend to him.

In such a situation the procedural counterpart of the law given in sections 188 and 189 CrPC shall come into play. According to section 188 when an offense is committed by a citizen of India on the high seas or anywhere outside India or by a non-citizen on an aircraft or ship registered in India then he will be dealt with as if he has committed the offense within India. However, the trial of such offense shall be with the sanction of the GOI.

424. A comparison of Sections 4 and 188 as mentioned above would reveal that section 188 (I) is logical and procedural supplement to section 4(1) while section 188(2) is the logical and procedural supplement to section 4(2). The word "found" does not mean where the person is discovered but where he is actually present.

§4. Extradition and Judicial Cooperation

425. Extradition is the handing over of the accused to his native country for purposes of prosecution. Computer-related crimes being generally cross-border crimes extradition will ultimately help in investigation and prosecution of the cyber criminal. Extradition presupposes a treaty between the two relevant countries. The extradition laws are formulated in such a fashion that they instead of facilitating the legal process often impede it. The*McConnel Report 2000* showed that the countries are lethargic in updating their criminal laws on technological lines and thirty-three out of fifty-two countries were found not to have updated their laws on the subject. [284]

§5. Electronic Evidence

426. The first computer evidence offered in the Court was information generated by businesses. Long before computers became a household appliance, telephone companies and banks were using them to record, process and report information that their businesses required. [285] But today computers are no longer the exclusive appliances of commercial domains. They have reached the common man's table and thus they cover mines and mines of information stored in it giving birth to legal issues. Internet evidence is unique in the sense that it is so easy to create, alter, distort, modify or even delete it in nanoseconds. Collection of Internet evidence and presenting it in the law court in its original form is yet another challenge faced by the law enforcers. The Model Law on Electronic Commerce[286] apart from other subjects deals with the admissibility and evidentiary weight of the data messages. (Article 9(1)). The Article contains the rule that in legal proceedings, rules of evidence would not apply to exclude a data message either solely because it is a data message, electronic in format, or if it is the best evidence that the person adducing it could reasonably be expected to obtain on the grounds that it is not in its original form.

427. Indian Scenario- India being signatory to the Model Law has imbibed most of the principles declared there in its legal provisions. Construction of new law provisions and amendment in existing laws continues. It not only attempts to define

284. "Cybercrime….and Punishment" (A report by McConnell International, December (2000) 5. http://www.mconnelllinternational.com/services/cybercrime.htm.

285. T.Vikram, "*Cybercrimes -- A Study with a Case*" July-September 2002 Indian Police Journal 80.

286. 51/162, Model Law on Electronic Commerce adopted by the UNCITRAL adopted on Dec. 16, 1996.

certain related terms but has given recognition to many of the electronic practices which lacked the same for quite some time. First, the traditional law defining the term "Evidence" has been amended to include electronic evidence as well by amending section 3 of the Indian Evidence Act 1872(1 of 1872) section 3 thus says:

> 3 'Evidence" means and includes –
>
> (2) all documents including electronic records produced for the inspection of the Court.

428. A separate section in the IT Act gives legal recognition to electronic records for the purposes of evidence. Legal Recognition of Electronic Records- says that if law requires any matter to be in writing or in the typewritten form or printed form then even any information or matter which is contained in electronic form and is accessible shall be deem to satisfy the requirement of the section (section 4). Thus, the section is an attempt to supplement the traditional provisions requiring a document to be in "writing" by allowing matter in electronic form to be treated as "written" if the need arises. This is a commendable step as it will solve a good number of problems in the application of procedural laws as it is quite common that these traditional laws have known the paper documents and intangible or digital evidence are causing hardships in the path of investigation.

429. Apart from this the IT Act 2000 has also added a new section 65-B to the Evidence Act regarding admissibility of electronic records. The section says that any information in electronic form whether printed on a paper, stored, recorded or copied in optical or magnetic media produced by a computer shall be considered as document and shall be admissible in evidence if it satisfies the conditions; First, the computer output containing information was produced by the computer during the period over which the computer was used regularly to store or process information for the purposes of any activities regularly carried on over that period by the person having lawful control over it. Second, the information of the kind contained in electronic record or of the kind from which the information so contained is derived, was during that period regularly fed into the computer in the ordinary course of the said activities. Third, throughout the material period if the computer was not functioning well or at all then such electronic record should have remained unaffected by such non-functioning, etc. Fourth, the information in the electronic record should have been fed into the computer as a regular activity. (Section 65-B) Thus, this amendment will help the prosecution and the defense where the evidence produced is electronic in nature. The applicable law for adducing Internet Evidence is section 65-B of the IT Act and the relevant amended provisions of the Indian Evidence Act 1872 (1of 1872). The cumulative effect of both these provisions is that certain computer outputs of the original electronic record are now made admissible as evidence in law courts without proof or production of the original record. Thus, the matter on computer printouts and floppy disks and CDs though original or downloaded from the Internet are now admissible in law courts.

Selected Bibliography

Government Publications

India 2014-Publications Division, Ministry of Information and Broadcasting, Government of India. New Delhi.

National Telecom Policy 2012-Ministry of Telecommunications, Government of India

The information Technology (Electronic Service Delivery) Rules 2011-Notification GSR-316 (E)-[Part II sec. 3(i)] The Gazette of India Extraordinary-Dated11-4-2011.

The Information Technology (Amendment) Act 2008-[Part II Sec.I]. The Gazette of India Extraordinary-Dated 5-2-2009.

The Information Technology (Procedures and Safeguards for Interception, Monitoring and Decryption of Information Rules 2009.Notification G.S.R. 780-(E)-Dated October 27, 2009. Clarification on the Information Technology (Intermediary guidelines) Rules 2011. Department of Electronics and Information Technology –Ministry of Communications and Information Technology- Dated March 18, 2013.

Clarification on IT (reasonable Security Practices and Procedures and Sensitive Personal data or information) Rules 2011.-Press Information Bureau- Government of India – Ministry of Communications and IT- New Delhi dated August 24, 2011.

Books, Journals and Papers

Chaudhary RN & Singh SP- *Law Relating to Telecommunications and Broadcasting*- 4th ed. Reprint 2013-Orient Publishing Company –New Delhi-Allahabad.

Chris Reed- *Computer Law*- (Cambridge University Press, 2003)

Fatima Talat –*Cybercrimes* –1st ed. 2011-Eastern Book Company-Lucknow

Kamath Nandan- *Law Relating to Computers Internet & E-Commerce*- 2nd ed. 2005-Universal Law Publishing Company Pvt.Ltd, Delhi.

Rachhoya RN- International Technology Law& Cybercrime-2003-Kirti Publications-Jaipur.

RaghavanVikram- *Communications Law in India*. 1st ed. Lexis Nexis Butterworths.2007.

Rashid MA. *Law Relating to Electronic Transfer of Money.* 1st ed. Lexis Nexis. ButterworthsWadhwa Nagpur. 2010.

Singh Avtar- *Company Law*

Singh Avtar- *Competition Law*. First edn. Eastern Book Company. 2012.

Singh Avtar- *Law of Contract*.

Verma & Mittal- eds *Legal Dimensions of Cyberspace*-2004- Indian Law Institute-New Delhi.

Papers

Bhattacharyya Manas- *Telecom sector in India: Vision 2020*- Background Paper submitted to the Committee on India: Vision 2020.

First Analysis of the Personal Data Protection Law in India –Final Report –Prepared by CRID-University of Namur- Report delivered in the framework of contract JLS/C4/2005/15 between CRID and the Director General Justice, Freedom And Security.

Selected Bibliography

Gopalakrishnan Veena- *Government Contracts*- Legal Service India.com

Gupta Apar- Protection of Databases in India: Copyright Termination sui Generis Conception- Journal of Intellectual Property rights – Vol. 12, July 2007, pp.422–427.

Gupta Atul- *Integrated Circuits and Intellectual Property Rights in India –Journal of intellectual Property Rights* –Vol 10, November 2005, pp 474–479.

Maggon Harsh-*Legal Protection of Databases: An India Perspective* – Journal of Intellectual Property Rights- Vol II- March 2006 pp 140–144.

Nollen Stanley- *Intellectual Property in the Indian software Industry: Past Role and Future* (June 2004) International Intellectual Property Institute-George Washington University- McDonough School of Business, Washington DC. U.S.A.

Rai Gulshan- *Our IT Rules are not Draconian*-Business Standard- July 27, 2014.

Securus—Strategic Trade Solutions- Copyright Securus Strategic Trade Solutions, LLC.

Swarup Mridushi- *Protection of Databases-An Analysis of the International Scenario and the Indian Position-The Road Ahead*-Indian Journal of Computer Science and Technology Vol. 2 Issue 3. September 2011.

Telecommunications Regulations handbook-

Telecommunications Regulations-Competition-ICT Access in the Asia Pacific region –Prepared by Hon David Butcher- ESCAP- United Nations-February 2010.

Vaz Natasha- Privacy and Telecommunication- April 2012.

Verma SK-*IP Protection of Software and Software Contracts in India –A Legal Quagmire!* - Journal of Intellectual Property Rights Vol 17, July 2012. pp 284–295.

Index

The numbers refer to paragraph numbers.

Index

www.ingramcontent.com/pod-product-compliance
Lightning Source LLC
Chambersburg PA
CBHW071439230926
51846CB00001B/284
9789041187437